Sutherland Springs, Texas

Sutherland Springs, Texas

Saratoga on the Cibolo

Richard B. McCaslin

Number 2 in the Texas
Local Series

University of North Texas Press
Denton, Texas

10 9 8 7 6 5 4 3 2 1

Permissions:
University of North Texas Press
1155 Union Circle #311336
Denton, TX 76203-5017

The paper used in this book meets the minimum requirements of the American National Standard for Permanence of Paper for Printed Library Materials, z39.48.1984. Binding materials have been chosen for durability.

Library of Congress Cataloging-in-Publication Data

McCaslin, Richard B., author.
Sutherland Springs, Texas : Saratoga on the Cibolo / Richard B. McCaslin.
pages cm. -- (Texas local series ; no. 2)
Denton, Texas : University of North Texas Press, [2016]
Includes bibliographical references and index.
ISBN 9781574416732 (hardcover : alk. paper) | ISBN 9781574416855 (ebook)
1. LCSH: Sutherland Springs (Tex.)--History. 2. Small cities--Texas--Wilson County--History. 3. Ghost towns--Texas--Wilson County--History. I. Title.
LCC F394.S95 M33 2016
DDC 976.4/445--dc23
2016044207

Sutherland Springs, Texas: Saratoga on the Cibolo is Number 2 in the Texas Local Series

The electronic edition of this book was made possible by the support of the Vick Family Foundation. Typeset by vPrompt eServices.

For Jana

Who has never asked why

Contents

List of Illustrations

List of Abbreviations

CAH: Dolph Briscoe Center for American History, The University of Texas at Austin
DRT: Daughters of the Republic of Texas Library, San Antonio
NA: National Archives, Washington
SHQ: Southwestern Historical Quarterly
QTSHA: Quarterly of the Texas State Historical Association
RG: Record Group
THC: Texas Historical Commission, Austin
TSLA: Texas State Library and Archives, Austin

Introduction

Cibolo Creek rises in the Texas Hill Country and meanders through a varied landscape until it empties into the San Antonio River southeast of San Antonio. Many towns have been established on its banks to take advantage of this fairly reliable source of water, with some building dams to enhance its utility. But along its course there was only one site that became well known for mineral springs, and that place before the Civil War attracted Anglo settlers who created a community and gave it the enduring name of Sutherland Springs. For six decades this settlement grew on the Cibolo, becoming an agricultural town and briefly serving as a political center before Reconstruction-era conflict derailed persistent efforts to make it the permanent seat of Wilson County. Some leaders, eager to secure a more prosperous future, tried to promote Sutherland Springs as a resort. The speculations of Texas real estate developers, most of whom were initially more interested in potential oil wealth, brought Sutherland Springs to its greatest peak as a resort during the early twentieth century, thanks in part to its proximity to San Antonio. They failed, however, to effect a permanent change from farming community to resort town. The decline in Texas water tables during the remainder of the twentieth century, as the growing population tapped deep into local aquifers, reduced the mineral water flows at Sutherland Springs to a trickle, and the community, like so many in Texas, could not survive on agriculture alone. Although several hundred people still live there, it became known as a ghost town. Sutherland Springs's history thus provides a great insight into the importance of water in shaping settlement through a discussion of the many ways that Texans sought to capitalize on this precious resource at a unique place on Cibolo Creek.

A constant theme in the history of the settlement of Texas, as geographer David W. Meinig has aptly noted, is that a town was not a "primary, formal and administrative creation but was a secondary, speculative response to commercial opportunity." What sets Sutherland Springs apart from most other small towns in Texas is the effort by local leaders to promote it as a resort. Historian Janet Valenza has written that there were three phases of resort development in the Lone Star State that focused on springs. The initial period lasted from 1830 to 1869, when the interest in mineral waters was primarily for medical reasons and structural improvements were minimal. From 1877 to 1899, Texas resort development enjoyed its golden age. More than one hundred operations opened, emphasizing both health and social activity. The peak decade was the 1890s, when more than half of these welcomed their first visitors. Thanks to the emphasis of the Progressive movement on health, visitation reached its highest levels during the next ten years, the first decade in a third phase of development that lasted from 1900 to 1940. Most of this era, however, was marked by a gradual decline in the number of mineral water resorts in the country and Texas. Their popularity faded as modern medicine began curing more ailments and opportunities for entertainment became more diverse. Sutherland Springs was one of the few communities in Texas to experience all three phases of resort growth. Unfortunately for several generations of residents, the town never developed a lasting identity as a resort, and ultimately the springs that brought the visitors stopped flowing, ending any pretensions at growing beyond its persistent role as a farm community in spite of its proximity to San Antonio, one of the largest cities in Texas.[1]

The dream of capitalizing on the springs along the Cibolo by developing a resort persisted through the first century of Sutherland Springs's history as a community. The first Spanish explorers apparently paid little attention to the mineral waters, but Indians lingered on the banks of the creek, and Mexican and Anglo settlers followed suit. Joseph H. Polley settled near the springs with the idea of expanding his agricultural operations, while John Sutherland Jr. saw the potential for increasing his profits as both a doctor and a land developer. They represented the dichotomy that defined Sutherland Springs until after World War II: a community that served as an economic focus for both local farmers and those who dreamed of making greater profits by building a resort. The arrival of railroads and oil prospectors promised commercial opportunities that remained largely unrealized, but farmers and land developers persisted in Sutherland Springs as long as the waters continued to flow. A flurry of resort development during the early twentieth century ultimately lasted only a few decades, and then the springs began to disappear as the growing regional population depleted the groundwater. Like so many farming communities in Texas during the twentieth century, Sutherland Springs faded away, its local leaders' ambitions for being something more vanishing like the mineral waters that no longer flowed from the banks of the Cibolo. Sutherland Springs thus offers a great opportunity to consider the life and death of a small town in Texas, with a special perspective on the importance of water in settling the Lone Star State.

The history of Sutherland Springs also offers interesting insights on black life in rural Texas. Market agriculturalists in the antebellum community relied on slaves for labor, but perhaps not always in a way familiar to modern readers. Cato Morgan, who was owned by Polley, battled with Indians, carried weapons while herding cattle, and even traveled unescorted as far as San Antonio. After the Civil War, Morgan and other blacks in Sutherland Springs moved apart and developed their own community, Doseido, while they also became pawns in the power struggle between William B. Longworth and other local leaders. As the resort aspect of the community developed, it is interesting to note that Sutherland Springs hosted ring tournaments and other social events for blacks, and it also served as a site for political rallies for black farmers. The community boasted a black high school at the beginning of the twentieth century, but racial threats and the decline of local black schools before World War II reflected the hard fact that separate was rarely equal. There were few black businessmen and landowners in Sutherland Springs proper, and the integration of the county schools during the 1950s forced the reassignment of far less than a handful of black children who lived in the shrinking community on Cibolo Creek. In sum, blacks were a more visible part of Sutherland Springs in the nineteenth century when it was an agricultural community; efforts to convert it into a resort town focused on recruiting whites, and blacks apparently moved elsewhere.

Women were always an integral part of the history of Sutherland Springs, as they were in any small town, and the documents they left behind have provided much crucial information for this study. Many of them, however, never played prominent public roles as either business or political leaders. Instead, their strong influence can be seen in the management of family matters and the development of social institutions such as schools. Mary Bailey Polley capably managed Whitehall, the stately home that also served as a vital headquarters for her husband Joseph's farming operation, and then after his death apparently took part in managing cattle and later opened her home as a boarding house. Her contemporaries who worked outside of their homes were most often teachers, though the census indicates that some black women served as domestics or laundresses. Ann Dickson Sutherland, the third wife of the community's namesake, John Sutherland, allegedly also operated a boarding house after separating from her husband. As New Sutherland Springs developed, Perdie Busby arrived and, with the help of her father, built and operated another boarding house. She came the closest to being a business leader, serving as the chair of the local women's commercial auxiliary organization. Later, Elizabeth Williams continued to open the local pool each year for more than a decade after her husband, developer Thomas J. Williams, died.

It should be noted that those who developed Sutherland Springs as a resort community apparently always focused on creating a family-oriented operation, not one that catered exclusively to men. Men and women swam in separate pools in the late nineteenth century, and while that practice ended during the Progressive Era of the early twentieth century, the strong influence of women could be seen in the continued ban on alcohol and gambling in Sutherland Springs. The community before the Civil War did boast a horse track and alcohol was readily available, but fifty years later the emphasis was on baseball and family picnics under the shady trees by the pools where men and women, boys and girls, could swim together soberly and chastely. This was in step with the surging tide of Progressive reform that would climax with the adoption of a statewide ban on alcohol in 1918, two years prior to national prohibition. While Valenza remarked that "the watering holes at Sutherland Springs particularly seemed to attract religious zeal," another writer who lived there during its heyday recalled that the community tried to be a fashionable place not only to try "taking the waters," but to be seen with the "right people."[2]

A close reading of this work will reveal that the sources used evolve as the story progresses. That reflects both the subject matter and how this project has grown through a process of about thirty years. The genesis came in a graduate course at the University of Texas at Austin, under the direction of Terry G. Jordan and Robin Doughty. This first monograph focused on the early years of Sutherland Springs, and it relied heavily on the family papers of Joseph H. Polley and John Sutherland Jr., which can be found in several archives and in the hands of family members. Other document collections contemporary to them, and government records such as tax rolls and censuses, helped to corroborate the information taken from these papers. For the Civil War, much was found in the material on the Texas Brigade of the Army of Northern Virginia, notably the published letters of Joseph B. Polley, the son of Joseph H. Polley. The post-Reconstruction narrative in the original monograph admittedly suffered from a lack of sources until the advent of the Internet, which enhanced access to newspapers, official records, and even more personal collections of documents made available by thoughtful descendants and local archivists. The personal papers largely disappear from the narrative and from the sources, replaced by newspapers, government records, and commercial publications. This in truth revealed a fuller history of Sutherland Springs embracing the events of the twentieth century, such as the foibles of the development companies, the impact of the Great Depression, and the decline of the community. A series of conversations with residents, who also provided great images, helped to preserve some of the personal history of the town, which might otherwise have been lost as personal paper collections dwindled.

One simple question needs to be addressed before this work progresses further: how do you pronounce Cibolo? Texans are noted for their unique abilities to alter the pronunciation of words and names. Cibolo is a Spanish word that means buffalo, which were encountered on the banks of the creek when the first European explorers arrived. Henry H. Field rode through the area before the Civil War and recorded that local settlers enunciated Cibolo as "Sea Willow." Fannie Amelia Dickson Darden visited the springs in the late 1870s and wrote that the proper way to say the word was "sewilla." Long-time residents of Sutherland Springs, who should perhaps know best, say "see-wil-low," and so that is the way all visitors should learn to say it. It is their place, after all.[3]

As mentioned earlier, this project has been a long time coming. It began as a research paper in a geography course taught by professors Jordan and Doughty in 1985. They escorted me and other students in a van throughout the San Antonio area searching for topics, and I spotted Whitehall. Perhaps they were overwhelmed by the length of the paper I produced, but they were gracious enough to praise it and share it with colleagues who encouraged me to continue. Among the latter was Randolph B. Campbell, who introduced me to the treasures in Texas courthouses and whose fine work on Harrison County greatly influenced this study. L. Tuffly Ellis, Carl H. Moneyhon, and the late Barry A. Crouch provided more information and kind words of encouragement. I can never repay Donaly E. Brice for the invaluable assistance he gave me many times. A grant from the Summerlee Foundation kept me fed during a summer of research in 1998.

Many people generously took the time to speak with me or share their own collections of family papers or local records. I owe a great debt of gratitude to Fred and Mittie Williams Anderson, Katherine Berger, George B. Everts, Elise Kidd, Lillian Williams Masters, Karen Mack Smith, Ruth Smith, Louise Stadler, and Barbara J. Wood. A special thanks goes to Elizabeth Lester, Diane Perry, Tambria L. Read, and Hannah Houston Spivey for providing images for this work. Most of all, I thank Shirley Grammer, who worked enthusiastically with me at several stages of this long project. Every community should be blessed with people who are just as interested in preserving their past. I hope they are satisfied with the result.

I am a lucky man because I have many supportive friends and family members. If I named everyone to whom I feel indebted for this project, my editors would likely lose patience with me. You who have helped me, talked with me, or simply tolerated me until I was in a better mood certainly know who you are. I treasure your friendship and your love, and I thank every one of you.

Richard B. McCaslin
University of North Texas

1

Setting a Pattern

Like much of modern Texas, the springs along Cibolo Creek southwest of San Antonio did not attract permanent settlers until after the Texans won their independence from Mexico. The pattern for future development became clear with the arrival of Joseph H. Polley and John Sutherland Jr. in the late 1840s. Polley, a Yankee farmer who raised livestock and cotton as one of Stephen F. Austin's original colonists, regarded the springs and the rich soil around them as great resources for market agriculture. Sutherland, a Virginia-born doctor who had some success with homeopathic methods, saw the springs as a great place to practice medicine and develop a spa devoted to the healing powers of the mineral waters. Both men had experience in buying and selling land for profit, and they understood that developing a community would enhance their enterprises. When Sutherland platted a town on his land west of the Cibolo, Polley supported its growth from his homestead on the eastern bank. These men, together with a growing number of settlers in the area, put Sutherland Springs on the map by 1860 as the seat of the newly created county of Wilson. More than just a farming settlement, their community also served as both a political center and a resort that focused on the Cibolo and its springs.

Cibolo Creek begins in the Texas Hill Country approximately forty miles northwest of San Antonio, near the town of Boerne, and flows southeast almost one hundred miles until it runs into the San Antonio River, thus forming the eastern boundary of that stream's broad watershed. Fed within its upper drainage basin by numerous springs and streams that bubble up through the porous limestone of the Edwards Plateau, the Cibolo runs off the plateau through several small canyons, which brings it much closer to the groundwater that lies underneath the grassy prairies and woodlands east of San Antonio. The site that later became Sutherland Springs lies upon the eastern edge of an underground swath of water-bearing sand that stretches from the Texas border with Louisiana to the Mexican boundary. These are the Carrizo sands of the Carrizo-Wilcox Aquifer, which end abruptly near a subterranean fault just east of Sutherland Springs. This subsurface interruption, coupled with the erosive effect of the Cibolo flowing across the Carrizo sands, creates the perfect situation for groundwater to be pushed to the surface, and as the water percolates upward, it brings with it various minerals such as alum, iron, manganese, and several varieties of sulfur. Other sites around San Antonio benefitted from similar circumstances, and some were developed as well when mineral springs were popular in Texas and elsewhere in the United States, but Sutherland Springs as a resort location developed early and lasted longer than most of its competitors.[1]

Polley and Sutherland were certainly not the first settlers at the springs on Cibolo Creek. One of the richest sources of pre-Columbian artifacts in Texas lies near modern-day Sutherland Springs, and both the Coahuiltecans and Tonkawas lived along the Cibolo, which they called Xoloton and Bata Coniquiyoqui respectively, during historic times. But the stream first appeared in historical records when Spanish authorities rode into Texas in response to the French intrusion during the late seventeenth century. Alonso de León, governor of Coahuila, probably camped on the Cibolo, which he called the Arroyo del Leon after finding a dead mountain lion nearby, in 1689 during his fourth expedition to find French intruders. Father Damien Massanet traveled with Alonso de León and returned to the area during 1691 with Domingo Terán de los Ríos. Massanet referred to the Cibolo as Santa Crecencia, while Terán called it the San Ygnacio de Loyola. Domingo Ramón, who led another entrada to build missions in East Texas, named the creek San Xavier in 1716. Five years later, the Marqués de San Miguel de Aguayo, who greatly expanded the number of missions and presidios in Texas to certify Spain's claim to the province, gave the waterway its enduring title of Rio Cibolo. He probably named it for the bison that still grazed along its banks at that time, although there is an intriguing similarity to Cibola, the name of a city of gold that appears among the Spanish mythology well-known to these explorers.[2]

The Spanish did not establish permanent settlements on the Cibolo, but several missions located in the future city of San Antonio, most notably Concepción, were granted lands near the springs to pasture livestock, which were tended by herders who built adobe shelters. Comanches and Lipan Apaches raided into the region where the springs flowed from the banks of the Cibolo during the first decades of the eighteenth century, when the missions were being founded at San Antonio. Apache attacks in the 1730s prompted the construction of more substantial outposts to the south and east, such as Rancho de las Cabras near modern Floresville and El Fuerte de Santa Cruz del Cibolo near present-day Cestohowa, but no further development occurred at the springs. Individuals later established ranches between the Cibolo and the San Antonio River, but the most successful clustered near the latter, and the number of these estates dwindled as the eighteenth century drew to a close. The region lay outside of the *empresario* grants given by Mexico after it gained its independence, and by the mid-1830s the few Hispanic families who had settled in the area abandoned their homes and moved elsewhere. C. B. Stevenson, who moved to Sutherland Springs in 1858, remembered the San Antonio River valley, to the south of the

Cibolo, as being like Mexico in its settlement, while Anglos had settled along the Cibolo and remained dominant until long after the Civil War. Joseph B. Polley, who came with his father in 1847, remembered that a small ruin, which appeared to have been a two-room building of red sandstone, stood near the springs, but by the time Stevenson arrived, this relic of Spanish settlement had collapsed and rocks from it were used to build chimneys in the area.[3]

The springs on the Cibolo attracted some official attention during the period that Texas was a Mexican province. Juan N. Almonte in his 1834 report of his inspection tour noted that they lay eight or nine leagues from San Antonio "on the west bank of the Arroyo del Cibolo." He described them as "thermal springs held in great regard for rheumatism and other ailments of this nature." What he did not record, perhaps because he did not know, was that the site of some of the springs had been claimed. José Alejandro Treviño, a former Spanish officer who also owned property just downstream on the eastern side of the Cibolo, confirmed his title to the tract that included the future site of Sutherland Springs in December 1833. Just a few years later there were skirmishes nearby during the Texas Revolution. The first clash occurred when Stephen F. Austin's scouts encountered Mexican cavalry on the Cibolo in late 1835. A brief fight ensued before the Mexicans retreated and Austin continued his march to San Antonio. Juan N. Seguín camped with a small force on the Cibolo downstream from Treviño's grant, greeting men of James W. Fannin's command coming from Goliad in February 1836 and fighting Tonkawas in March and April. Volunteers from Gonzales crossed the Cibolo near Treviño's springs as they marched to join the Alamo garrison. Allegedly Santa Anna's army crossed the Cibolo on its march to defeat at San Jacinto; in 1891 a farmer near Sutherland Springs unearthed an "iron pot" filled with "doubloons of gold" worth $17,000, which some believed had been left by Mexican troops in 1836.[4]

Across the Cibolo from Treviño's claim were other springs, which began to draw more attention after the Texas Revolution. George Bonnell in his *Topographical Description of Texas*, published in 1840, wrote that these "white sulphur springs" on the Cibolo were "celebrated" and "the most beautiful springs in the world." He saw a bowl carved in the rock on the east side of the Cibolo, about twenty feet in diameter and filled with water from a spring that emerged in its bottom, with the excess water flowing away in a "bold stream." William Kennedy mimicked Bonnell in his own book on Texas, printed in 1841, by writing that "near the Cibolo, just below the crossing of the Gonzales road, are the white Sulphur Springs of Bexar, celebrated for their medicinal qualities. The water boils up from the bottom of a large basin in the solid rock, and flows off with a bold current." At about this same time, Ludovic Colquhoun did more than just write about these springs—he bought them. Manuel Antonio Santiago Tarín, a veteran of the Álamo de Parras Company whose father resigned his Spanish commission to join the Gutiérrez-Magee Expedition in 1813, served under Seguín at San Jacinto and received a land grant for his service. He sold it to Colquhoun in January 1838, and it was surveyed across the Cibolo from Treviño's grant, on the east bank alongside Treviño's other claim.[5]

The Texan victory at San Jacinto did not end the fighting with Mexico along the Cibolo. Seguín returned to the stream in 1842, but this time as a soldier in the service of Mexico against the Texans. He commanded a detachment that rode east from San Antonio as part of Mexican general Adrian Woll's raiding force in September 1842. When some of Seguín's troopers found three Anglos and a Mexican at the springs on the Cibolo, a sharp skirmish ensued that ended with the Anglos killed and the Mexican joining Seguín. The most prominent of the three dead men was Launcelot Smither, who escaped the Alamo as a courier and later served as treasurer and mayor pro tem of San Antonio, ironically when Seguín left the city while serving as mayor. Smither and the others allegedly were ill and went to the springs to seek some relief, as an increasing number of people apparently did.[6]

Among the prisoners taken by Woll and sent to Perote Prison in Mexico was Colquhoun, who resumed his speculation in Texas property after his release. He apparently never settled on the grant he bought from Tarín; instead, he sold it to Gideon Lee Jr. in September 1848. Lee was born in Putnam County, New York, in 1824. His father was a prominent politician who served as a mayor and alderman for New York City, a legislator, and a United States Congressman. The younger Lee came to Texas in 1846 to fight against Mexico. He served as a lieutenant in Henry W. Baylor's company of Maj. Michael Chevallie's Battalion, then after his discharge bought land on the road from San Antonio to Indianola, including the property that contained the springs on the eastern bank of the Cibolo. Lee reportedly planned to construct a resort and contracted with developer Joseph F. Johnson of nearby Seguin to build cabins by the pools to board patients when a cholera epidemic tormented San Antonio in the spring of 1849. Patronage was good, especially when well-known families from the city such as the Mavericks came to the springs seeking relief. Lee himself actually settled on Salado Creek to the west, where he raised cattle and worked unsuccessfully to have the San Antonio and Mexican Gulf Railroad cross his Cibolo property. He moved to New York City as the Civil War approached, but long after that conflict he returned to San Antonio and died there in 1894, still the absentee owner of the springs on the east bank of the Cibolo.[7]

Lee's purchase precluded anyone else from developing the springs east of the Cibolo, but his absence meant that an enterprising person could use the unfenced land for his own purposes. In 1847 Joseph H. Polley bought the adjacent grant, which had originally been given to Felipe Luar, from his son-in-law John James, a San Antonio land developer who had recently married Polley's daughter, Emeline. Polley had been born in 1795 at Whitehall in upstate New York. His father, Jonathan Polley, was a Connecticut native who fought in the American Revolution and later prospered as a dairy farmer. Young Joseph at age fifteen became a teamster in Capt. Samuel Brown's company of New York militia during the War of 1812. Discharged, he traveled west with, according to family lore, fifty cents and a horse. Somehow he found Moses Austin. Several sources, most notably Polley himself, assert that

Polley accompanied the Missouri land speculator on his 1820 journey to San Antonio. Austin died before he could reap the benefits of his *empresario* grant, but his son Stephen F. Austin, only one year younger than Polley, took charge of the project and sought the approval of the newly independent Mexican government. Austin noted that as he traveled to San Antonio, Polley joined him. After confirming his grant, Austin returned to Louisiana to recruit. Polley stayed with Josiah H. Bell, who had settled on the Brazos River and for whom Polley had previously worked. They thus became some of Austin's first colonists.[8]

Polley did well in Austin's Colony. He got a league in Brazoria County as a partner of Samuel Chance, then claimed a league of his own in nearby Fort Bend County. He remained on his individual headright long enough to settle the title, then relocated to Columbia and later San Felipe, the capital of Austin's Colony. In 1826 he married Mary A. Bailey, seventeen-year-old daughter of fiery James B. Bailey, for the first time; they repeated their wedding vows before Father Michael Muldoon in 1831 and again before a Presbyterian minister at Mary's insistence. The newlyweds lived for a few years in San Felipe and then returned to Brazoria County, settling on land inherited from Bailey, who died in December 1832 during a cholera epidemic that struck Austin's Colony. By the time Mary lost her father, she had three children: Mary Augusta, James Bailey, and Emeline Elizabeth. James died in 1834, at the age of four, but Mary had six more children before she and her husband settled on the Cibolo in 1847: Susan Rebecca, Sarah Adell, Catherine Sayre, Joseph Benjamin, Harriet Roxanna, and Abner Hubbard. Two more sons were born at the Polley home on the Cibolo: Jonathan James and Walter Webster.[9]

Polley thus gained land and a large family in Texas, and he worked hard to support them. During the early years he made good money by laboring or hauling goods for others, including Austin, but he also raised crops and livestock. The latter must have included dairy cattle; when Mary opened their home as a boarding house in San Felipe, welcoming dinner customers as well as lodgers, the Polleys were noted for serving butter and cheese. Polley even had a neighbor buy a set of molds and Mary made tallow candles for sale. Most important, he invested his profits in more land, paying taxes on nearly ten thousand acres scattered across southwestern Texas by 1837. Most of this was agricultural land, but he did invest in the development of towns such as Bolivar, which failed, and Brazoria, which later served as the seat of Brazoria County. He would resell land if an opportunity arose to increase his proceeds, but much of it supported his farming operations. He began raising cotton, which Austin encouraged, about 1835, and his increasing purchases of slave clothing, along with larger ploughs and sturdy steel hoes, indicate a serious investment in slaves and the potential profit of a cash crop. He contracted with Galveston cotton factor Robert Mills and sold four bales in December 1843 for almost six hundred dollars. Prices fluctuated wildly, however, and when two bales in 1844 brought less than seventy dollars, Polley abandoned the fleecy staple.[10]

Polley's enduring agricultural interest, which brought him to settle on the Cibolo in 1847, was beef cattle. He received cattle from estates that he probated as an executor and bought more when he could do so at a good price. He paid for most of his purchases of personal goods with beef and hides. His contributions to the revolutionary army of Texas were beef and draft oxen, which he sold at a fraction of their value to his embattled neighbors during the summer of 1836. The following year, when he paid taxes on land scattered in seven counties, he registered his first brand, a linked JHP, in Brazoria County. Cattle made Polley's fortune. The 1840 census reported that he had three slaves (whom he had purchased at New Orleans in 1836), twelve horses, and a silver watch. When he moved west seven years later, he was reputedly one of the richest men in Texas, paying taxes on nine slaves, twenty horses, and six hundred cattle. His livestock holdings were probably more extensive than he admitted to the tax man, because he told the census taker that he was worth $20,000 in 1850.[11]

Polley thus arrived on the Cibolo as a prosperous man who had done well in market agriculture. He also had a well-demonstrated interest in community development and had held political offices. He was listed among the voters of San Felipe in 1824, and just two years later became the first sheriff of Austin's Colony. His tenure proved uneventful, and everyone seemed to like the "slow-moving, quiet Yankee." He then became involved in the movement for Texan independence. Meetings of the fledgling government took place in his home where, according to his son Joseph B. Polley, Gov. Henry Smith used a button from his coat as the first lone star seal. Another relative wrote that the lone star flag was created there. These assertions have not been verified, nor the claims that he assisted anyone other than his family in the Runaway Scrape when Texas settlers fled before Gen. Antonio López de Santa Ana's advancing Mexican army, but they indicate continuing political involvement. Polley lost an election for coroner in 1837, but he served on steering committees for meetings at Brazoria that endorsed the annexation of Texas by the United States. With him were Robert Mills, with whom he had traded in cotton, future Texas governor Elisha M. Pease, whose legal services he had retained to settle the Bailey estate, and other prominent persons whom he knew. Polley of course voted with them for annexation.[12]

Polley's agricultural enterprises, despite his early success, actually began to suffer from a lack of good land at his Brazoria homesite, pushing him to look elsewhere. When he left, he sold the property to Thomas Robinson, who discovered that his predecessor's efforts had exhausted the soil. Robinson also found that the buildings erected by Polley were collapsing, and within two years he had demolished the last original building. His wife chided Polley in a letter, "you may remember you ran away from this place because you did not want to rebuild all the houses." At the same time, the open range to the west of Austin's Colony offered Polley the opportunity to expand his cattle herds onto vast tracts of public property. He was encouraged in this idea by his new son-in-law. His daughter Emeline married John James in 1847. A native of England raised in Canada, James had arrived in Texas in 1837 and became the chief surveyor of Bexar County. Like his father-in-law, he prospered with land and livestock. He wrote to Polley about the great potential of Mexico as a market for cattle, an idea mentioned earlier in a letter Polley's nephew wrote while he was serving with the First Regiment of Texas Mounted Riflemen during the war with Mexico. Polley and his wife walked with James over the league of land originally granted to Luar near the Cibolo, adjacent to the Tarín grant with its springs, and he purchased half of the tract from James in the late summer of 1847.[13]

The Cibolo land chosen by the Polleys well suited their needs and concerns. It lay on the prairies just west of the East Texas timberlands, which was where adequate rain for agricultural production gave way to a drier climate. To supplement the rain, there was the Cibolo. Springs near the Polley property replenished the stream, and it flowed strong from there until it joined the San Antonio River, providing Polley's herds with a reliable source of water. There was abundant building material. Along with plentiful limestone, timber stood nearby, with post oaks scattered over sandy sections and pecan, elm, and live oaks on the Cibolo. Surrounding plains were good for stock because they were almost entirely covered in a "splendid coat of grass." Polley chose the east side of the Cibolo to settle because it sloped gently away from the creek, unlike the west bank which had high bluffs. Anticipating floods, he settled on a small knoll, which also situated him several miles from the marshy lands that directly bordered the Cibolo. Disease, especially cholera, was a prevalent concern. Allegedly eighty people died of cholera in December 1832 at Brazoria in the epidemic that also claimed the life of Mary's father. A common treatment was laudanum and camphor, and the Polleys frequently purchased both. Despite their efforts, they had lost their son James in 1834 at the age of four. On the Cibolo, they had a cistern to catch rainwater for human consumption, used their well only for watering stock and irrigation, and resorted to the nearby springs to help cure maladies, including Joseph's recurring neuralgia.[14]

The Polleys moved to their new homesite on the Cibolo in the late summer of 1847. With them traveled slaves, cattle, horses, and six children ranging from twelve to almost two years of age. Mary Augusta, the Polleys' oldest daughter, had married her cousin in 1842 but was now a widow and came with the caravan, tending her two young children, Joseph Egbert and Eleanor Adelia Polley. Emeline, the Polleys' second daughter, presumably was already living with her husband, John James, in San Antonio. Tragically, she died in childbirth at the age of sixteen in December 1848, just a week after the birth of her brother, Jonathan James Polley. Her daughter, named for her, joined her in the new family cemetery in August 1850, after only twenty months of life. It was a sad start for the Polleys on the Cibolo, but they would do better.[15]

Within a few months of the Polleys' arrival on their new land, another former resident of Austin's Colony bought the Treviño grant, with its springs, on the western bank of the Cibolo. John Sutherland Jr. was born in 1792 at Danville, Virginia. In 1805 he moved to East Tennessee with his father, who immigrated to the United States from Scotland and fought in the American Revolution. Young John first entered business in Knoxville, starting as a store clerk and quickly advancing to partner while also serving as an assistant postmaster. He married Diana Kennedy in 1816 and migrated to Decatur, Alabama, in 1824, establishing himself as president of a bank. That enterprise failed, so he moved to Tuscumbia in 1826 and became partners with his older brother George, a veteran of the War of 1812, in a mercantile business. There John also served as a trustee of LaGrange College. When the brothers' operation folded, George left for Austin's Colony. John was contracted in January 1830 to be among those brought to Texas by George, but he chose to stay in Alabama. Diana had died in 1827, and he married Ann Bryant Lane and began a new family. His father joined him in Tuscumbia, and the younger Sutherland would not leave him. He studied medicine and opened a lucrative practice, but the lure of Texas persisted. In the fall of 1835, John decided to visit George to look for a new home. He found that his brother had become a leader in the growing unrest against Mexico, and in fact George was among the Texans who stormed into San Antonio in December.[16]

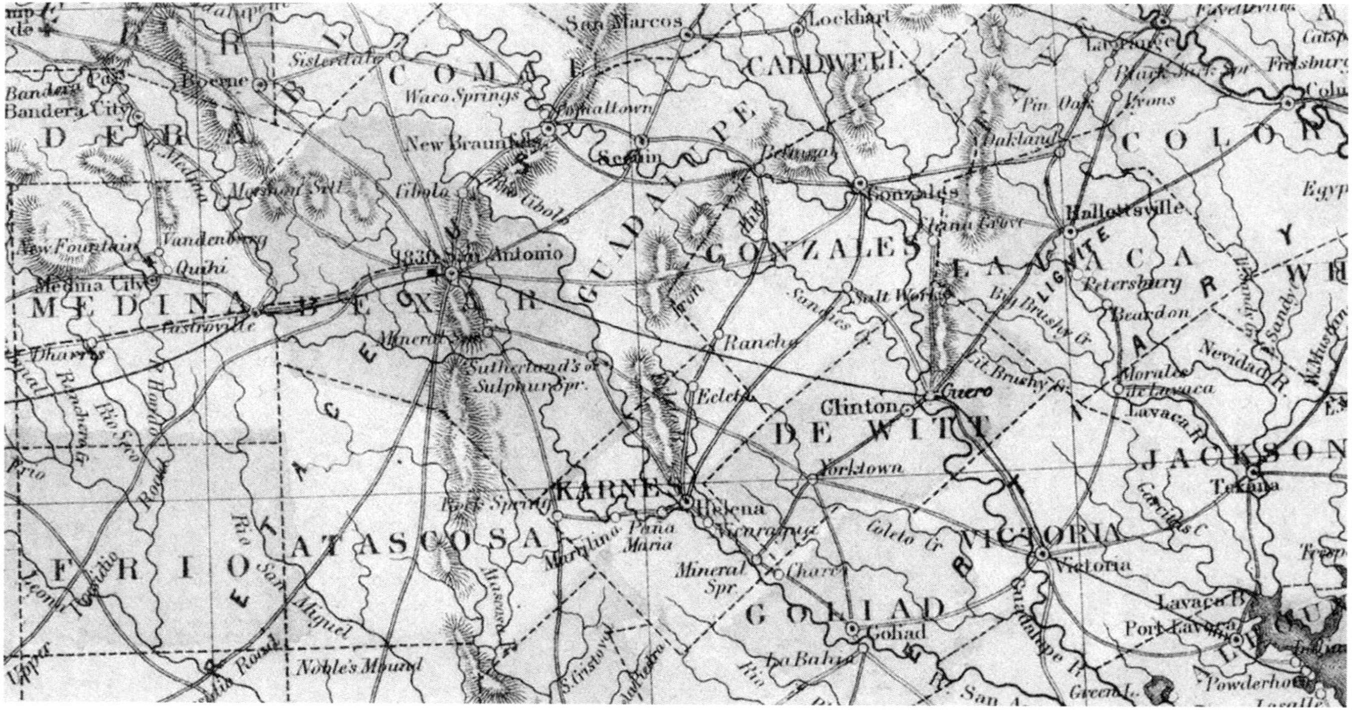

1.1 Excerpt from Charles Desilver, *Richardson's New Map of the State of Texas, Including Part of Mexico* (Philadelphia, 1859). Courtesy of University of Texas at Arlington Library

1.2 Placido, Chief of the Tonkawas. From Homer S. Thrall, *A Pictorial History of Texas* (St. Louis: N. D. Thompson & Company, 1879)

1.3 Juan N. Almonte. Courtesy of Prints & Photographs Division, Library of Congress

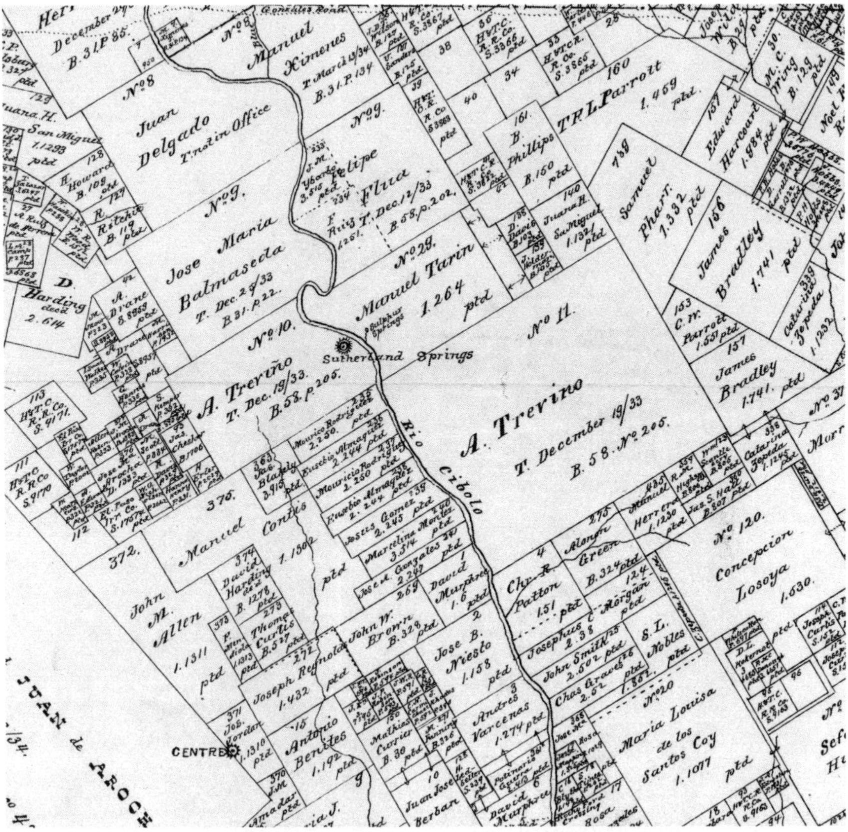

1.4 Excerpt from Texas General Land Office, *Wilson County Land Grant Map* (Austin, 1879). COURTESY OF PRINTS & PHOTOGRAPHS DIVISION, LIBRARY OF CONGRESS

1.5 Joseph Henry Polley. From "Capt. Joseph Henry Polley," http://www.findagrave.com/cgi-bin/fg.cgi?page=gr&GRid=28057356 (accessed Aug. 24, 2016)

1.6 Mary Augusta Bailey Polley. Courtesy of Author's Collection (Provided by Shirley Grammer)

1.7 John Sutherland Jr. Courtesy of Author's Collection (Provided by Shirley Grammer)

1.8 Whitehall, April 1936. Courtesy of Prints & Photographs Division, Library of Congress

1.9 Kitchen at Whitehall, April 1936. Courtesy of Prints & Photographs Division, Library of Congress

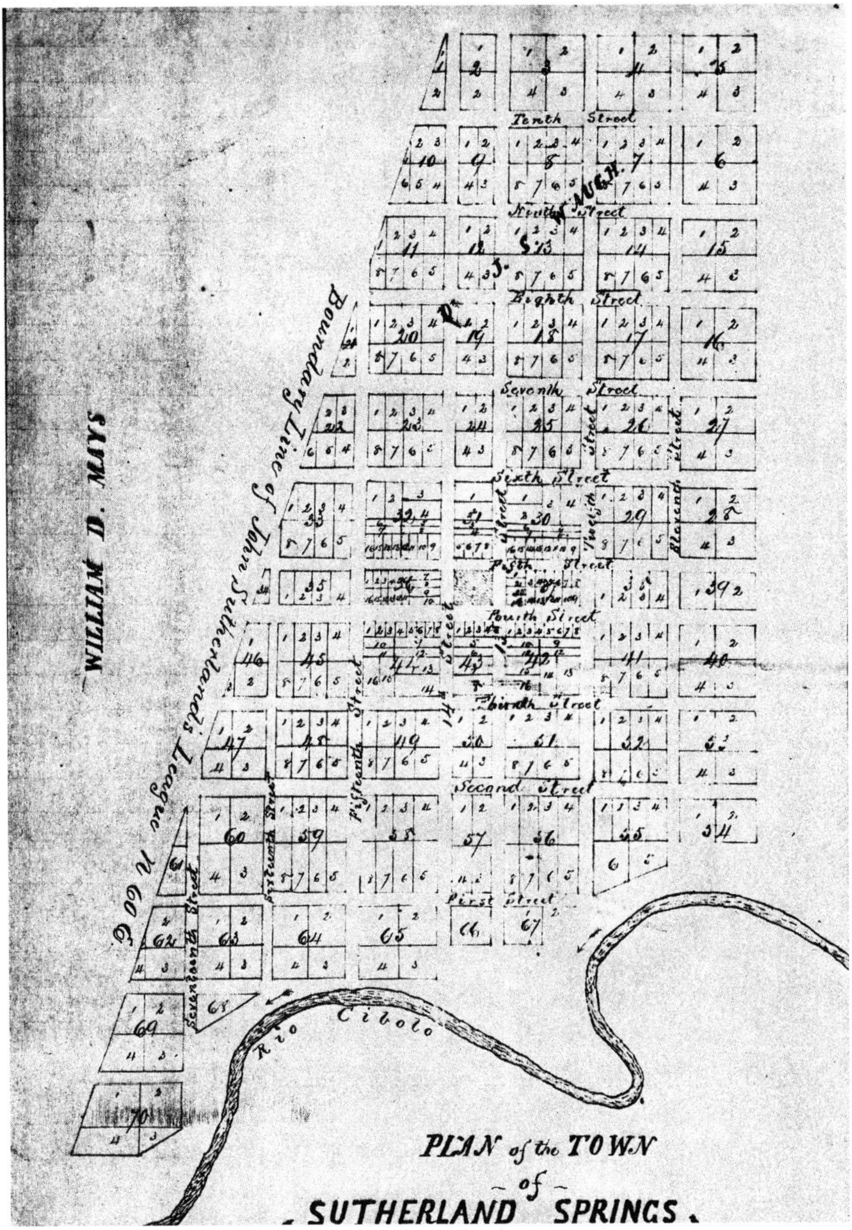

1.10 Thomas Pooley, *Plat of Sutherland Springs* (ca. 1854). From Plat Records Volume 1, page 76, County Clerk's Office, Wilson County Courthouse, Floresville, TX

John embraced the Texans' cause and joined Capt. William H. Patton's company, which was traveling to San Antonio. The company included William D. Sutherland, George's son and thus John's nephew. Patton, a veteran of the fights at Velasco and San Antonio, had been told by Sam Houston, as the commander of the Texas forces, to assemble volunteers and forward them for service. The company arrived by mid-January 1836 at the Alamo, where Patton delivered his recruits and departed. John and his medical kit were welcomed by the Alamo defenders, and he was also generous with his money, paying troops and buying supplies. He soon had a chance to play an even greater role: when Gen. Antonio Lopez de Santa Anna's Mexican army approached, Alamo commander William B. Travis sent Sutherland and John W. Smith, a future mayor of San Antonio, to scout the enemy. While returning at a gallop, Sutherland's horse slipped in mud and fell on him, injuring the doctor's leg. Unable to stand and fight, Sutherland became a courier. He left the Alamo for the last time on February 23, riding with Smith to Gonzales to bring more reinforcements. While leading a group to San Antonio, the two couriers noticed that the daily signal gun at the Alamo was no longer being fired. Among the men who died at the Alamo was John's nephew, William. Sutherland, still crippled, reported to the Constitutional Convention at Washington on the Brazos River and became a secretary to Pres. David G. Burnet. He remained with Burnet until after the Texans' victory at San Jacinto in April 1836.[17]

John Sutherland returned briefly to Alabama. His father died in September 1836, and the next year Sutherland settled with his family on the Colorado River near the community of Egypt, Texas. When his second wife died, he married again in 1841 to Ann Margaret Lucas Dickson, the widow of Abisha Dickson, who was among those massacred with James W. Fannin at Goliad in 1836. The union produced three children, just like each of Sutherland's other marriages. John J., David K., and Sarah Agnes were the children of his first wife while his second had three sons: George Quinn, Levin L., and Jack, the first of whom was born in Texas. Mary F., William T., and Alexander H. were the children of Sutherland's third marriage to Ann Dickson, who had children from her previous union as well.[18]

Like Polley, Sutherland worked hard to support his big family. He joined his brother George in purchasing land grants throughout Bexar County, which included much of west Texas. The Republic of Texas allowed settlers to claim or buy millions of acres, and the Sutherlands worked with those who wanted to swap acreage for cash. John purchased seventeen tracts from grantees, plus another grant from his Alamo comrade Smith, who bought it from a homesteader. Sutherland acquired other lands later, and he got a grant in his own name in 1845, although his 1854 petition for another grant as a veteran of the army of the Republic of Texas was apparently ignored. He also tried other enterprises, such as operating a ferry on the Colorado like his father had done on the Clinch River in Tennessee, establishing a stage line from Houston to Victoria by way of Egypt, and trading in livestock. Adolphus Sterne, a Nacogdoches businessman, noted in his diary that Sutherland drove a herd of mules from Bexar County to Nacogdoches in the fall of 1840. George Sutherland nominated John to be the tax collector at Lavaca, but he did not get the appointment. One scheme almost cost John his life. He and Philip Dimmitt began selling goods together at the mouth of the Nueces River. Their prospects appeared good until Dimmitt and three others were arrested in July 1841 by Mexican troops under the command of Gen. Pedro de Ampudia. Sutherland was detained soon afterward in Matamoros, but protests to the British consul secured his release. He was expelled from Mexico while Dimmitt and about two dozen prisoners were marched south under guard. Tragically, Dimmitt committed suicide when he learned that he was to be used as a hostage to compel the return of companions who escaped.[19]

Sutherland like Polley was also pushed to move to the Cibolo by shifts in his fortunes. He tried to grow cotton like Polley, but wrote to his daughter Sarah, who had gone to Tennessee for school and there married James P. N. Craighead, that his crop in 1842 was "almost an entire failure" after a long drought was followed by fifty days of rain and then an infestation of pests. Friends and relatives moved away, but he returned to land speculation, apparently focusing on planters moving into his region to plant sugar cane but also spending time marketing his western lands. He did not become as prosperous as Polley, but in 1850, soon after moving to the Cibolo, he paid taxes on 4,500 acres, eight slaves, six horses, and 110 cattle, for a net worth of $10,000. As a doctor, Sutherland certainly shared Polley's concerns over disease. A note to Sarah from her stepmother Ann shortly before the move to the Cibolo recalled the death of several neighbors from influenza, yellow fever, and flux. Ann also complained bitterly about her husband's long absences, leaving her alone to tend the children. A new home closer to his business interests within Bexar County might alleviate that problem. And finally, John quarreled with George and his family over business matters, clashes that may have been enhanced by lingering accusations of John having abandoned his nephew William in the Alamo. After George's death in 1853, his widow and children struck a deal, agreeing to pay John $2,000 "for the purposes of peace and quiet" and ceding the rights to land on Rosillo Creek in Bexar County, just ten miles from his new home on the Cibolo.[20]

Sutherland had numerous tracts in Bexar County, but he settled on the Treviño grant to take advantage of the springs there. He was schooled in the theories of medicine propounded by a self-taught doctor from New Hampshire, Samuel Thompson, who advertised the use of steam treatment and vegetable compounds as the cure for most ailments (although Sutherland also used popular medications such as quinine and blue mass, an opium compound, in treatments as well). He was certainly not the only visitor to central Texas who believed that the springs offered not just healing but a financial opportunity. George Bonnell in his 1840 work had remarked that the springs on the east bank "will no doubt become a place of considerable resort." Edward Stiff, the author of a guide book for Texas immigrants published that same year, declared that "the little creek of Sobolo [*sic*] ... is hereafter to be the great rendezvous, and its banks the promenade [*sic*] ground for invalids in body, and heart sick lovers—the veritable Saratoga of Texas."[21]

The springs on the Cibolo may have initially attracted Sutherland's attention in 1836, when he led reinforcements from Gonzales that failed to reach the Alamo, but he apparently was not financially able at that time to capitalize on his find. He was also greatly concerned about the chance of Mexican raiders; after the attacks on San Antonio in 1842 he wrote to a friend that he was very concerned about the vulnerability of the "western settlements" and thought that it was "altogether probable" that Mexico would invade Texas in the spring of 1843. When that did not happen, Texas was annexed by the United States, and epidemics persisted in the new state, Sutherland decided to move. He reported to his daughter Sarah in May 1849, just eight weeks after he settled on the Cibolo, that his new home site was "handsome," "healthy," and a "place of great resort." He added, "We have quite a variety of waters close at hand to wit—white & black sulphur, calibrate [*sic*], magnesia & alum springs within one hundred yards of my dwelling."[22]

The Tarín grant on the eastern bank of the Cibolo, which contained the springs that had enthralled Bonnell, had already been acquired by Gideon Lee Jr., but useful springs still bubbled from the Treviño league on the west bank. There was ample opportunity for a resident doctor, and Sutherland during September 1848 purchased what was described as the "Sulphur Spring League" from Treviño's sister, Francesca María de Jesús Treviño, who had inherited the property after his death. Settling on the Cibolo gave Sutherland yet another business opportunity. He located his home at the intersection of two important roads. The Chihuahua Road ran from the Gulf of Mexico at Indianola west to San Antonio. This was one of only a handful of principal roads in antebellum Texas, and two stages each week already traveled from San Antonio to the coast. The Goliad Road ran south through Sutherland's land, then east along the San Antonio River to Goliad before angling north to intersect the Chihuahua Road again at Victoria. Traffic moved regularly along both roads, so their intersection by the Cibolo was a great location for the ambitious Sutherland. The doctor arrived with his family in the spring of 1849. With him came his third wife Ann and their three children, Mary, William, and Alexander, as well as Jack, the youngest child of Sutherland's second wife. Eight slaves came with the Sutherlands to their new home.[23]

It may not be a coincidence that Sutherland settled within just a few miles of Polley. They had several mutual acquaintances. Samuel Chance, Polley's erstwhile business partner, apparently marched to the Alamo with Sutherland in Patton's company. John James, Polley's son-in-law, was the chief surveyor of Bexar County for many years and certainly became well acquainted with Sutherland. The most important link may well be Claiborne Rector, who was related to both men. Rector and his brother Pendleton were Alabama natives who were distant cousins of the Sutherlands by marriage. When George Sutherland came to Austin's Colony, the Rectors accompanied him. Claiborne fought alongside George at San Jacinto. The Rectors later moved to Brazoria County, where Claiborne married Mary Polley's sister and therefore became Joseph Polley's brother-in-law. Both men served as executors of James B. Bailey's estate, and Polley employed Rector as his agent in buying land. Rector traveled to the Cibolo area in the early 1840s and filed a patent for 4,000 acres there in 1845. When the Polleys moved to the Cibolo in 1847, Claiborne Rector came with them, and his brother Pendleton followed soon afterward. Claiborne became a valuable partner for several years, working as both a driver with the family cattle herds and a business agent before moving to his own land further up the Cibolo, near his brother Pendleton's property.[24]

While Sutherland explored his financial options on Cibolo Creek, Polley expanded his agricultural operations. Even after his daughter Emeline died only a year after marrying James, the two men remained close business associates. James was Polley's broker in San Antonio for selling cattle to Mexico and California. Polley and his widowed daughter Mary Augusta Polley registered brands when they arrived on the Cibolo, and afterward James hired men to reopen the road from San Antonio to the Rio Grande. James gave Polley power-of-attorney over property that he controlled on the Cibolo in 1849, adding to the land under Polley's direct control. Mary Augusta Polley remarried in 1852 to Walker K. Baylor, who had served with Gideon Lee Jr. in Chevallie's Battalion under the command of Capt. Henry W. Baylor, a brother to John R. and George W. Baylor, both of whom became famous as Texas Rangers and political leaders. All three men were Walker's uncles. Walker became his father-in-law's chief lieutenant, struggling to keep accurate records of herds that multiplied rapidly and wandered far. In 1854 James trailed cattle to California, accompanied as far as Bandera, Texas, by Abner H. "Hub" Polley, Joseph's nine-year-old son who tended his father's stock. The four-month trip proved too costly, so the drive was not repeated. Nonetheless, by 1859 Polley reportedly owned more cattle than almost anyone else in Texas. Ed Trewes, who worked for him, estimated that Polley's herds that year numbered about 150,000, and they ranged from the Cibolo as far south as the Rio Grande and as far east as Corpus Christi. Trewes declared that he participated in branding 3,500 Polley calves in Guadalupe County that same year, and at least that many the previous year in Bexar County. Baylor recorded the branding of about one-sixth the number of cattle claimed by Trewes each year, but Polley obviously did well.[25]

Even as Polley's cattle herds grew, he diversified his economic interests. He raised hogs, and the annual yield from his stock increased from about 4,000 pounds in 1849 to nearly 23,000 pounds by 1856. He sold fodder to neighbors, including Sutherland, and also horses. He got a lucrative contract from the United States Army to provide corn to troops traveling between San Antonio and the coast in 1851, but by 1857 he had so much livestock that he had to buy corn from as far away as Victoria and Port Lavaca. He tried raising sheep, selling the wool in New York City through his younger brother, Jonathan Polley, and then spent the proceeds on Kersey cloth to clothe his slaves. The high price of cotton at the end of the 1850s, as well as the success of neighbors as a "series of good seasons" created a "heyday of prosperity" in the area, tempted him to plant that staple once more, and he contracted with James to sell several bales through a Mexican factor in San Antonio in 1860 and 1861. Polley invested a lot of his profits in land. He sold much that he acquired, but his holdings increased from nearly 8,000 acres in 1848 to more than 13,500 acres in 1860, exclusive of the approximately 2,000 acres he managed as an agent for James. These tracts were scattered from Fort Bend and Brazoria counties in the east to Uvalde and Medina counties in the west, and as far north as Burnet and Llano counties. Each parcel of land included reliable water, allowing his herds to graze freely. Polley by 1860 also paid taxes on nineteen slaves, 120 horses, 1,800 cattle, and 25 sheep. He told a census taker that he was worth more than $135,000, which made him one of the wealthiest men in Texas.[26]

Polley's financial success allowed him to build the home that would become one of the best-known landmarks in the Sutherland Springs area. His brother Jonathan visited from New York and drew the blueprints for Whitehall. It took two years to finish the shell, from 1853 to 1854, and Joseph and Mary spent the next five years completing the inside and furnishing the rooms. Framed in cypress, the walls were of limestone blocks eighteen inches thick. Slaves quarried the limestone nearby, and burned mussel shells from the Cibolo for lime to mix mortar. The cypress was cut at a sawmill on Curry Creek near Boerne and hauled to the Polley estate. Additional lumber, such as dressed ceiling and floor material, was imported through Port Lavaca and carted overland. Doors and frames, windows, sashes, and cabinetry were sent by Jonathan from New York City. He assured Joseph that the doors were "the most fashionable, four panels and beveled, instead of mouldings [*sic*], which our folks like the best." Even panes for windows and tin solder to seal them were bought and shipped in New York. Joseph also had Jonathan send the proper roofing tin to shelter his new home. Within a few years, Jonathan filled orders from several of Polley's neighbors for similar materials.[27]

Whitehall served well as the grand home and headquarters of Joseph's farming operation, but its details and daily operations clearly reflected the influence of Mary, whose sole domain it became during his long absences on business. The exterior of the house evidenced an attempt at classic lines, with a two-story veranda supported by columns covering the entire front. Inside were eight rooms, four each upstairs and down averaging sixteen by seventeen feet, connected by halls twelve feet wide and thirty feet long that ran from the front to the back of the home. Mary named each room for a color, except two she called the Star Room and the Bridal Chamber. The furnishings came from New York, including parlor and bedroom furniture crafted of rosewood, and carpets and tapestries made by Northern mills. A rosewood piano, inlaid with figures and fitted with mother-of-pearl keys, provided a fine centerpiece for the house. An iron stove was installed in the separate log kitchen, and Mary also probably welcomed the gift of a sewing machine from her brother-in-law Jonathan. She used it herself, refusing to let anyone else near it. But sewing (at which Mary excelled) was just one of her many tasks. There were many guests who joined the Polleys' large household, and Mary had to supervise butchering, soap-making, cleaning, ironing, and many other endless jobs. That included tending a large yard sodded with Bermuda grass and planted with oleander, crepe myrtle, pomegranate, mock orange, and other flowering shrubs. The pride of the gardens was an almond tree, highlighting a grove of fig, apple, and peach trees transplanted from New York. It must have been exhausting, but at least one relative, Jonathan, wrote enviously of his plans to join them.[28]

Whitehall was surrounded by outbuildings, which increased as Polley's family and his slaves grew in number. In 1850 his household included eight children, two grandchildren, and two young laborers who were not relatives. Two daughters married and left home during the next decade: Mary and her younger sister Susan, who became the wife of Connally F. Henderson in 1858. By 1860, though, Polley's house still held seven children, two grandchildren, and five employees. His slaves also increased, from ten in 1850 to nineteen men, women, and children ten years later. Polley later explained that he never "traded in slaves." He purchased "only those I thought would suit me" and sold "only when those I bought failed to suit me." Many of the men tended fields, but several were taught to drive cattle. One of these, Cato Morgan, was one of the three men that Polley bought in 1836. He became a favorite. When Morgan married a woman from a nearby estate, Polley acquired both her and her child. She and Cato later had five more children at Whitehall. Among the women were maids for each Polley daughter. Each family had a cabin and garden plot to supplement rations provided by the Polleys. Field hands cooked their own food, but house servants ate from the family kitchen.[29]

Life on the Cibolo was not all work. One of the Polley daughters, Harriet, wrote to her future husband, David H. Houston, in 1859 about the "fine dance" that was held at the springs to celebrate the Fourth of July despite heavy rain and standing water that stained the long dresses. She also reported spending much time harvesting pecans from the many trees along the creek. Of course, it was not just the Polleys who took advantage of the natural resources in the area. John Sutherland's daughter Mary, who was attending a boarding school in Seguin, wrote to her friend Harriet in 1858, "Have you been in bathing lately? That is one pleasure that I miss very much." While not all of the region's abundant flora and fauna were to be enjoyed—Harriet wrote to David once that nine rattlesnakes had been killed in a single morning at Whitehall—the new settlement of Sutherland Springs offered a very attractive quality of life.[30]

While Polley and many others prospered on the Cibolo, life was not always peaceful. Lipan Apaches visited the Polley farm in 1848, while he was absent. Mary had a slave woman blow a horn to sound the alarm and met the Lipans, providing them with food while hoping her husband heard the blasts. He did, and soon arrived with Claiborne Rector and two slaves, "each well armed." One of the two slaves served as interpreter with the Lipans, some of whom could speak a little Spanish. They left without a fight, but Indian raiders claimed lives and property during the next few years. Indians stole three horses from the Polleys in 1848 and 1849. In 1854, Lipans charged two of Polley's slaves, Jim Bailey and Cato

Morgan, as well as William Skinner, a white youth who lived with the Polleys and was sent to herd horses with the two men. Cato, waving a big knife, and Skinner rode through the Indians and escaped, while Bailey took advantage of his faster horse and raced for home and safety by another route. Accounts differ as to whether Bailey eluded his pursuers and lived, but apparently the Indians got the horses. The next year, another group of Indians, reportedly Comanches, killed Jouette S. McGee, the son of Methodist circuit rider John S. McGee, and a slave woman named Lucy Elam near Sutherland Springs. The boy's uncle, Pendleton Rector, was with him, but he eluded the attacking Indians and sounded the alarm. It may have been about this time that Cato began carrying a shotgun when he was away from the Polley home, traveling as far as San Antonio on errands.[31]

Across the Cibolo from the Polleys, John Sutherland also prospered. He benefitted from several cholera epidemics in San Antonio and became well known for curing the disease with his treatments. The most severe outbreak occurred in 1849, but each time the malady struck, people came to the Cibolo, boarding with Sutherland or in the "comfortable houses" erected by Joseph F. Johnson near the springs on Gideon Lee's property. Among the celebrities who came seeking a cure was Ben Leaton from the Big Bend, who died while traveling home. Walker K. Baylor came as Lee's agent and became Polley's son-in-law. Stories of cures were numerous, despite skeptics such as Mary Maverick. She insisted that the springs did little good but returned each year with friends and relatives to sit in or drink the waters. As Sutherland expected, the location became, in the words of a Polley relative, a "place of resort." He expanded his business interests, virtually abandoning ranching and building a stage stop at the crossroads on his land. Here he received and forwarded freight and travelers several times each day, and he also sold supplies to the Army. Anglo and Mexican drivers battled for contracts and struggled with poor equipment and mud, but Sutherland prospered. Perhaps recalling his experience as an assistant postmaster, he opened a post office in his stage stop in 1851. The location had earlier been known by several names, including Cibolo Springs, Mineral Springs, and Sulphur Springs, but Sutherland renamed it for himself and served as the local postmaster intermittently until 1866. By 1860 he was worth $42,000, almost twice the average for farmers who owned slaves in the area. Most of this wealth came from his control of nearly 18,000 acres located in Llano and Bexar counties, deeded in his own, his children's, and his grandchildren's names.[32]

Sutherland had moved to the Cibolo both to enhance his business opportunities and to provide a better quality of life for Ann, his third wife. He spent little to improve his house, much to her disgust. She complained to her stepdaughter Sarah that her grown children were building nice homes while nothing was being done to improve hers. She resented being left alone while her husband traveled on business, and she was appalled at the crude life of the Texas frontier. Her mood did not improve when her stepson Levin stabbed and killed George Galbraith after a quarrel, even though Levin was tried and acquitted. Sutherland's solution was to have Thomas Pooley, an English schoolteacher, plat a town site on his land in 1854 and offer the lots for sale, trying to develop a more settled community for his wife and, of course, make money. It worked. Joseph B. Polley, Joseph H. Polley's son, later recalled that Sutherland Springs by the mid-1850s boasted "half a dozen residences, one hotel, and two or three stores." The 1860 census listed about four dozen heads of households in the community. More than half were farmers or stock raisers, but there were four merchants, three carpenters, two brothers who were wagon drivers, a blacksmith, and a gunsmith. Sutherland shared the medical business with R. Stevenson, from New York, and Thomas M. Batte, a Mississippian who actually settled on the Cibolo east of Sutherland Springs. More important for Sutherland, thirteen people paid taxes on town lots they had purchased, while Columbus M. Reese was assessed for part of the Treviño grant, which he had apparently bought from Sutherland as well.[33]

With Polley's support, the new community gained a school. The legislature in 1854 set aside $2 million for public education, but distribution of these funds proved sporadic. Schools had to be built by churches, organizations, or concerned individuals. Polley in 1855 hired Sarah Ann Lillie Bumstead Hardinge, a Boston native, to settle with her husband George, an English-born lawyer, at Whitehall and teach. She soon had more than a dozen students, and produced a lovely watercolor of the Polleys' home, but the threat of Indian attacks and the birth of a third son led Sarah and George to leave Texas in 1856. After she left, Polley learned that Sutherland had a small rock building, which he briefly rented to a merchant, on his town site. Sutherland had been a trustee for LaGrange College in Tuscumbia, Alabama, and Alamo College in San Antonio, both of which failed, but a partnership with Polley succeeded. The Cibolo Institute opened in January 1857. Parents could supply books in lieu of paying tuition, which could also be paid with crops. Polley at one time had five children enrolled and provided compilations of Cicero and Ovid, three books on Latin and another on Greek, a mathematics text and two on algebra, a geography textbook with an atlas, a grammar text, a book on world history, and a compilation of English plays. Thomas Pooley and Edward J. King served as the core of the academic staff, with other teachers and apprentices serving one or two years before leaving. In 1860 one teacher, John Roger, and a schoolmistress, Mary Butler, taught about sixty children in a new concrete building built by Sutherland and William D. Mayes, who settled in Sutherland Springs after prospecting for gold in California.[34]

The students at Sutherland Springs studied many subjects: algebra, composition, declamation, drawing, English grammar, French, mathematics, geography, geometry, Greek, history, Latin, painting, philosophy, reading, rhetoric, Spanish, spelling, and even surveying. Some appreciated the little schoolhouse—Mary F. Sutherland wrote that it was located in a "beautiful place," and described the building itself as "pleasant" and spacious. Harriet R. Polley was more critical of King, complaining that "I cannot bare him he is so cross sometimes." But she also added, "I generally manage him he keeps me in sometimes and then I keep him in for laughing for just as sure as he laughs during school hours I keep him in." Joseph H. Polley may have been concerned at the flirtatious tone of this relationship, because by the spring of 1859 Harriet and her sister Eleanor joined Mary Sutherland at a boarding school in Seguin.[35]

Polley and Sutherland also co-founded a church in Sutherland Springs. The former had sponsored a Sunday school in Austin's Colony and at Whitehall. His preferred denomination is not clear, but his wife was a Presbyterian and he met the Hardinges at a revival sponsored by Southern Methodists, the most numerous denomination in Texas on the eve of the Civil War. On the other hand, Sutherland was a "zealous" Methodist who had served as the president of the Colorado County Bible Society when it organized at Egypt in 1839. The community had been served previously by Methodist circuit riders such as John S. McGee, but now Sutherland and Polley had the small rock schoolhouse. Together they co-sponsored the installation of the Sutherland Springs circuit within the Rio Grande (later West Texas) Conference of the Methodist Episcopal Church, South. Alexander A. Smithwick of North Carolina became the first assigned pastor, arriving shortly before 1860. Smithwick died in September 1860 at the age of 29, but his place was quickly taken by John S. Gillett, who in 1861 ministered to 86 white and 21 black members of the Sutherland Springs circuit.[36]

Apart from Sutherland's and Polley's efforts, the new town became a social center for the community. Pooley had surveyed it with a meeting ground in the center, but most newcomers bought lots near Cibolo Creek, so the public square actually lay just outside the main settlement. It served as a good place for gatherings of all kinds. Sutherland Springs also had the common vices of antebellum Texas: drinking, horse racing, and gambling. Joseph B. Polley remembered that grocery stores, the most common source of alcohol in many Texas towns, "sold rotgut by the bottle and kept it on tap." He also wrote that the "most influential citizen ... but not the most respectable, by any means, was a horse racer of some little note." This was John D. Wyatt, who raised horses and built a mile-long racetrack just south of town. His partner was Creed Taylor, a colorful veteran of the Texas Revolution and a fixture on south Texas racetracks. Taylor had come to the Cibolo area in 1848, then bought town lots in Sutherland Springs and built a house and buildings that he rented for various purposes while also working with Wyatt. A concrete store built by Taylor actually served as a courthouse after Sutherland Springs became the seat of Wilson County, which was carved from Bexar County in 1860.[37]

Despite its flaws, the new town provided Sutherland's wife Ann with the community that she craved. She moved out of her husband's home and established a boarding house near the stage stop, where she lived with her three children Mary, William, and Alexander until her death in early November 1862. Her stepsons Jack and Quinn lived nearby, working as "trailers" for merchant William P. Hughes. She took all of the family slaves, which had increased to eleven in number, with her, allegedly declaring that her husband did not need them or treat them well enough. The couple remained friends and attended church and community events together; apparently she simply could not live with him. Sutherland stayed in his house a half mile from the town he had platted. There he was joined by his daughter Sarah, now a widow, who came from Tennessee in 1857 with four children, and his daughter-in-law Emily, who had been widowed by the death of Sutherland's son David in 1852, perhaps from scarlet fever. Emily brought a daughter and four slaves with her, completing a full household near the springs on the old Treviño grant.[38]

Sutherland remained at the center of affairs as his town became a political center. When border troubles alarmed San Antonio in the fall of 1855, he served on the committee that drafted a call for volunteers. Two of his sons, Quinn and Levin, as well as others who lived along the Cibolo, joined William R. Henry's company after James H. Callahan's disastrous expedition into Mexico. Sutherland also served as a justice of the peace in the same period, and he twice penned petitions to the legislature asking for the creation of a new county with Sutherland Springs as its seat. Despite opposition in San Antonio, the legislators approved his proposal in February 1860, naming the new county for James C. Wilson, an Englishman who had survived the ill-fated Mier Expedition to become a state senator. Sutherland wrote a note to a "dear old friend" at that time, Sam Houston, asking him to forward a certified copy of the act "at as early a day as convenient." Sutherland Springs became the temporary county seat, and Sutherland and other town residents filled the county offices. Andrew G. Pickett, who had come in 1855 and succeeded Sutherland as justice of the peace, won the election for county clerk in 1860 despite the gloomy prediction of his wife Susan, who declared he was "wasting time & money" campaigning against King, the teacher. After all, she declared, "Who ever heard of a poor man out of the Methodist Church beating one in it and who is well off?" Pickett was elected county clerk again in 1864, after Sutherland took his place in 1862, when Pickett was in charge of the local militia. Sutherland and Pickett were also elected as justices of the peace in 1860, but only Sutherland was reelected in 1862 and 1864. Merchant Daniel H. Bird was chosen to be a county commissioner in 1860, 1861, 1862, and 1864, while Hughes became the county treasurer in 1860 and 1862. Jack Sutherland was elected as district clerk but his father had to serve in his place during Wilson County's first murder trial in the fall of 1861. Jack had become a Confederate soldier.[39]

Sutherland Springs on the eve of the Civil War had become a community that was a bit different from most of the others that dotted the antebellum Texas landscape. Thanks to Polley and Sutherland, and many others, it had many of the usual amenities of a town on the southern frontier: a church, private school, hotel, and a variety of businesses that served the farmers who lived in the area. Men such as Polley raised cattle and cotton for the market economy with the assistance of dozens of slaves. Many other towns even had stage stops, saloons, and a track for racing horses, like Sutherland Springs. But not every town was a county seat, and very few had well-known medicinal springs like those that flowed from the banks of Cibolo Creek. Events during the Civil War and Reconstruction eras would bring great changes to Sutherland Springs, which disrupted the development efforts of local leaders such as Polley and Sutherland. But the springs continued to flow along the Cibolo, and so dreams of a better future persisted.

2

Losing a Generation

The voters in Sutherland Springs on the eve of the Civil War were about evenly divided between Upper and Lower Southerners, with a small fraction who had come from the north. A significant number owned slaves, with a few claiming the status of planter with twenty or more.[1] Obviously, if those from the Upper South divided on the issue of secession, as voters in their native states did, there would still be strong support in Sutherland Springs for leaving the Union to protect slavery and the political, social, and economic system based upon it. Yet it was not that simple for many residents. John Sutherland Jr., a slaveholder from Virginia, remained a Unionist throughout the Civil War, although several of his sons fought for the Confederacy. Joseph H. Polley, a native of New York who owned twenty slaves, tried to remain neutral but ultimately supported the South, for whom several of his sons also served in the military. In truth, the decisions made by these two men mattered little. Most of their neighbors voted for secession, the young men marched off to war, and the national conflict left Sutherland Springs with reduced hopes for a prosperous future. Marketing agricultural products proved difficult during the war, few visitors came to enjoy the springs on Cibolo Creek, and new taxes further reduced profits. After the war, emancipation and the creation of the Bureau of Refugees, Freedmen, and Abandoned Lands (commonly known as the Freedmen's Bureau), along with federal efforts to support Republican Party rule in Texas and the other former Confederate states, set the stage for a political battle. Ambitious newcomer William B. Longworth, a Freedmen's Bureau agent and Republican politico, failed to secure lasting change in favor of blacks, Republicans, or himself, but he stripped Sutherland Springs of its status as a county seat, further reducing its potential for development.

Polley's transformation into a Confederate illustrates the struggle of many conservative agricultural entrepreneurs. He opposed radicals, both abolitionists and secessionists, before 1860. He generally voted Democratic, although he explained that he "never so closely adhered to that party as to prevent my voting for a good honest and capable man." Such sentiments may have prompted his support of the American Party, or Know-Nothings, in the mid-1850s. They won many offices in nearby San Antonio, but their swift demise pushed him back into the Democratic Party, where he found that he fit better as sectional conflicts intensified. When the *San Antonio Ledger* became ardently Unionist, he complained to a friend in New York, who sent him a copy of the *Whitehall Times* from Polley's home town. The editor of that newspaper assured Polley that he held "broad Democratic principles, which, as we understand it, is for every one to mind his own business and let his neighbor alone." The election of 1861 and the secession of Texas apparently convinced Polley to support the South. In May, his brother Jonathan wrote to him, "Brother, I am not going to argue on the crisis because we cannot mend matters." He added, "I believe our views coincide in all things but right of secession." By 1862 Joseph was taking the Houston *Telegraph*, which was edited by Edward H. Cushing, like Polley a Yankee transplant who supported slavery.[2]

Polley's eldest son also underwent a similar political transformation. Prior to the election of 1860, Joseph B. Polley wrote home from Florence

Wesleyan College in Alabama that he and most of his fellow students supported John Bell, the presidential candidate of the Constitutional Union Party who mostly avoided the slavery issue. In Wilson County, Bell lost to the Southern Democrat, John C. Breckinridge, by a vote of just 47 to 40, making Wilson one of only a half dozen counties in Texas that gave Bell such strong support. After the election, when Republican Abraham Lincoln had clearly won, young Polley declared to his father, "I am glad to hear that Texas has an idea of availing herself of the right received at the time of her annexation and stepping out of the union as an independent republic—I think she can do better out of it than in it." For the younger Polley the issue appeared clear: he would follow the state of his birth, even out of the Union, to protect a way of life that he believed was threatened by Republican abolitionists.[3]

The Polleys' shift in political sentiment mirrored that of many Texas voters who embraced the radical leadership of prominent Democrats in favor of secession. A majority of those voting in Sutherland Springs proved quite willing to accept such leaders. Claiborne Rector, Polley's brother-in-law and former employee, was elected to represent Wilson County in the Secession Convention, which met at Austin in early 1861. When he and his fellow delegates, most of whom were born in slave states and three-fourths of whom were slaveholding farmers like Rector, endorsed secession, voters in Wilson County, as well as the rest of the state, overwhelmingly agreed in a referendum held in late February 1861. The vote was 92-21 in favor of secession in Wilson County and 314-22 in favor of secession in neighboring Guadalupe County, where Joseph H. Polley and others lived on the east bank of Cibolo Creek. Ironically, Sutherland opposed secession but was appointed as a notary that same month, just in time to certify the vote in favor of disunion.[4]

Robert E. Lee stopped at the Sutherland Springs boarding house kept by Sutherland's wife Ann on his way to the Texas coast from San Antonio in February 1861. There he wrote a poignant letter to an associate, declaring that he was "unable to see a single good that will result" from the secession of Texas and the other southern states. Ironically, by 1862 many men from Sutherland Springs served in Lee's Army of Northern Virginia. They were members of the Mustang Grays, which became Company F of the Fourth Texas Infantry, initially led by and forever associated with John Bell Hood, its first colonel and a West Point graduate who served under Lee in the Second United States Cavalry in Texas before the Civil War. Joseph B. Polley graduated from Florence Wesleyan College in the spring of 1861 and joined a military company organized at Sutherland Springs, along with Sutherland's son Jack. The new unit called itself the Mustang Grays, probably in honor of a legendary Texas Ranger leader who was the subject of a popular song and at least one published biography before the Civil War. An older Sutherland sibling, George Quinn, allegedly also served in the Texas Brigade in Virginia, at least for a short time. Regardless, then, of when or if they supported the Confederacy, the families of Sutherland Springs sent their young men to fight for the South.[5]

The recruits for the Mustang Grays gathered with many others during July 1861 at Camp Clark on the San Marcos River in central Texas. By the late summer, the Mustang Grays arrived in Virginia, where they mustered into Confederate military service as Company F of the Fourth Texas Infantry. Their captain was Edward H. Cunningham, a "fine, large two-hundred-pounder," while among their lieutenants was Lemuel P. Hughes, who had clerked for Sutherland Springs merchant and incumbent Wilson County treasurer William P. Hughes. Sgt. Edward R. Crockett's wife was Jack Sutherland's cousin. Sgt. Haywood W. Brahan, Cunningham's brother-in-law, had attended Florence Wesleyan with Polley. In the ranks were Polley's future brother-in-law David H. Houston and his brother Russell, who had served with Quinn and Levin Sutherland in William R. Henry's volunteer company in 1855. The Houstons' father, Ross Houston, later secured a position for David in the Eighth Texas Cavalry, popularly known as Terry's Texas Rangers, but Russell stayed with Company F until 1863, when he went home because of persistent illness. During April 1862, Connally F. Henderson, another Polley brother-in-law, arrived with Benjamin Goodwin, a forty-year-old Irishman who had worked for the Polleys. In sum, the Sutherland Springs recruits had many familiar faces around them.[6]

The people who remained at home were dismayed to hear the initial news from Virginia. The Fourth Texas joined the First and Fifth regiments of Texas infantry in the only Texas brigade that served in the eastern theater. Their first brigade commander, firebrand former Congressman Louis T. Wigfall, worked closely with his men, but he could offer little more than sympathy while 20 percent of the Texans died or were discharged due to illness by March 1862. Among the Mustang Grays, four died and six returned to Sutherland Springs during this period. Warm weather brought little relief; one more original Mustang Gray succumbed to illness before the summer's end and another four left for home. An infantry company was supposed to have one hundred members, but the Mustang Grays initially mustered just eighty-four. After disease, transfers, and desertions thinned their ranks, the Fourth Texas, like other regiments, sent recruiters home during February and March 1862. Two visited Sutherland Springs: Lieutenant Hughes and Sgt. J. T. "Tom" Cunningham. They sent forty more men to join the Mustang Grays, including Henderson and Goodwin. Unfortunately, these recruits also fell ill: four died in June 1862, and Goodwin departed when lumbago and rheumatism forced his discharge. Wigfall meanwhile became a Confederate senator and a vocal opponent of Jefferson Davis, but he introduced the president's successful bill for military conscription in April 1862. This brought five more into the ranks of the Mustang Grays as the first year of service for the original members drew to a close.[7]

Despite hardships, the members of the Fourth Texas insisted to people at home that morale remained high. A private in Company E wrote in April 1862: "I have seen none half so anxious for a fight as the Texas Brigade. We have got a great reputation to sustain and we will not only sustain our reputation but add new glory to the name of Texan." Much of that confidence came from the selection of a new brigade commander. Hood was appointed as a brigadier general to succeed

Wigfall in command of the Texas Brigade. As a gesture of respect, the men of the Fourth Texas joined with others to buy their former colonel a horse. The Mustang Grays did not have to wait long to follow their new general into combat. The Union Army of the Potomac, led by Maj. Gen. George B. McClellan, landed on the Peninsula between the York and James rivers, southeast of Richmond, in April 1862 and advanced upon the Confederate capital. On May 7 the Texas Brigade was surprised by a Union division at Eltham's Landing. Recovering quickly, the Texans chased the Federals to the cover of their fleet's big guns. Hood lost about two dozen killed and at least that many wounded, but Federal losses were greater. Families in Sutherland Springs were relieved to learn that the Mustang Grays suffered no casualties. Hood later wrote that Eltham's Landing was "a happy introduction to the enemy" for his men, but Polley recalled that he was "thoroughly content" that others did the fighting. The Texans also escaped virtually unscathed from the Battle of Seven Pines on May 31, enduring an artillery barrage before gorging on food left by retreating Federals.[8]

Sutherland Springs lost its first sons in combat less than a month after Seven Pines. Hood allegedly declared that he "could double-quick the 4th Texas to the gates of hell and never break the line." He tried that on June 27, 1862, at Gaines's Mill, where the Federals held a strong position behind a creek, protected by abatis and supported by artillery. Hood, as he promised when he took charge of the brigade, led the Fourth Texas forward. Other regiments advanced under the cover of some trees, but the Texans trotted through a large field under heavy fire. They delivered a volley when they were just thirty yards from the Federals, then drove their foe from two lines of trenches and captured fourteen cannons before repulsing a cavalry counterattack. They thus won glory by being the first to break the Union line, but they paid a tremendous cost. Maj. Gen. Thomas J. "Stonewall" Jackson inspected the field the next day and praised the Texans, but others noted that during their assault "men fell like leaves in an autumn wind." Lee in his official report recalled that "the dead and wounded marked the way of their intrepid advance, the brave Texans leading, closely followed by their no less daring comrades." Of the men in the Fourth Texas, almost half were killed, wounded, or captured. The Mustang Grays had fifty-six men and officers at Gaines's Mill. Of these, ten were killed or died from wounds, while another fourteen were wounded but recovered (only half of these ever returned to the company). Polley, knocked unconscious by a splinter from a rail fence that struck him in the forehead, rejoined his comrades, but his brother-in-law, Connally F. Henderson, was among the dead.[9]

More Mustang Grays fell in their next battle, Second Bull Run. Lee drove the Federals back from Richmond in a series of engagements that became known as the Seven Days Battles, of which Gaines's Mill was the second. Lee then took the opportunity to raid into the North, which led him to the field at Bull Run and a battle with Maj. Gen. John Pope. Jackson's Confederates arrived first and settled into a railroad cut to endure a series of Union assaults. Lt. Gen. James Longstreet, whose troops included the Texans, came up on the Federal left flank on August 29, 1862. The next day, Longstreet's Confederates drove the Union troops for several miles in a near rout, with Hood's Texans in the vanguard. The Fourth Texas captured a battery after its defenders, brightly uniformed Zouaves, fled. Again the Texans paid heavily for their zeal, as Hood reported that he lost almost half of his effective strength. Sutherland Springs residents must have been relieved to learn that casualties among the Mustang Grays were relatively light. Only three privates were wounded, one of whom later died. Polley, who escaped this battle unharmed, was jaunty in his report of it to a lady friend, writing that the fallen Zouaves "gave the scene the appearance of a Texas hillside in spring, painted with wild flowers of every hue and color."[10]

Lee, having defeated Pope, marched into Maryland in September 1862. McClellan hurried north with his troops, forcing the Confederate leader to concentrate his units at Sharpsburg, behind Antietam Creek. For the Texans, the battle there began at nightfall on September 16 when Federals pounded them with artillery and probed their lines with infantry. The following morning, Hood led his brigade and another commanded by Brig. Gen. Evander M. Law to the Confederate left. The Texas Brigade advanced into a cornfield, pushed two Union corps back, and held "their ground against many times their own number of the enemy." It was a stand that prompted a reporter for the New York *Herald* to declare, "That those ragged and filthy wretches, sick, hungry, and in all ways miserable, should prove such heroes in the fight, is past explanations." Almost two-thirds of the brigade became casualties. One Texan recalled that gunfire was "cuting [*sic*] us down almost like Grain before a Cradle." Another wrote, "Legs, arms, and other parts of human bodies were flying in the air like straw in a whirlwind." Over half of the Fourth Texas were killed or wounded, a casualty rate eclipsed within the brigade only by the First Texas, which lost 82 percent of its members killed or wounded. Lieutenant Hughes led thirty-two Mustang Grays into the fighting; six were killed or died of their wounds while a dozen were wounded but recovered. Two of the wounded were among the five Mustang Grays captured by Federals. Hughes was one of these, and he had his shattered left arm amputated by a Union surgeon. Like most of the others who were wounded or captured, he did not return to service. Polley was on duty elsewhere during the battle. When he rejoined the Mustang Grays, he recalled that "looking about me for the faces of men endeared to me by common suffering and danger, I missed many."[11]

Jerome B. Robertson became the new commander of the Texas Brigade after Hood was promoted to command a division in the fall of 1862. He led the Texans at Fredericksburg, where they played only a minor role in the battle, then marched with them into southern Virginia for the Suffolk campaign. This operation's main importance for the Mustang Grays was that it kept them out of the Battle of Chancellorsville. Lee won perhaps his most impressive victory there, then led his army north again after Longstreet's corps, which included the Texas Brigade, rejoined him. Lee strictly forbade pillaging, but the Texans ate and drank well with supplies smilingly purchased with Confederate money as they marched through Pennsylvania. When Lee ordered his scattered army to concentrate, it converged at Gettysburg and collided with the Union Army of the Potomac once more under a new commander, Maj. Gen. George G. Meade. The Confederates drove the Federals back on the first day, July 1, but the latter settled on the hills and ridges south and east of the town. The next day, Lee tried to prod his generals into a coordinated assault on both ends of the Union line. When Longstreet led his troops, including the Texans, to the Federal left, Hood protested his order to attack, explaining that his flank would be exposed to heavy gunfire. Longstreet stubbornly insisted that he do as he was told. Val C. Giles of the Fourth Texas remembered, "There seemed to be a viciousness in the very air we breathed." Men "commenced falling rapidly" as the Texans advanced on Little Round Top. Hood was shot from his horse, as was Robertson. The Texans did not scale the rise; instead, they retired to the shelter of nearby rocks and trees. They charged twice more, then endured a sniping gunfight through the next day, after which Lee ordered a retreat.[12]

The Mustang Grays had only a few months to recover from heavy casualties at Gettysburg before they fought again at Chickamauga. Two privates died at Gettysburg, one accidentally shot by one of his own colleagues, and another succumbed after his arm was amputated. Two wounded privates went home, while seven other Mustang Grays became prisoners of the Federals. Only four of the latter returned to the company. Those still in the ranks followed Longstreet to reinforce Gen. Braxton Bragg in Georgia. Maneuvered out of Tennessee by Maj. Gen. William S. Rosecrans, Bragg counterattacked at Chickamauga Creek in September 1863. On September 19, the Fourth and Fifth Texas drove their foes from a fortified house and occupied a hill. When artillery fire forced them to withdraw, they held their new line against Union assaults until after nightfall. The next day, they and other Confederates advanced again and encountered a hole in the Federal line created by the mistaken withdrawal of a division. Southerners poured through, but in the confusion the Fourth Texas was hit by friendly fire and had to scramble for cover. The people of Sutherland Springs, while they mourned their dead, also had more than two dozen disabled or maimed men to tend by late 1863. Some who stayed in the ranks were not in much better shape. Jack Sutherland was gouged by a shell fragment at Chickamauga and received only cursory care in a field hospital before returning to his company.[13]

After enduring a disastrous winter campaign in the cold mountains of East Tennessee, the Texans returned with Longstreet to Lee's Army of Northern Virginia in the spring of 1864. Their new brigade commander, Brig. Gen. John Gregg, led them into the Wilderness, where Lee faced yet another new opponent, Maj. Gen. Ulysses S. Grant. When the Federals advanced on May 5, Lee attacked and pressed until darkness ended the fight. Before he could launch a morning assault, Union troops smashed into his unprepared line. Just as his men began to waver, Longstreet's corps, led by Gregg's Texans, arrived. Lee excitedly tried to lead the Texans into battle, but they refused to advance until he retired to the rear. With Lee safe, they charged and held the position, but once more they paid dearly for their success. Almost 63 percent of the men in the Fourth Texas were killed, wounded, or captured. Two officers and seventeen men of the Mustang Grays participated in the advance, during which two of them were killed, six wounded, and one captured. Three more Mustang Grays were wounded, and three more were captured, during several more weeks of hard fighting before Lee settled his army into the trenches that protected Richmond.[14]

The Mustang Grays, like the rest of Lee's army, were slowly crushed in the defensive works at Richmond. A tremendous blow fell at Darbytown Heights, where on October 7, 1864, "the old battle worn Texas Brigade made a desperate charge on the enemy's heavy work & was repulsed with considerable loss." The Federals used breechloading rifles to deliver a rapid and deadly fire; among the dead was Gregg. One Texan noted in his diary, "Brigade pretty well used up." Both Joseph B. Polley and Jack Sutherland were crippled at Darbytown. Polley took shelter behind a tree to escape the deluge of Union gunfire but realized it provided little shelter. As he ran he was hit in the right foot, his third wound of the war. He called to Sutherland for help, then saw that he had been shot in the shoulder. Polley had his foot amputated, and both men departed for home. In Texas, their former brigade commander, Robertson, wrote to Gov. Pendleton Murrah in October 1864 that, of about 4,000 recruits sent to the Texas Brigade, there remained no more than 300 in service. Approximately 1,200 had died from disease, while almost a thousand had died in combat and another 1,500 were disabled. He asked Murrah to demand recruiting furloughs or the Texas Brigade would cease to exist. He had made the same plea in late 1863 after Gettysburg. Now he got the same answer: Lee could not spare anyone to go home and recruit.[15]

If a recruiter had visited Sutherland Springs in 1864, he would have found few eligible men who had not yet enlisted. When the war began, Robert W. Brahan, Haywood W. Brahan's father who served as a delegate to the Secession Convention and as the brigadier general of the Thirtieth Militia District, considered disbanding Claiborne Rector's Cibolo Guards. He believed they were overage and unfit. Instead, Rector's organization expanded its rolls. The Cibolo Guards by the late summer of 1861 enrolled sixty-seven officers and men. Among them were Connally F. Henderson, who later died at Gaines's Mill as a Mustang Gray, and Joseph E. Polley, who subsequently joined the Thirty-Third Texas Cavalry. Brahan was replaced in February 1862 with James Duff, who later that same year earned infamy for his attacks on German Unionists. Duff reorganized the militia in Wilson County. Rector's Cibolo Guards apparently disbanded, but two other units remained. The Wilson Guards had mustered at Sutherland Springs in November 1861 under the command of John W. Lilly, a local merchant and former postmaster. Among its forty-two members was Walker K. Baylor, Joseph H. Polley's son-in-law and business partner. Another company was led by Creed Taylor, but no muster roll survives. Duff placed these two units under the direction of Andrew G. Pickett, who served as the lieutenant colonel of the Fifth Battalion of the Thirtieth Brigade of Texas State Troops. Elected to his new military post, Pickett decided not to run again for county clerk, so John Sutherland took his place. Pickett confessed to Adjutant General Jeremiah Y. Dashiell that he was a "novice" and asked for advice, but fortunately his term as a state officer proved to be quiet.[16]

The persistence of militia units in Sutherland Springs until late in the war indicated the great concern of residents for local defense. Harriet R. Polley, whose brother Joseph B. Polley served in the Mustang Grays, wrote to her future husband David H. Houston in early July 1861: "You are all leaving the state and just as soon as you get off far enough the Lincolnites, Indians, and Negros will come in and murder all they can get." Rather than have Houston, who was then with the Mustang Grays, think that she was just being silly, Harriet added, "older heads than mine think so, too." But no invaders of any color reached Sutherland Springs during the war, while the imposition of a draft to sustain the armies of the embattled Confederacy eventually forced the dissolution or enrollment into regular service of most militia companies in Texas by 1864, when Taylor led his remaining state troopers south to join John S. "Rip" Ford's expeditionary force on the Rio Grande, where Federals had in fact established a beachhead.[17]

The draft became the focus of much discontent in Texas as almost every able-bodied man in communities such as Sutherland Springs had to enlist. Mary F. Sutherland confessed to Harriet R. Polley in May 1863, when a young man left Sutherland Springs to join the Mustang Grays, that she "felt so sorry to see him start for I thought of the time when my brother [Jack] left and who knows when they may return to us." Some found a solution in serving closer to home. Joseph B. Polley's younger brother Abner H. "Hub" Polley and their nephew Joseph E. Polley were not old enough to serve in 1861, but they both later joined the Thirty-Third Texas Cavalry, which remained for the duration of the war in Texas and Arkansas. Jack Sutherland's brother Levin became a captain in the Second Texas Cavalry (Arizona Brigade), led by Walker K. Baylor's uncle George W. Baylor in New Mexico, Texas, and Louisiana. The youngest Sutherland brother to serve, William T., and John Sutherland's grandson, John S. Craighead, joined Border's Texas Cavalry in 1864. Craighead went home due to illness, but his uncle William allegedly served until the end of the war in Texas. John Sutherland as county clerk in January 1864 had to request an exemption for L. D. Stimson, a fifty-five-year-old widower with three children who worked as a gunsmith. There is no record of active service for Stimson, but he enrolled in the Texas Reserve Corps. At least one wife in Sutherland Springs protested the draft. Telemachus S. Wyatt, formerly a member of Lilly's militia company, either enlisted or was drafted into the Thirty-Second Texas Cavalry. In 1864 his wife, Nannie E. Wyatt, wrote to Governor Murrah asking him to let her husband come home under the exemption provided for those who owned more than fifteen slaves. Wyatt's father, John D. Wyatt, who built the racetrack in Sutherland Springs, had died, apparently leaving her in charge of more than five dozen slaves, and there were no other white men around "except those that are too old & they all have as much as they can attend to." Her letter was sent to Confederate authorities along with a petition signed by her neighbors, but her husband came home only after he was shot in the chest and disabled.[18]

The draft was not the only hardship for Texas families during the Civil War. New taxes had to be imposed by both state and Confederate governments to support the war effort. For Wilson County, Manuel C. Herrera, who lived south of Sutherland Springs, collected the levies for the state throughout the war, while young Samuel Ross Houston, brother to David H. and Russell Houston, served as the tax collector for the Confederate government until he joined the Thirty-Third Texas Cavalry about 1863. When Lemuel P. Hughes, who had his left arm amputated while he was a prisoner after the battle of Antietam, returned from the war, he continued to serve the Confederacy by collecting its taxes in Sutherland Springs during the last two years of the war. Regardless of position and sentiment, all had to pay. Both Jack Sutherland, as a soldier in Virginia, and John Sutherland, his father at home who struggled to survive financially while muting his Unionism like all prudent opponents of secession, paid their share. An additional tax-in-kind, collected by

Robert W. Brahan as the Confederate quartermaster for the district that included Wilson County, added to the financial burden.[19]

Joseph H. Polley's financial troubles illustrate how the war undermined the agricultural enterprise of Sutherland Springs. Polley marketed cattle, wool, and cotton as the war began. He contracted with buyers for cotton in New Orleans, but the Federal capture of the port city in April 1862 ended that venture. He found credit was almost impossible to get and scrambled for cash to feed his family. This included his son in Lee's army, who was always grateful to get money from home. A drought that actually began before the war plagued Polley and his neighbors for most of the conflict; as early as June 1860 Susan J. Pickett noted that the crops were dying from lack of water and added, "I have never seen every thing and every body look so gloomy as they do here."

Polley did produce some cotton to sell in Mexico, tying bales with rawhide because hemp was not available. He realized little profit because Mexican duties had to be paid in specie, which became scarce. If he avoided duties by selling to agents in San Antonio, they often paid with Confederate currency, which fell to 2 percent of its 1861 buying power by late 1864. Efforts by Confederate authorities to restrict the export of commodities only made the problem worse. He sold to Walker Baylor the portion of their cattle herds judged to be his in 1862, then during 1864 asked the district commander for permission to sell another 150 head of cattle in Mexico. State property taxes that increased fourfold and county property taxes that swelled tenfold, in addition to Confederate taxes, further drained Polley. State and county taxes fell after the war's end, but the federal government collected internal revenue taxes, which of course were in arrears.[20]

Reduced finances and the war apparently slashed the number of visitors to the springs, so John Sutherland eagerly welcomed any who made their way to his boarding house. He was too old to serve in the military, and he stepped down as postmaster in favor of William P. Hughes in April 1862, but he remained active as a justice of the peace and Wilson County clerk. As a representative of Sutherland Springs, he signed a petition calling for the creation of frontier defense units, which was later done. His unhappiness over the war was compounded by the death of his estranged wife Ann in November 1862. After she died, he allegedly freed their slaves and operated the boarding house alone. One traveler who came was an English businessman and amateur ornithologist, Henry E. Dresser. After landing with a cargo intended to be traded for cotton at Matamoros, where he lost most of his belongings overboard, and then making his way across the Rio Grande border in the parched summer of 1863, Dresser combed south Texas for specimens. He arrived at Sutherland's place in September and learned that his host shared his zeal for hunting. Sutherland showed his curious young visitor two decaying deer heads with the horns interlocked. Apparently they had become entangled during a fight and met a sad end. Intrigued, Dresser offered a box of percussion caps for the grisly trophy, which Sutherland "eagerly" accepted. Caps were scarce for civilians, and hunting with them would bring more food to the family.[21]

The war undermined social institutions as well as families in Sutherland Springs. The tiny school closed, and the church almost did so. The Rio Grande (later West Texas) Conference of the Methodist Episcopal Church, South, endorsed the Confederate war effort at its annual convention in November 1861, and congregations met regularly in the rock building in Sutherland Springs during the war under the direction, in turn, of ministers Thomas F. Rainey, John S. Gillett, and Thomas T. Leach. The community hosted the Conference convention in November 1863, three years after that honor had been requested. Unfortunately these efforts did not lead to a significant increase in the size of the Methodist congregation; in fact, the number of members fell, as it did in many other places throughout Texas. While the Methodists managed to keep their church open, the community school in the nearby concrete building apparently closed. The Methodists in Sutherland Springs asked their Western Conference in November 1864 to allow the trustees to use the rock building for a school. This request was granted by a special committee "in view of the present distracted state of our county," and "in view of the obligations we are under to further the education of the children of our absent soldiers." The members of the committee lamented that no other accommodation could be made for the school, but this arrangement continued for several years after the war.[22]

State administrators were not entirely insensitive to the plight of families in communities such as Sutherland Springs. The legislature chartered the San Antonio Mutual Aid Association, one of many such organizations within the state, in March 1863. They operated like any incorporated business, buying and selling property to achieve their goal of providing financial assistance to the families of Confederate soldiers. A later act set aside $1 million to support aid societies. Joseph H. Polley served as treasurer of the San Antonio organization in Sutherland Springs, which by March 1864 was the seat of a county that reported 57 indigent soldiers with 157 minor dependents. These numbers of course increased during the last year of the war when the faltering Confederacy could not pay its soldiers.[23]

Interestingly, both the young men of Sutherland Springs at war in Virginia and many of their fathers at home apparently continued to support the Confederacy even in its last days. Robert W. Brahan—erstwhile Secession Convention delegate, militia commander, and local Confederate quartermaster—purchased Confederate bonds in June 1864, when Lee's Army of Northern Virginia settled into the trenches at Richmond. In January 1865, his son Haywood W. Brahan served as the secretary for a meeting of what remained of the Texas Brigade. Brahan and his comrades adopted resolutions declaring both their commitment to the Confederacy and unwavering support for Lee and Davis. They defiantly added, "Our final triumph is certain and inevitable, and our subjugation is an impossibility." Less than three months later, Lee's thin lines broke under renewed Federal attacks. He led a remnant of his army west until Grant's forces surrounded them. Five privates and a sergeant from the Mustang Grays surrendered together at Appomattox Court House, while seven other members of the company who had been assigned to other duties, or wounded like Brahan, signed paroles separately from their comrades.[24]

Sutherland Springs welcomed its surviving young men home when the war ended. Jack Sutherland arrived from Virginia, followed by Joseph B. Polley, who had spent weeks recovering from the amputation of his right foot while three Mustang Grays who served in the Fourth Texas band tended him. Others who served closer to home found the trip easier; William T. Sutherland recalled that he walked to Sutherland Springs from Seguin when the war ended. There he found his nephew, John S. Craighead, who had earlier left the unit in which they both served, Border's Texas Cavalry. Polley's brother Abner (or Hub) and nephew Joseph E. Polley were discharged from the Thirty-Third Texas Cavalry during June. That same month, Maj. Gen. Gordon Granger landed at Galveston and initiated a parole system for Texas Confederates. Jack Sutherland and Joseph B. Polley were included in the parole of the Fourth Texas at Appomattox, but Hub and Joseph E. Polley signed their paroles at San Antonio in September 1865, when Hub also surrendered four Enfield rifles and a mule. Levin L. Sutherland of the Second Texas Cavalry gave his parole at San Antonio that same month.[25]

One of the first concerns for many ex-Confederates was securing a pardon. Under President Andrew Johnson's proclamation of May 29, 1865, most could simply sign loyalty oaths and thus avoid legal retribution. Some had to ask for executive pardons, including anyone who owned at least $20,000 in property in 1860 or who served in the Confederate government. Joseph H. Polley fell in the first category. Upon the advice of his business associate and former son-in-law John James, Polley wrote to Johnson in September 1865 and again in April 1866. William P. Hughes also had to write to Johnson because he succeeded John Sutherland as postmaster for Sutherland Springs in 1862. Polley and Hughes had endorsements from Gov. Andrew J. Hamilton, a well-known Unionist and former Congressman appointed by Johnson to be the provisional governor of Texas, but their pardons were not delivered until 1867, after both signed a second oath. James got a pardon much sooner after meeting with Hamilton, enlisting the support of prominent Unionist and two-time Texas governor Elisha M. Pease, and assuring Johnson that he supported the Union and had joined the Confederate reserve forces only after he was drafted.[26]

While waiting for a pardon, Joseph H. Polley, like others in Sutherland Springs, had to support his family. Polley's fiscal predicament was typical of that endured by many rural elites in post-Civil War Texas. Specie was rare, and Confederate bills could not be used to settle federal or state tax debts. Emancipation, bad weather, and falling prices hindered cotton production, which dropped 19 percent in the 1860s after increasing 643 percent during the previous decade. Disrupted transportation networks, including roads and railroads, further depressed land values. Polley grew cotton and sold some land, but nothing seemed to bring much money. Federal tax receipts indicate that his income fell by about one fourth from 1864 to 1866. His growing cattle herds, meanwhile, expanded beyond his capacity to manage them and the available markets. He contracted first with Walker Baylor, then with others to oversee some of his livestock for a share of the profits. When he died in March 1869 he left little to Mary, his widow, and their children except Whitehall and its furnishings, a lot of hungry livestock, and real estate scattered across southern Texas. Similarly, John Sutherland continued to practice medicine but also sold much of his land to pay debts before he died in late 1867, having apparently never applied for an executive pardon.[27]

Emancipation complicated the postwar economic recovery of market agriculturalists such as Polley, who reported to Johnson that he owned "about twenty slaves" when the war ended. He set them free after June 19, 1865, when Granger promulgated the Emancipation Proclamation in Texas, as soon "as the order of that date reached me." He then signed a contract with six former slaves, all men. The agreement bound them to work through December 1865, when Polley purchased forty head of cattle from one of the six, Cato Morgan, who bought the animals while in bondage with money earned hauling goods for James and others. Morgan and some of the older blacks continued to work for the Polleys, while Theresa Moore, a former house slave who left, wrote to Mary, asking her to keep in touch because she missed the family and their home "by the Springs." More often, freed blacks in Wilson County moved a short distance from their former owners, and some of them organized colonies. Polley and Gray Jones Houston supported one such effort by providing land on Cibolo Creek for a settlement near Sutherland Springs, which came to be called Doisedo Colony (pronounced, and often spelled, "Dō-See-Dō"). Polley provided farmland along the creek, while a hamlet developed on Houston's donation. It had stores, a school, and a brush-arbor church where Morgan, although apparently illiterate, delivered a sermon every Sunday. The *Western Chronicle* of Sutherland Springs in early 1877 praised "Do-See-Do" as the most progressive colony in Wilson County. The article described the "fine farms" and "numbers of good substantial houses" there, each "neatly whitewashed or painted" with glass windows shaded by Venetian blinds. It noted that the corn cribs and cotton pens of the former slaves "overflowed," and that each year their enterprise brought thousands of dollars to Sutherland Springs.[28]

What was not clear was whether the removal of blacks from Sutherland Springs to Doisedo Colony was a process of accommodation or exclusion. Whites later wrote that black men, apart from the few who made a living as blacksmiths and carpenters, preferred to work as sharecroppers rather than for wages. But that also implies that the blacks lost ownership of their land, or that they never had it. The 1870 census reports that the precinct in which Sutherland Springs lay had 128 residents, 44 of whom were black, but the tax rolls reveal that none of them owned any town lots or any part of the old Treviño grant. The same records indicate that twenty-one white heads of households paid taxes on town lots or the Treviño grant. One reason for the removal of blacks from Sutherland Springs may have been an inability by many whites to accept emancipation, which led to violence in Texas counties with substantial black populations. Sutherland wrote to his daughter-in-law Emily that not having slaves was a hardship. Three years later, his daughter Sarah reported that they had hired "a freedman to cultivate a part of the field but he is too lazy to do much." She did note that her brother Jack—who farmed, worked as a carpenter, and operated a store in Sutherland Springs—was doing better with his black laborers. Other whites agreed with the bigoted claim of legislator Joseph A. Durand that blacks in Wilson County were "not to be relied upon; they are lazy and worthless." Perhaps just as troubling to them was the support of Wilson County blacks for the Republican Party, for which they voted consistently during Reconstruction.[29]

Racial tensions, and even clashes, provided the context for a political battle that ended with Sutherland Springs being replaced as the seat of Wilson County. The community avoided becoming the principal setting for a bloody feud when Creed Taylor moved away. Taylor, remembered by many as a rough character, apparently could not accept defeat nor emancipation, and his extended family and other allies joined him in a violent campaign against Union authorities. Among the atrocities committed by Taylor's clan from his ranch east of Sutherland Springs was the murder of a freedman at La Vernia in April 1867. Official protests ensued and Taylor was questioned, but he provided an alibi for himself and an explanation for those involved in the killing. The violence escalated with the killing of several black soldiers by Taylor's sons and became a ten-year melee known as the Sutton-Taylor Feud that claimed more lives. Taylor was repeatedly detained before he relocated west during the early 1870s. His son Philip G. Taylor, known as "Doughboy," was less fortunate; after being arrested in Sutherland Springs in April 1871 for a murder indictment, he went west like his father but was shot to death in Kerrville.[30]

The struggle for Sutherland Springs was more often fought with pens rather than pistols. The enemy was not a gunman but William B. Longworth, a native of Ireland who came to the area from Karnes County during the war. According to at least one historian, Longworth was a Quaker, opposed to slavery and devoted to equality, and he had experience as a law clerk. Upon the advice of Thomas A. Stribling, a San Antonio Unionist, Governor Hamilton appointed Longworth as the chief justice of Wilson County in September 1865. Stribling told

Hamilton that Longworth was "universally known as one of the most reliable Union men," for which he has "suffered much." Be that as it may, Longworth's appointment soon prompted more than two hundred voters, including many from Sutherland Springs, to sign a petition calling for his removal. Longworth nominated others, endorsed by Stribling, for appointments, which Hamilton accepted, but Longworth then quarrelled with his own appointees. He wrote to Joseph Spence, Republican clerk of the Texas Secretary of State's office, that several should be replaced. Daniel H. Bird, an ex-slaveowner appointed to the county commission in place of Claiborne Rector, had "failed to qualify," and George Bird "refused to qualify" for his appointment as the district clerk. Longworth especially disliked "John Sutherland, in whom I have been deceived." Longworth wrote that Sutherland as a county commissioner "has three separate times laboured [sic] to pack the Grand Jury, but thus far I have succeed[ed] in offsetting him." He asked that Sutherland be suspended, which apparently was done. Longworth subsequently was appointed justice of the peace for Sutherland Springs to secure him against challenges from Sutherland and others.[31]

Hamilton wanted civil rights for blacks, and Longworth focused on that issue to obtain the governor's support. He wrote to Hamilton in October 1865, "Slavery is as absolute yet in the state as I ever knew it to be." Decisive action was "imperative," especially in cases of kidnapping, of which there were more than twenty such incidents "almost within my sight since your arrival." As proof, he sent an affidavit recounting the taking of a freedwoman from the home of a white woman by former district clerk Andrew G. Pickett and other men in October 1865. Pickett's wife Susan sent a note to Hamilton a few months later, recalling mutual friends and claiming that Longworth tried to have the county commissioners illegally take a black servant from the Picketts. Longworth had told them that Susan was a "severe mistress," recounting how a black maid tried to poison her two years earlier. The commissioners, among whom at that time were Bird and Sutherland, refused to support him, and a provost marshal returned the young girl to the Picketts.

2.1 Joseph B. Polley. From J. B. Polley, *Hood's Texas Brigade: Its Marches, Its Battles, Its Achievements* (New York: Neale Publishing Company, 1910)

2.2 Robert E. Lee. Courtesy of Prints & Photographs Division, Library of Congress

2.3 Lemuel P. Hughes. From J. B. Polley, *Hood's Texas Brigade: Its Marches, Its Battles, Its Achievements* (New York: Neale Publishing Company, 1910)

2.4 Harriet R. Polley and David H. Houston. Courtesy of Hannah Houston Spivey

2.5 Mary A. B. Polley and Walker K. Baylor. Courtesy of Shirley Grammer (Gift of Janice Frost)

2.6 Creed Taylor. Courtesy of Robert G. McCubbin Collection

2.7 Lemuel P. Hughes (standing far left) behind Andrew G. Pickett (seated on left, with hat and cane) and Jack Sutherland (seated on Pickett's left) in group. Courtesy of Wilson County (TX) Historical Society

2.8 Telemachus S. Wyatt. Courtesy of Diane Perry

2.9 Henry E. Dresser. Courtesy of Prints & Photographs Division, Library of Congress

2.10 Joseph B. Polley, John McDaniel, and Lemuel P. Hughes of the Fourth Texas Infantry (left to right), with Benjamin G. Rosser of the Second Texas Cavalry (second from left). COURTESY OF TEXAS HERITAGE MUSEUM, HILL COLLEGE

Two months later, the Picketts were dismayed when Longworth became the local agent for the Freedmen's Bureau, a federal executive agency created to provide education, legal support, and economic aid to the freed slaves. He had pressed for the post since June and was finally accepted in December after agreeing to serve without pay. William Green, an ex-slave, recalled how Longworth then confronted ex-slaveholders about unfair contracts. Green declared, "He was a little man but he tole de boss just where matters stand." Susan saw matters differently. In her letter to Hamilton, she reported that he took black children from former masters because he believed no child was truly free until they were removed from their slave homes. She added that he urged blacks to sue for all wages due to them since Granger declared the Emancipation Proclamation to be in effect in Texas. She also claimed that Longworth pushed black couples who had lived for years as married to file for a license so he could keep the fee, and that he told blacks to donate money to buy a homestead for him.[32]

Susan J. Pickett asked Hamilton to remove Longworth or at least curb his excesses. The governor sent her note to Maj. Gen. Edgar M. Gregory, assistant commissioner of the Freedmen's Bureau for Texas. Gregory's subsequent inquiry brought a hostile response from Longworth, who had often complained about the whites in his district, his lack of supplies, and the troops sent from San Antonio to assist him because there was no federal garrison in Sutherland Springs. Longworth had already written to Gregory that someone might "attempt to poison you against me." Now he wrote that he only had eight or ten soldiers "of the lowest order" to help him. As for conciliating the local whites, "You might as well try to conciliate a pack of Hyenas by throwing one of four children to them with the hope of saving one." Longworth declared that his plans for a school for blacks failed because he could not find an instructor, but he intended to open a hospital for former slaves at Sutherland Springs. Longworth then sparked another conflict in April 1866 by arresting James L. Dial, an ex-slaveholder. Isaiah A. Paschal, a Unionist friend of Hamilton and the Picketts, had warned the governor that Dial had "peculiar views" about blacks, and a note from Dial critical of Longworth later arrived in Austin. Longworth in turn accused Dial of making deadly threats and kidnapping blacks, and he had soldiers imprison Dial at Sutherland Springs "in an old house filled with vermin" for days. Gregory supported his agent, but residents of Bexar, Wilson, and Guadalupe counties signed a petition demanding Longworth's removal. They wrote that he was a "stranger" and "arbitrary, vindictive, and unjust," as well as corrupt. Furthermore, they added that his efforts were "calculated to demoralize the freedmen and to prevent the working of crops," while his use of troops was unnecessary. Among the petitioners were Abner H. "Hub" Polley and two veterans of the Fourth Texas Infantry, one-armed Lemuel P. Hughes and Haywood W. Brahan, as well as the latter's father, Robert W. Brahan.[33]

Longworth responded vigorously to the charges against him. He explained to Gregory that in the Dial case he was forced "to make an arrest or acknowledge that I was a useless machine." In a second note, he ridiculed the charge that he demoralized blacks: "If to send them home elated and buoyant with a knowledge of the fact that they could safely go to work and expand their muscle and intelligence over and on their crops, with a hope of getting paid therefor[e] is demoralization, then I am guilty." The assertion by some that all was peaceful until he arrived was ludicrous. That "peace was all on one side," and it was "peaceable as the volcano smothered up until it got air." He then made the mistake of relocating his office to Seguin, which allowed William C. Wiseman, an ex-slaveholder serving as chief justice of Guadalupe County, to arrest him for false imprisonment and financial fraud. Dial was subsequently freed upon Wiseman's order, but Longworth appealed to Gregory, who again supported him in posting his bond and rearresting Dial. While free on bail, Dial added a civil suit for $20,000 to Longworth's troubles. Seeking more substantial assistance, Longworth continued to send letters to possible sympathizers, including Sen. Charles Sumner, one of the most prominent Republicans in Washington.[34]

Gregory was replaced as assistant commissioner in May 1866 with Maj. Gen. Joseph B. Kiddoo, who initially tried to placate the former slaveowners. He removed Longworth, in spite of his protests, in July 1866. Kiddoo preferred military agents, and he was upset to get a letter from Sumner about Longworth. Matters quickly became worse for Sutherland Springs. Longworth's successor as the local agent for the Freedmen's Bureau, Lt. James B. Moore, was removed for drunkenness and embezzlement. The next agent, Capt. Samuel A. Craig, arrived in Seguin after being implicated in the burning of Brenham in September 1866. Under orders from Maj. Gen. Samuel P. Heintzelmann, commanding at San Antonio, Craig scoured the files of the district clerk in Guadalupe County in October 1866 for court records concerning Longworth's indictment and civil suit and Moore's many indiscretions. The district clerk resisted at first, but Craig threatened to arrest him and send him to San Antonio. The clerk, afraid of the cholera then ravaging that city, capitulated. Craig was eventually arrested by Guadalupe County officials but Heintzelmann rescued him and he mustered out. His successor, Maj. George W. Smith, allegedly directed the burning of Brenham. He served as the Freedmen's Bureau agent for the district that included Sutherland Springs from late December 1866 until he was removed for fraud in 1869. Although the agency continued to operate in Texas for another year, there is no further record of an agent assigned to Sutherland Springs.[35]

Sutherland Springs residents welcomed Longworth's removal as a Freedmen's Bureau agent, followed by his displacement as chief justice of Wilson County. No delegate from Wilson County attended the Constitutional Convention of 1866, but it and the elections that followed were a conservative triumph. James W. Throckmorton, who opposed secession but became an officer for the Confederacy, was elected governor, while his conservatives swept Wilson County, where Confederate veteran Telemachus S. Wyatt was elected chief justice and Daniel H. Bird returned to the county commission. Wyatt resigned in February 1867, but Walker Baylor, who was elected as a county commissioner and justice of the peace in 1866 but refused to accept either office, took his place. Sutherland Springs merchant John Lilly, who had been the captain of the Wilson Guards when Wyatt and Baylor joined, and had become Baylor's business partner in September 1866, was elected county treasurer.[36]

Longworth tried but failed to reject some of the votes cast in June 1866 "from some little irregularity." His vindication came during 1867, when Congress passed the Reconstruction Acts. Ten southern states were put in five military districts, each to be administered by a general who could remove officials deemed to be impediments to Reconstruction as defined by the Republican-led Congress. When Maj. Gen. Philip H. Sheridan took charge of the Fifth Military District, which included Texas, the impact was immediate. Chief Justice Baylor reported to Throckmorton in May 1867 that more than a dozen Wilson County offices were vacant, in part due to Sheridan's ban on elections. That summer, Sheridan replaced Throckmorton with Elisha M. Pease, while Maj. Gen. Charles Griffin, the commander of the Department of Texas, and his successor, Maj. Gen. Joseph J. Reynolds, replaced more than 400 Texas officials with Unionists and Republicans. The requiring of a test oath adopted by Congress led to more dismissals because officeholders had to swear that they had never supported the rebellion. Many could not do this and were replaced in April 1869 by Maj. Gen. Edward R. S. Canby, who succeeded Reynolds after he was promoted to command the district.[37]

The removal of conservative Democrats by the military, together with the requirement that voters also sign the test oath, allowed the Republican Party to take charge in Texas. Longworth did not wait long to capitalize on this. He sent a "list of officials to be decapitated" to Joseph Spence in August 1867. Baylor, Bird, and Lilly in Sutherland Springs were among his targets, and Longworth asked that he succeed Baylor. He warned that the contest between the conservatives and Unionists would become a "life or death grapple, and unless we make it war to the knife we will be defeated, certain." This request was apparently given to Pease, who also received a letter from Baylor and Bird asking him not to be deceived by "evil or zealous minded persons" into removing officials who were "competent and worthy." But Baylor went too far. He wrote to Griffin, asking what to do about vacant county offices. Sheridan still barred elections, while some who had temporarily filled posts, such as Jack Sutherland as county clerk, had been disqualified as ex-Confederates. Incensed, Griffin agreed with Pease that trouble makers such as Baylor had to go. Almost every Wilson County official was replaced in accordance with Longworth's suggestions during the fall of 1867. Apparently only Claiborne Rector, who was elected as a justice of the peace in February of that year, survived the purge. Longworth took Baylor's place as chief justice. He resigned that post in 1868, shortly before it was abolished statewide, but in 1869 he got appointments as county clerk and justice of the peace for Sutherland Springs, which made him the chair of the new county board under the Constitution of 1869. Elected as district clerk in December 1869 and December 1870, he also became the county surveyor in January 1871. For much of the time that he held these offices, according to his own reports, he dominated Wilson County.[38]

Longworth had his fill of Sutherland Springs and as the chief justice could settle the county seat issue to suit himself. In December 1867 he validated the result of an election that designated a site south of Sutherland Springs as the seat, to be called Floresville. He thus took legal advantage of the 1860 legislation that created Wilson County, which mandated that the county seat should be near its geographical center. The commissioners had discussed relocation, and Sutherland lobbied for his town, but they made no decision. Allegedly Longworth in 1867 asked Lilly to pay him $250 not to move the court from Creed Taylor's concrete building, where it had met since 1860, but Lilly refused. Longworth arranged to have the county records hauled to Lodi, just south of Sutherland Springs on the Goliad Road. Older than Sutherland's town, Lodi had never flourished, and it later disappeared. Nevertheless, Longworth settled in rented rooms there until permanent quarters could be built at Floresville.[39]

Reshaping the Texas electorate was a key part of the Republican reform push. Longworth not only removed the county seat from

Sutherland Springs, he ensured that the list of voters little resembled the group that approved secession in 1861. Under his supervision, 407 voters registered in Wilson County. Of these, almost one fourth (98) were blacks registering for the first time, while one fourth (75) of the white voters were from Mexico. Nearly one third (130), black and white alike, had come to the area since 1865. While only four newcomers came from the North, and just five were Union veterans (two of whom were Mexican), clearly Longworth hoped to displace the antebellum leaders, few of whom registered. Of these, William D. Mayes and Daniel Bird were perhaps the best known, while Walker Baylor signed the list but was removed. Interestingly, in Guadalupe County, where Longworth had no authority, Confederate veterans Joseph B., Abner H., and Joseph E. Polley registered to vote. Longworth's efforts closely reflected the statewide result for Texas as almost all eligible blacks but only half of potential whites registered to vote. Many whites then boycotted the election for delegates to another constitutional convention, while 89 percent of black voters cast ballots. Wilson County elected no delegate. Longworth wrote that those who refused to vote did so "out of pure hatred to the Government and laws of the country." He boasted to Secretary of State D. W. C. Phillips in April 1868 that in future elections, "Wilson County is safe for Congress and the constitution, should I have the managing as I had last time." Edmund J. Davis, leader of the Radical Republicans, won the subsequent governor's race, which many whites again boycotted while his own party members quarreled among themselves. He thus took office with only a narrow majority and many enemies, including influential Republicans.[40]

Davis soon ran afoul of Longworth. Before Pease left office as governor, Longworth asked him for support in the post-convention election. Infuriated at being ignored, Longworth wrote, "I can do as well without the Republican party as the party can without me." He added nastily, "Of all the Radicals in all the counties in the states I have the smallest party to back me in the County—Collectively the party have not a spoonful of brains. With me out of the way it would be a walk over [for the Democrats]." His tone did not improve by August 1869, when he wrote to James P. Newcomb, a leading Republican, that he alone kept the party alive in his county. In January 1870, Longworth wrote to Davis, "I am worth something, and should be upheld ... If I am allowed to be snuffed out away goes the county. I am the Republican party, in the county." Davis in fact decided to find out exactly what was happening in Wilson County. Longworth asked the Army officer sent to investigate him to tell him the result, and he triumphantly forwarded the officer's report to Davis with a mocking letter that crowed, "You will easily perceive by the tone of it that I am unsullied in reputation, and as bright as your hopes and wishes could well desire." Longworth added again that he needed Davis's "active interference" to be retained in office so that he could "maintain the party" and win the elections as he had done previously.[41]

After another blast at Davis, Longworth settled for the office of district clerk in 1870, a banner year for the Republicans in Texas as they dominated the legislature and Congress formally readmitted the state to the Union, thus ending the military phase of Reconstruction. That summer, Davis signed a hotly debated bill creating a State Guard. Andrew McClung mustered Company D of the Seventh Regiment at Sutherland Springs in November. In it were Confederate veterans such as William T. Sutherland, Telemachus S. Wyatt, and John S. Craighead, and familiar family names such as Dial, Bird, and Wiseman. They were intended to work with the State Police, also created during the summer of 1870. The police company organized in Wilson County during October 1870 included among its members McClung and Fourth Texas Infantry veteran Haywood W. Brahan. Denounced for corruption elsewhere, the Guard and Police in Wilson County helped maintain security—a member of McClung's Guards arrested "Doughboy" Taylor in April 1871 during the Sutton-Taylor Feud—and actually became a factor in the unseating of Longworth, although they could not keep the county seat from moving away from Sutherland Springs.[42]

Longworth's decline began in 1871. Sutherland Springs became the county seat again after an election held in response to a petition signed by forty men, including Joseph B. Polley, Jack and William T. Sutherland, and Walker Baylor. After the commissioner's court refused to meet there, however, the seat was moved back to Lodi. In October, Longworth complained about the recent election, even though he got all but one of the votes cast for chief justice. He may have resented serving on the election board with James L. Dial, whom he had earlier arrested, and William T. Sutherland, the Confederate veteran whose father, John Sutherland, had defied him. More important, leniency in barring ex-Confederates meant that many more like William T. Sutherland voted. Wilson County Democrats reorganized at a barbecue in Sutherland Springs in September 1871, and black voters began to disappear. Six years later, the Sutherland Springs *Western Chronicle* quietly noted that local blacks had learned not to vote for Republicans. In November 1872, Longworth as registrar refused to register many voters but lost the district clerk race to Andrew G. Pickett and that for surveyor to William T. Sutherland. At the same time, Democrat Ashley N. Denton, a former Confederate surgeon who had recently moved from Sutherland Springs to San Antonio, was elected to represent Wilson County in the legislature. Longworth protested his losses, recalling that when the electoral judges asked for the keys to the courthouse in Floresville, which had become the county seat, he did not surrender them. The judges conducted an election in Lodi, guarded by State Police, but Longworth insisted the 1869 Constitution required polls to be in the county seat, even if, as the sheriff testified, Floresville was "almost as much a place of the imagination as of reality." Matters became stranger when Dial repudiated his signature on a petition that asserted the legality of the election, declaring that he was drunk when he signed it. Despite the chaos, Davis accepted the election results and Longworth was out. By 1874, he had left the area.[43]

Longworth was gone, but Sutherland Springs had lost, too. When Chief Justice Wyatt in the fall of 1866 had raised the issue of a permanent county seat, John Sutherland pushed hard for his town. Instead, the site that would become Floresville won in a special election held in January 1867 and again in 1871. A courthouse was completed in time for Longworth to lock the electoral judges out in the fall of 1872, and in 1873 it officially became the seat of government for Wilson County. The next year, when Wilson County was enlarged by adding the portion of Guadalupe County that included the Polley estate, rumors flew of another election concerning the county seat. In 1883, when plans were laid to construct a more substantial courthouse in Floresville, about 200 people signed a petition demanding that it be constructed in Sutherland Springs, but once more they lost an election. Pickett, the former resident of Sutherland Springs, began holding court as county judge in a newly constructed brick courthouse at Floresville in 1885. With him was county clerk Lemuel P. Hughes, who had lost his arm while leading the Mustang Grays of Sutherland Springs at Antietam. The San Antonio and Aransas Pass Railway reached Floresville a few years later, assuring its economic ascendancy as well.[44]

The political bitterness engendered by the Civil War and Reconstruction lingered for many years in Sutherland Springs. Editor August Siemering of the *San Antonio Express,* a Republican, noted that a “Specimen Democrat” had been appointed postmaster for the tiny community by late 1874. He referred to Fourth Texas veteran Joseph B. Polley, who had personally taken the disputed election results to Davis in 1872. The hostility was mutual. When Siemering asked Polley about the whereabouts of a former judge, presumably Longworth, the postmaster responded that he was probably in the state penitentiary, “the same as that of hundreds of his radical friends.” Siemering, in reporting the incident, opined that Polley should be in the state prison, adding, “He may be an escaped convict, for aught we know.” Not to be outdone, a Democratic editor in Austin printed his own version of the exchange, expanding Polley’s comments to include the remark that Longworth in the state prison was “for the first time … doing his county good and proper service.”[45]

Reconstruction ended with Sutherland Springs stripped of its prominence as a county seat and local farmers and businessmen still struggling to recover from the disruption of the Civil War. Recovery was hindered as well by the deaths of the two original founders of the community, John Sutherland and Joseph H. Polley, the impact of which was enhanced by the loss of many young men in the conflict, as well as the fact that many more survived but suffered crippling injuries. Emancipation and the racial tensions it engendered further complicated the situation. Numerous Texas towns did not survive the turmoil, especially communities that relied entirely on agriculture for their prosperity. But Sutherland Springs was not one of those places, because while economic and political affairs fell into disarray, mineral-laced waters continued to flow from the banks of Cibolo Creek. As long as that was true, there was always the possibility of a better future for the community.

3

Another Start Uphill

Susan J. Pickett wrote in 1860, when Wilson County was created, that if the county seat was not located permanently at Sutherland Springs, "I believe after a year or two this place will be only known as having once had an existence." In truth, the population grew substantially in spite of losing its status as a county seat during Reconstruction, which effectively ended by 1874 in Texas. Local leaders also invested in economic expansion, especially after railroads were built into the area. Pickett actually enjoyed a lively business after the Civil War, boarding "judges, lawyers & jurors" when the courts met in Sutherland Springs, as well as sick people who came to town to partake of the mineral springs. By 1870 she reported that her growing community was "settling up quite rapidly." A new school and church were almost completed, while the number of residences being constructed indicated "considerable progress." By 1877, the editor of the newly established *Western Chronicle,* a weekly newspaper in Sutherland Springs, declared that he was pleased to see his town "taking another start up hill." Despite Pickett's glum prediction, the town survived not only as a farming community but also as a locally popular resort, focusing on the springs that flowed from the banks of Cibolo Creek. Unfortunately for local leaders, funding proved insufficient to support more ambitious plans until after the turn of the century.[1]

Sutherland Springs by 1871 had an economically diverse populace that was significantly larger than what it had been ten years earlier. In 1860, thirteen people had paid taxes on town lots, while John Sutherland and Columbus M. Reese were assessed for parts of the old Treviño grant. By 1865 the number of lot owners apparently had declined to seven, while Sutherland had deeded parts of the Treviño property to three of his sons. William A. Waugh, an itinerant cattle rancher who eventually settled in South Texas, replaced Reese as the taxpayer for the remainder. Six years later, in 1871, thirty people were assessed for town lots, of whom all but three listed Sutherland Springs as their post office. Eight people paid taxes on portions of the Treviño tract, one of whom was Jack Sutherland, the veteran of the Fourth Texas Infantry and a son of John Sutherland. There were many other familiar names as well. Andrew G. Pickett (who owned 83.5 lots and part of the Treviño grant) was the local magistrate, while Walker K. Baylor was the postmaster. John W. Lilly (who owned or served as agent for 30 lots) sold groceries, as did James W. Anderson. Joseph B. Polley (who along with his relatives owned or managed 69.5 lots) was the resident attorney, while Ashley N. Denton was the sole doctor. Jack Sutherland, who had sold much of his father's land to Lilly, Pickett, and several Polley family members but retained ownership of a substantial estate, had two competitors as a carpenter (one white, one black), while a gunsmith, stonemason, wagon maker, and wheelwright also lived in town.[2]

If Sutherland Springs was going to continue growing, it needed an economic boost. Just as before the Civil War, cattle became a primary source of substantial profit for many residents, although the methods for marketing substantially changed. The Polleys during the late 1860s branded thousands of calves for which they needed a market. Abilene, Kansas, was built about that time as a depot for the

Kansas Pacific Railroad and became the focus of tremendous growth when about 1.5 million Texas cattle arrived between 1865 and 1873. Abner H. "Hub" Polley in 1866 led a thousand head up the Sedalia Trail to Missouri. He traveled the Chisholm Trail to Abilene and then Dodge City in successive years and bought more farmland in Wilson County, though he married Belle Beverly in 1870 and settled briefly in nearby Karnes County. Cattle drives from Texas began to decline after 1873, when railroads reached the state and quarantines excluded longhorns from markets due to a fear of Texas Fever ticks, but Hub persisted through the end of the 1870s with the help of his brother Walter, as did many of their neighbors. Several times bad prices and other obstacles forced Hub to attempt other businesses, such as operating a store or working as a stock driver for other ranchers, but he returned to cattle and Sutherland Springs, where many of his neighbors also raised livestock.[3]

Cattle remained a principal source of income for Sutherland Springs even as cotton production recovered statewide after the Civil War. A newspaper correspondent writing under the pseudonym of "Saxet" noted that fluctuating prices in cotton and corn pushed local farmers to continue to invest in livestock, especially improved breeds of cattle. By the late 1870s, cattle and horses began to be surpassed by hogs as the primary livestock being raised for sale. At the same time, farmers diversified their crops on farms around Sutherland Springs, growing corn, potatoes (Irish and sweet), sorghum, and grains such as wheat, rye, and oats. Apparently much of this production came from new settlers who bought small tracts carved from the large early grants. Cotton became such a popular commodity that men such as Joseph B. Polley, who had pressed for introducing new breeds of cattle, invested in steam plants that could grind grain, gin cotton, and saw lumber. His mill began operating in 1873. Just three years later, perhaps after Polley decided to focus more on his law practice, brothers David and Anton Oppenheimer, Bavarian-born Confederate veterans from San Antonio, built a mill for grinding grain, ginning cotton, and sawing lumber in

Sutherland Springs. They in turn were succeeded in 1878 by Alfred Griffin, whose improvements for that fall were announced in an article in the *Western Chronicle* that told the readers to "listen for the whistle!" This activity, coupled with that of other businesses in town, prompted another newspaper writer to declare that "Sutherland Springs is getting to be quite a village."[4]

John Sutherland's daughter Sarah wrote in 1869: "We have no preaching now nor school. I fear the children will grow like heathens." She was not wrong about lacking a church. Thomas T. Leach served the Sutherland Springs circuit during the last years of the Civil War, when the membership reached 109 whites and 21 blacks. After he moved to another post, he rocked the West Texas Conference with his avowal of Republican ideals, which led to his suspension in 1868. When he declared his intention to ally with the northern Methodist Church in 1869, his suspension became permanent. He returned to Sutherland Springs and joined Longworth on the Wilson County election board, but he was rejected in his efforts to become a "fraternal delegate" from his new church to his old conference. The Methodist Church membership in Sutherland Springs had declined to twenty-five whites and twenty-five blacks by 1867, when a teacher read the service at Sutherland's funeral because there was no minister. While it recovered to 283 white and 19 black members by 1875, when Washington Goodwin served as minister, it was abolished the next year in favor of a new circuit centered on Floresville, the county seat. Sutherland's son, Alexander, became a Methodist minister, but he worked in circuits along the Texas coast and Rio Grande. Itinerant pastors from the Episcopal, Cumberland Presbyterian, and Southern Methodist organizations did hold services in Sutherland Springs, and revivals co-sponsored by the latter two denominations were often held during the summer on Cibolo Creek outside of town, but apparently no established churches survived more than a few years during the first few decades after the Civil War. The Amateur Dramatic Association produced a show in Sutherland Springs, with the proceeds to be spent on erecting an Episcopal church so that the congregation did not have to continue meeting in the old rock building, but this did not prove successful.[5]

Sarah was less correct about schools. According to the 1870 census, two teachers tended thirty-one children in Sutherland Springs. All of these were white; the Freedmen's Bureau never had a school for blacks in the town. When a public school was founded in Wilson County under the 1869 constitution, it opened at Lodi. The Democratic majority that took control of the Texas legislature in 1872 dismantled the Republican public school system, giving the responsibility for education to local boards. This was confirmed by the state constitution adopted in 1876; as a result, public education remained poorly funded and segregated in much of Texas well into the 1900s. In Sutherland Springs, trustees for the Cibolo Hall and Female Academy purchased a lot from Joseph B. Polley in 1871. This may have been the high school for which Edward R. Tarver served as the principal in 1872. Tarver had left the Eighth Texas Cavalry to join the staff of his brother-in-law, Brig. Gen. Hamilton P. Bee, during the war, and fled to Mexico after the war, but he later settled briefly in Sutherland Springs and married Joseph B. Polley's sister-in-law, Julia C. Legette. In January 1877 the Male and Female School opened in the small rock building used before the war. It was operated by W. B. Cross, an ardent Democrat who prospered as a teacher and moved the following semester into a concrete structure that had previously been used as a store. His former location was occupied by Stephen G. Burton, a graduate of Indiana University and former Episcopal deacon who established the Sutherland Springs Academy. By 1885, when Sutherland Springs had been assigned to the ninth school district in Wilson County, there was a school for whites directed by Fleetwood White and a school for blacks taught by Sarah Wilson.[6]

A growing town needed a newspaper, and in January 1877 the *Western Chronicle* first appeared in Sutherland Springs. Its proprietor was James W. Anderson, the grocer who described himself as a "Texas Cowboy" who "laid down the lariat for the pen." Tarver, who had opened a law office in Floresville and only came to Sutherland Springs twice a week, served as the first editor. It proved to be an important year for the community, with much for Tarver to report. The Galveston, Harrisburg, and San Antonio Railway reached San Antonio in 1877, bringing a flood of freight traffic into the surrounding region. The rails passed north of Sutherland Springs, but Tarver noted its impact by announcing that his community was "taking another start up hill." Six months before, hardly one wagon had passed through along the stage roads for San Antonio. Now he reported that freight shipments were becoming heavier each day. As many as thirteen wagons drawn by ten mules apiece came through in convoys several times daily. Regular stage service to San Antonio began again. Other new businesses opened as well. Walker Baylor, who had been succeeded by Joseph B. Polley as postmaster in 1874, began selling groceries, as did Jack Sutherland. While Tarver stepped down after just one year as editor and was succeeded by John W. Callahan of Navasota, Anderson continued as the owner of the newspaper while also operating his store. Lilly's grocery remained open as well, indicating that trade in Sutherland Springs may have doubled in 1877.[7]

The railroad's arrival increased the flow of visitors to the springs on Cibolo Creek, which had provided a steady but not substantial amount of revenue to the community since the end of the war. Correspondents such as "Saxet" helped to advertise the waters, which were described as containing twenty different minerals that could cure a wide variety of ailments. Saxet insisted that at Sutherland Springs the "finest body of mineral waters in the world bubble up from dozens of springs that nestle here and there under the tall boughs of stately oaks and the drooping foliage of weeping willows." These waters, he or she added, had already accomplished "astonishing cures." In another letter, readers were told that there were two sulfur springs, one of which fed a pool "twelve feet square," flowing at a rate of 300 gallons per minute with a temperature of 45 degrees. Those who were not interested in bathing or drinking these chilly waters were informed that the hunting for deer, turkeys, quail, ducks, and passenger pigeons in the area was very good, too, depending on the season. As for nighttime entertainment,

Saxet reported in May 1874 that a ball and midnight supper had been hosted by James A. Sharpless, the proprietor of a local hotel, with music provided by "Prof. Docedo's band." Presumably the bandleader was Harry Doisedo, a black farmer noted for his fine fiddle playing who lived in Doisedo Colony (named for him) near Sutherland Springs. Three years later a writer for the *Western Chronicle* of Sutherland Springs reported that Doisedo was skillfully directing the band in "Bailey's Hall," where a sign over the door to the ladies' dressing room read "Be merry while you stay."[8]

Saxet assured his readers that efforts were being made to increase accommodations for lodgers, who at that time often stayed in tents due to limited facilities in town. Several people opened their homes to boarders, including Susan J. Pickett and Joseph H. Polley's widow, Mary. Her son Walter still raised cattle and regularly trailed them to Kansas, and his brother Abner or "Hub" joined him in this work, but Mary supplemented that income by operating Whitehall as a boarding house. She did not advertise, but word-of-mouth brought many visitors, often filling her home to overflowing, with some sleeping on pallets laid on the floor. She of course fed her guests and for an extra fee would have them conveyed to the springs. Sometimes she hosted a dance or other social event. It was reminiscent of her many years in Austin's Colony, when she and her late husband boarded guests at their home. An enthusiastic niece gushed in 1877, "I think that soon Sutherland Springs will be a bigger resort than Lampasas." Most of the visitors came from Texas towns. Among the most prominent was Maj. Gen. Edward O. C. Ord, who came with his family in November 1877. As an Army officer in Texas before the Civil War, Ord had served with Robert E. Lee and John Bell Hood, under whom the Mustang Grays, including Joseph B. Polley, fought in the Civil War. When he came to Sutherland Springs in 1877, he was serving as the commander of the Department of Texas.[9]

In town, the most popular establishment was the Hygeia House, which apparently was built before the war and later purchased by Daniel B. Messinger, a pharmacist and sometime doctor who had attended the University of Michigan. One traveler remembered the place as a "long, low, rambling old house 'under the hill,'" but Messinger constructed a two-story addition to accommodate more visitors, for whom he also provided transport to the springs on the far side of the Cibolo. Unlike the Polleys, he advertised in Galveston newspapers, assuring travelers that they would find "Superior Sour, Iron, Seltzer, and Sulphur Springs" near his place. He declared that ladies would especially enjoy the "cool sparkling waters of the White Sulphur beautifying the skin in color and velvety smoothness." He hosted frequent public events, including a "grand masquerade ball" on Christmas Eve in 1877, welcoming locals and visitors alike. Mail stages left San Antonio for his place three times a week, stayed overnight, then returned to San Antonio. Advertisements in Galveston newspapers informed passengers that they could get a return ticket for half price if they paid a round trip fare, and of course access to the springs was always free. A rival, Peyton T. Warren, opened the Sutherland Springs Hotel nearby and later served as a justice of the peace. Messinger probably did not worry; a Galveston newspaper in the summer of 1877 noted that all of the hotels in Sutherland Springs were filled with visitors who came to enjoy the "rock walled spring there under the willows, in whose clear sparkling waters health lies hidden despite the suggestive odor."[10]

Sutherland Springs residents responded to the growing interest in the springs by opening new businesses and refurbishing old ones that catered to the visitors. Stage lines to San Antonio and the coast were supplemented by hack companies and coaches outfitted to transport travelers in greater comfort. W. H. Lillie, who ran a grain mill in town, bottled ten varieties of local water for sale, including black and white sulfur. Those who wanted to drink something stronger got alcohol despite the imposition of prohibition in Sutherland Springs under enabling laws passed by the legislature in 1876. An anonymous letter in the *Western Chronicle* in 1877 crowed that the last "grocery" in town, which was a common source of liquor in Texas before and after the Civil War, had closed three years earlier, thereby eliminating the "drunken, odiferous, beastly negroes and ... whites" that filled the streets. He may have been referring to John W. Lilly, who had a license to sell liquor "by the Quart" in 1874. However, in 1877 Baylor advertised genuine lager from St. Louis, Sutherland sold a selection of wines, and F. M. Bailey offered whiskey and billiards. Tarver as the editor of the *Western Chronicle* wrote that same year, "We may not be a judge of mean whiskey, but we do profess to know a good article, and after testing the old Bourbon kept for medical purposes in the drug store of Doctor Messinger, we unhesitatingly pronounce it a fine article." Messinger advertised that he sold a "Carefully Selected Stock of Drugs, Medicines, Pure Wines and Liquors, for Medical Use." Temperance advocates, mostly women, met every Saturday night, but apparently they had little effect. Some ambitious women founded a literary society and tried to build an opera house and organize a brass band, intending perhaps to provide alternative entertainments, but there is no evidence that they succeeded.[11]

Sutherland Springs did offer other less refined diversions for the "throngs" of people that visited. Horse races were staged every Saturday. As early as 1874 the community boasted a "Stonewall Jackson Base Ball Club," which proved good enough to play in tournaments at San Antonio. Baseball of course became a national obsession and teams of grown men played at Sutherland Springs through World War I, but a peculiarly Southern sport that did not survive the nineteenth century also briefly flourished in the community. A ring tournament, in which teams of mounted men competed against each other for honors, was first held at Sutherland Springs in September 1876, with fourteen "knights" from the local area. The next summer, the "Knights" of Atascosa and Wilson counties met for another tournament, with the men from Atascosa County emerging as the victors. Sutherland Springs thus became the "unwilling grave yard of Wilson County's chivalric hopes." Eleven competitors from Wilson County and eight from Atascosa each made three runs on horseback at five rings, so a perfect score was fifteen rings snared on a lance. Albert Marion Turner, the "Knight of Wichita" from Atascosa, competed in goggles due to "sore eyes" but snared fourteen rings, the most of any competitor. He thus got the honor of crowning the "Queen of Love and Beauty." The day ended with a grand ball at which "the ladies were as fair and numberless as the wild flowers that grow on the banks of the lovely stream that beautifies and adds wealth to the town with its waters and springs." Allegedly a similar contest was staged with black competitors in nearby Doisedo that year, and the following year separate contests for both races were held at Sutherland Springs.[12]

As Sutherland Springs approached the end of its third decade as a community, there was much reason for optimism. The census taker in 1880 recorded that about one hundred people lived on the town site, while the tax collector noted that many more families lived on the old Treviño grant that surrounded it. Peyton T. Warren served as justice of the peace, while Zadok Brooks was the postmaster and also managed the Messinger Hotel. Brooks had been an early follower of Joseph Smith but apparently quit the Latter Day Saints over the issue of polygamy; since he was also later both a Baptist and Church of Christ minister, he may have led services for his neighbors in Sutherland Springs. His son Charles was a blacksmith, as was Absalom Reese. There were two carpenters, Jack Wilson and Josiah D. Brooks, black and white respectively. Lilly continued to operate a store, but Anderson listed himself as "retired," as did Baylor, who was Brooks's brother-in-law since both had married daughters of Joseph H. Polley. John D. Murray made saddles and Alfred Griffin had a grist mill and cotton gin. Erstwhile newspaper editor Tarver advertised himself as an attorney, while there were two doctors: Benjamin Francis and G. M. Devereux, who signed the by-laws of the revived Texas Medical Association in 1869. Devereux boarded with Warren, so he was perhaps only visiting from his home in Houston when the census taker found him in Sutherland Springs. Interestingly, Wilson was not the only black resident in 1880: John Sheppard worked as a herder to support a household of seven people, and Nat Henderson, a farmer with a family of three, paid taxes on two acres of the Treviño grant. Both Wilson and Henderson had been slaves owned by John D. Wyatt prior to emancipation.[13]

3.1 Ashley N. Denton. Courtesy of Denton (TX) Public Library

3.2 Abner H. "Hub" Polley (front row, second from left) as member of grand jury. COURTESY OF WILSON COUNTY (TX) HISTORICAL SOCIETY

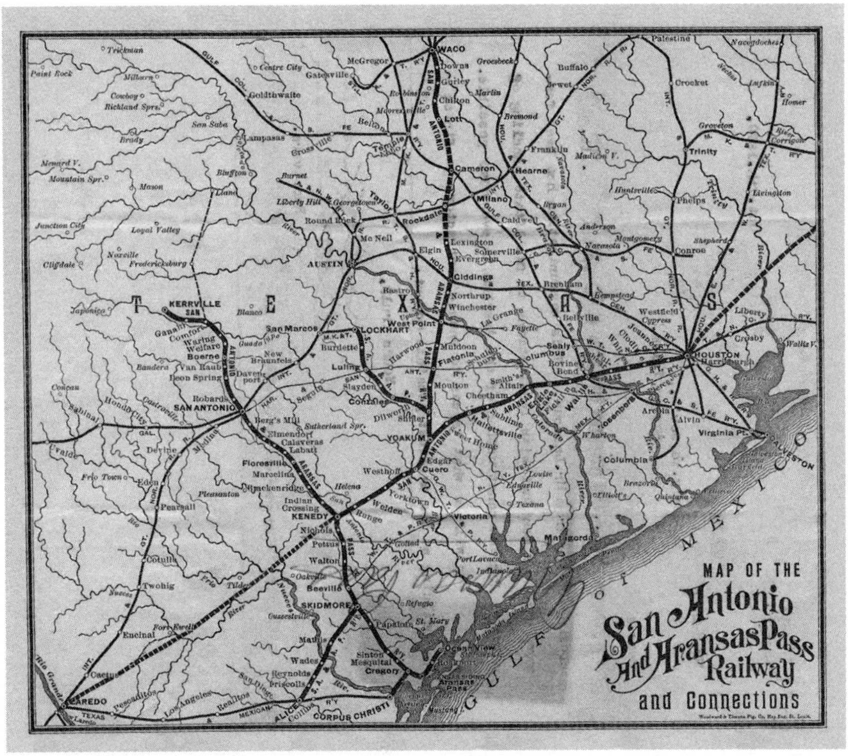

3.3 Woodward & Tiernan Printing Co., *Map of the San Antonio and Aransas Pass Railway and Connections* (St. Louis, 1890). Courtesy of University of Texas at Arlington Library

3.4 Walter W. and Ada Wyatt Polley. Courtesy of Diane Perry

3.5 Swimming in Cibolo Creek. COURTESY OF ELIZABETH LESTER

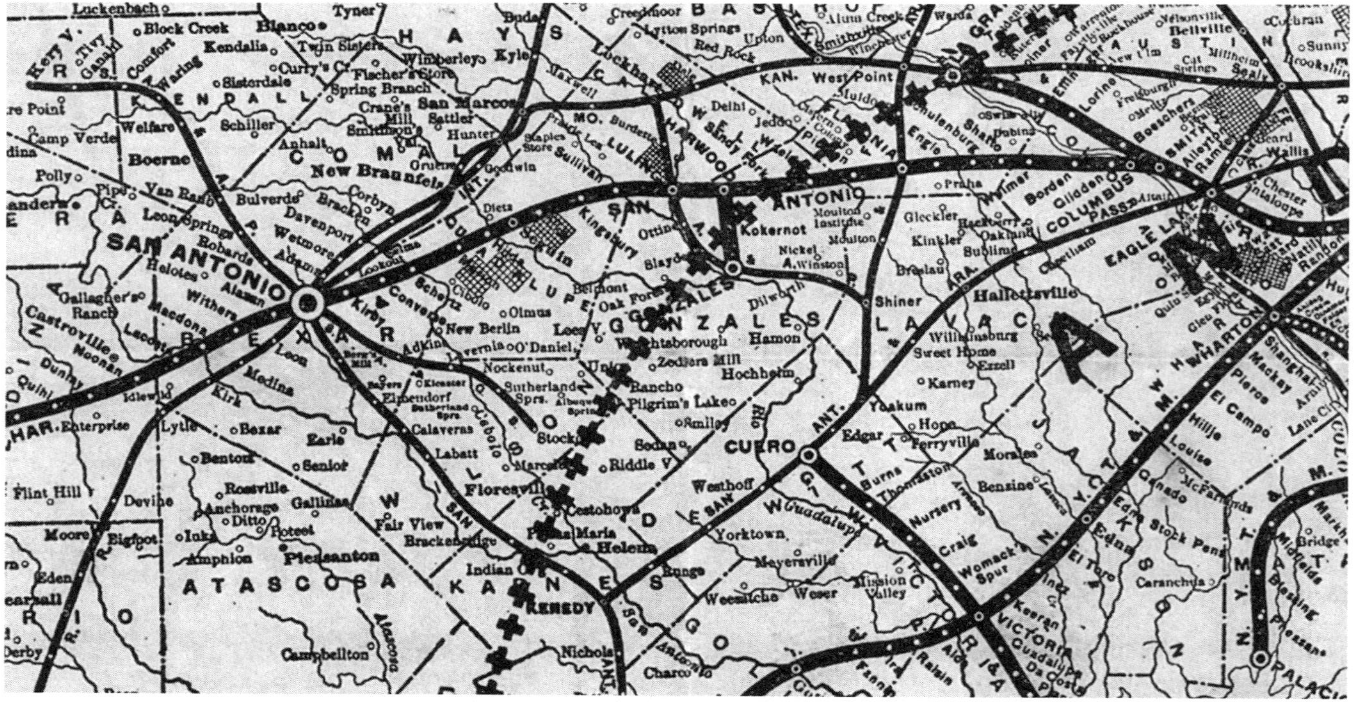

3.6 Excerpt from Southern Pacific Company, *Correct Map of Texas* (Chicago, 1903). Courtesy of University of Texas at Arlington Library

3.7 Diving in Cibolo Creek. Courtesy of Elizabeth Lester

3.8 Iron Pony Truss Bridge over Cibolo Creek. Courtesy of Elizabeth Lester

3.9 William L. Wright. Courtesy of Wilson County (TX) Historical Society

Despite its economic revival, an unkind writer for the *San Antonio Express* in 1877 declared that the community of Sutherland Springs remained "uninviting in appearance." What made it an "important place," he or she explained, was the mineral water. Some claimed there were more than one hundred springs still flowing within two miles of the town center. Warm and cold chalybeate (or iron) springs were good for drinking, as were seltzer and soda waters. The most popular for bathing were the black and white sulfur springs on the far side of the Cibolo from Sutherland Springs. A Galveston writer reported that "on crossing the Cibolo, upon whose banks the town is built, the olfactories [*sic*] are assailed by an unsavory smell from an immense black sulphur spring, ten feet in diameter, boiling up with gas, like a huge cauldron; and, to add to his surprise, he finds, upon jumping into this tempting bath, that the human body floats around, and is tossed about like a cork, and the astonishment is still more increased when he finds that to sink beneath the water is an impossibility." This experience was reserved for men. About a hundred yards away, and open to both genders, was the "beautiful White Sulphur, ten feet in diameter, four feet in depth, and discharging two or three hundred gallons of water per minute, as clear as crystal and as cold as ice." Some estimated the flow of each spring to be 500 gallons per minute. One visitor praised both pools, writing that each one left "a glow after bathing," but another was more truthful, declaring that the stench of the black sulfur water "forcibly reminds one of all the defunct embryo chicks in the infernal regions." Live oaks, elm, and pecan trees grew over each pool, providing some protection from the summer sun if not from the pervasive smell.[14]

Sutherland Springs' promoters stressed the health benefits of their water. Several types were colorfully described in an 1878 travelers' guide as "tonic, diuretic, cathartic, alterative and antibilious." The writer promised that the waters could help anyone who suffered from "dropsy, liver complaint, dyspepsia, consumption and all diseases of the kidneys." These claims must have referred to the waters that people drank, such as seltzer, chalybeate (or iron), "aperient" (or laxative), and soda (sour), but both the "white and black sulphur waters" could "give a delicate smoothness and a rich glow of health to the skin" for all who bathed in them. A popular history of Texas published in 1879 was more reserved, but even that writer agreed that the waters were "of good quality, and much resorted to by invalids." Many of the latter came to the springs to seek relief from arthritis and rheumatism, and they believed that they found it. The promoters' efforts were aided by the endorsement of at least part of the medical community. The American Medical Association published an extensive study of medicinal springs in the United States in 1880, but it stopped short of endorsing them. For Sutherland Springs, this was improved upon in 1884 when a doctor spoke to a meeting of the Texas Medical Association, urging them to use the medicinal springs in Texas. The American Climatological Society, organized that same year, issued a nationwide report in 1885 that stressed the healing powers of mineral waters, especially for those who suffered from tuberculosis and many other respiratory ailments. Joseph B. Polley, hired as a promoter for Wilson County in 1888, wrote a pamphlet that capitalized upon the other reports by praising the medical value of the waters in his community as well as its popularity as a resort. Eleven years earlier, in 1877, he had published an article in the *Western Chronicle* that claimed the local springs were "especially adapted to the cure of chronic female diseases."[15]

At least one visitor extolled the virtues of the "pure atmosphere" at Sutherland Springs as well as the medical waters found there. Gulnare H. Garrison, whose husband James B. Garrison was a doctor, included the community in her laudatory study of resorts in southwestern Texas published in the *Medical and Surgical Reporter* in 1881. Both she and others, many of whom had been advised by her husband to take the waters, had been cured of their various maladies at Sutherland Springs, and she insisted to readers that they would not need a hotel room. Because the air was so "health-giving," she explained, "A village of canvas will spring up, as if by magic, in the night." There invalids could sleep under the stars comfortably and with a great sense of security, "feeling that each day and night so spent gives a new lease of life."[16]

Despite the glowing endorsement of the existing facilities from visitors such as Garrison, the arrival of the railroad in San Antonio and the influx of new faces did prompt discussions of improvements at the springs themselves. Gideon Lee Jr. still owned the property but had made few changes. The small cabins built before the Civil War by his associate, Joseph F. Johnson, had collapsed by the 1870s, but renewed interest inspired Lee. He visited from his New York home several times and planned a "Resort City of the South." He negotiated with a Galveston company for capital to improve the springs, construct a bridge across the Cibolo, and build some bathhouses, but they wanted to buy the site. Several contemporary sources indicate that he did talk with these investors about selling 600 acres for the construction of a hotel, but that deal was never made. The residents continued to maintain the pools, keeping the springs and the trails to them open, laying pine boards across the bottom to use as seats, and erecting an arbor to screen the black sulfur pool.[17]

Before additional efforts could be made to raise money for substantial improvements, many businessmen moved away from Sutherland Springs, often settling in nearby Floresville. Joseph B. Polley moved in the late 1870s, and others followed after a conflict erupted one last time in 1883 over moving the county seat from Floresville to Sutherland Springs. County Judge Andrew G. Pickett ordered a referendum held to resolve the issue on July 9, 1883. Once again Floresville won in an election noted for a strong turnout, prompting Sutherland Springs residents to protest futilely while the construction of a new brick courthouse got underway at the county seat. Apparently amused, a writer for the San Antonio *Light* quipped, "We think if the citizens of Sutherland Springs and vicinity would rouse from their Rip Van Winkle slumbers that they would find that it is not absolutely necessary to have a court house and jail in order to make their town improve." He added that they had the materials to grow and make money if they would put their energy into those enterprises and not allow the removal of the county seat to settle upon them a "black pall of a disappointed hope and a crushed ambition." As a good example of what could be accomplished, the commentator mentioned J. S. Cox, who had relocated his grist mill and cotton gin to Sutherland Springs. The editor added that building another hotel would be a good idea.[18]

Cox was not the only new businessman in Sutherland Springs in 1883 because the town was rapidly changing. Saddler John D. Murray and black carpenter Jack Wilson remained in Sutherland Springs three years after they had appeared in the 1880 census, but others who were present in 1880 were not included in a Texas business directory published in 1884. Anderson sold the *Western Chronicle* to a Floresville publisher while his former editor, Tarver, moved to Laredo. Among local shop owners, John W. Lilly died in 1883 while Jack Sutherland moved to Floresville, leaving only his younger brother William on the Treviño grant. Zadok Brooks left the Messinger Hotel in 1883 and opened a restaurant in Floresville. His son, William F. Brooks, replaced him as the postmaster in Sutherland Springs, where he also sold pharmaceuticals and groceries with few competitors. John Waddell was a grocer, and newcomer B. E. Plunkett had a butcher shop, but the proprietor of the Messinger Hotel, Daniel B. Messinger, who had also sold pharmaceuticals, died in 1891, leaving Justice of the Peace Peyton T. Warren as the only owner of a hotel. The only blacksmith listed in the 1884 directory was Charles N. Vezey, a son-in-law of Walker Baylor. Two new doctors lived in town, J. R. Harmon and W. C. Carrington, and the 1884 directory also noted that the community still had a school and a church, indicating that it continued to provide important services to local residents.[19]

The 1880s exodus from Sutherland Springs did almost completely erase the last vestiges of the two founding families. John Sutherland's daughter Sarah had written to her niece in 1869: "The old people are falling off[.] Soon the old settlers will all be gorn to their long homes [sic]." Her father had died in 1867, followed by Joseph H. Polley in 1869, only a few months before his own daughter Sarah succumbed to tuberculosis. Among Sutherland's children, Quinn, Levin, and Sarah, all died within a few years of their father. Mary and Alexander moved away. Sarah's son, John S. Craighead, lived near his uncle William for many years and even served as sheriff of Wilson County, but he later died in the Confederate Soldier's Home at Austin. Of the Polleys, Joseph relocated to Floresville, where he served as county attorney and in 1879 became the first person from Wilson County to sit in the legislature since the war. The death of his mother Mary on January 21, 1888, and her will's direction that Whitehall be sold out of the family, displaced her sons Abner (Hub) and Walter. Hub, who had worked in Floresville and Dodge City before returning home to help Walter raise cattle, later lived in San Antonio and received a pension as a Confederate veteran in Comal County. Walter became a guard in the Arizona state prison before settling in Floresville, where he served as a justice of the peace and a deputy county clerk. The proceeds from the sale of Whitehall went to the Polley's daughter Catherine, who in 1875 had been sent to the state asylum for the insane. Two of her three sisters moved away: Susan with her husband Josiah D. Brooks, and Harriet with her husband David H. Houston. Only Mary, the wife of Walker Baylor, stayed with him in Sutherland Springs, where he died in 1891 and she in 1915. Her son by her first marriage, Joseph E. Polley, lived in Sutherland Springs until his death in 1908, but his sister Eleanor married Andrew G. Pickett in 1877 after his wife Susan died, and they settled at Floresville. Joseph H. Polley's youngest son, Jonathan, lived briefly with his sister Susan, but he later worked as an attorney in Floresville.[20]

Sutherland Springs was described in an 1887 newspaper as "a dilapidated village, with probably some dozen or fifteen inhabitants," but it was far from extinct. The San Antonio and Aransas Pass Railway was built through Floresville in 1886, and a stage line continued to bring visitors to the springs. The black and white sulfur pools, fitted for bathers, continued to flow on Lee's property, as did the sour springs and others suitable for drinking. A writer for another paper in 1888 insisted that "a bath in the pure white sulphur, and alternated by a dip in the black sulphur, interluded by a reading from Emerson and a draught from the chalybeate waters, is a pleasure to be envied, even by Oscar Wilde." The 1890 census reported that there were actually 164 residents, and many organizations found Sutherland Springs to be a pleasant place to meet. The Farmer's Alliance sponsored a barbecue there in August 1886 and returned in 1892 for a county-wide rally at which former governor John Ireland spoke. Confederate veterans who lived in Wilson County also gathered at Sutherland Springs for a reunion in 1892. Thousands of people attended a Fourth of July celebration hosted in 1893 by the People's Party, or Populists, which included a dance at the Messinger Hotel. One writer remarked, "The gathering showed the intense earnestness of the populists of this part. They are resolved not to let the cause go back, but are going to roll the old chariot along and not drag on behind." Jerome C. Kearby, the People's Party candidate for governor, attended a Populist camp meeting at Sutherland Springs in July 1896. Two militia units from San Antonio, the Belknap Rifles and San Antonio Zouaves, hosted a picnic and staged an exhibition at Sutherland Springs in 1897, one year before they mustered into the army for the Spanish-American War.[21]

The problem for Sutherland Springs after almost five decades of development efforts remained transportation. A traveler in 1878 noted that even when the dirt roads that led to the town were dry, they were still "rough enough to jolt a chew of tobacco out of your mouth." An iron bridge was completed across the Cibolo in 1892, providing the community with improved access to the springs and facilitating travel, but little effort was made to upgrade the local roads. The solution lay in railroads, and Sutherland Springs' developers worked hard for years to have one built to their town, beginning before the Civil War. The Texas legislature in 1850 issued a charter for the San Antonio and Mexican Gulf Railroad, which was intended to link San Antonio with Port Lavaca on the Texas coast, near the east end of the Chihuahua Road that ran through Sutherland Springs. Among the directors of the company were John James and Gideon Lee Jr. Joseph H. Polley bought stock in the company with the stipulation that the rails would "cross the Cibolo Creek at or above the Sulphur Springs," and Lee sold them a right-of-way across his land. Despite financial support from San Antonio and Bexar County, quarrels led to the completion of only five miles of track from Port Lavaca by the end of 1857. Three years later, the rails reached Victoria, but much was damaged by scavenging Confederates and had to be rebuilt after the war. Reorganization of the firm as the Gulf, Western Texas and Pacific Railway Company facilitated completion to Cuero by 1873, but this was far from Sutherland Springs, Polley had died, and Lee had moved to New York. Businessmen in Sutherland Springs supported proposals to build a narrow-gauge railway to connect Wilson County with Cuero and San Antonio after the railroad reached the latter city in 1877, but this project, if it was ever begun, was never completed.[22]

Rumors flew during the early 1890s that a railroad would be built in or near Sutherland Springs. Lee, who had moved back to San Antonio from New York City, lobbied hard to have the rails cross his property on Cibolo Creek before he died in 1894. By that time, the idea of building a railroad through Sutherland Springs, to connect San Antonio with Galveston, was being promoted by Nelson "Hurricane" Mackey, who had made a fortune in the production and sale of bricks in San Antonio. The proposal quickly gained support. When Populists gathered for the Fourth of July at Sutherland Springs in 1893, speakers mixed political talks with railroad promotions. That same month, William H. Brooker, a San Antonio attorney and prominent member of the United Confederate Veterans, and his business partner William Davis made a reconnaissance of the possible route for the line, stopping to speak in Sutherland Springs and other towns as they traveled. By December, Brooker and Davis secured a charter for the San Antonio and Gulf Shore Railway Company, with Brooker on the board of directors and Davis serving as president of the company.[23]

The San Antonio and Gulf Shore Railway had a troubled history, but its evolution had a positive impact on Sutherland Springs, which from the start was to be an important junction on the proposed line.

One possible obstacle to construction was cleared when it was announced that if the community could not raise the required financial contribution, the company would plat a new town site and sell the lots to raise money. Davis wrote to Judge Pickett in September 1894 that another problem had arisen: the railway would have to cross Lee's tract due to difficulties in acquiring a right of way in Sutherland Springs. The United States Trust Company of New York, as trustees for the Lee estate, sold Davis a right-of-way and a depot site, as well as one hundred acres to serve as a park and four hundred acres to be sold as town lots. The trustees retained a half interest in any profits made from lot sales. Crews began laying tracks on Halloween in 1894 after a ceremony that included remarks by former governor Ireland. By the spring of the next year, when the railway was completed to Sutherland Springs, Ireland had replaced Davis as the president of the company, which had gone into receivership. When the railroad was sold by a court order in July 1896, Oscar Bergstrom bought it for $150,000 as a trustee for the executors of Ireland's estate. Davis believed that Bergstrom acted on behalf of the original directors against him and declared that whoever purchased the railway had bought a lawsuit. He in fact did sue Bergstrom and the company for years. Meanwhile, the firm was sold to the San Antonio and Gulf Railroad, chartered in March 1897 by Bergstrom and his associates for the sole purpose of acquiring the San Antonio and Gulf Shore Railway. They operated until 1905, when they were consolidated with several other small companies by the Galveston, Harrisburg, and San Antonio Railway. This effectively made them part of the Southern Pacific Railroad's popular "Sunset Route," which carried passengers from New Orleans to California.[24]

A variety of factors delayed the impact of finally completing the railroad that connected Sutherland Springs to San Antonio, then the largest city in Texas. The 1890s were the heyday of resort development in Texas, and San Antonio became the premier destination in one of the most popular states for hordes of rail-riding health-seekers. There were a dozen or more communities within a hundred miles of that city competing for business, which may have been another factor that delayed the immediate development of Sutherland Springs. There were too many projects already underway. A second factor was the delay in settling lawsuits concerning the railroad. While trains were the best solution at that time for the problem of "getting there," as Mary B. Polley's grandniece wrote in 1877, there needed to be a destination for the travelers. As the rails approached Sutherland Springs, plans were laid for a new resort community located on the east bank of the Cibolo, but these were abandoned in the legal battles that raged from 1895 to 1905. The San Antonio and Gulf Shore Railway agreed in 1896 to build the depot, expecting to recoup its cost by selling the four hundred acres divided into lots to buyers lured by the one-hundred-acre scenic park situated around the springs. The "Sunset Depot" as completed was the largest between San Antonio and Houston for many years, but it stood in an empty field, nearly two miles from the original town on the far side of the Cibolo. Apparently the lack of development and lot sales subsequently led the United States Trust Company to repossess the Lee property, on which the depot stood.[25]

As the new century began, visitors continued to come to Sutherland Springs to bathe and drink the mineral waters, albeit not as many as local business men might have desired. Since the railroad company had not yet fulfilled its promises of development, accommodations remained minimal. J. M. Shaw quit the hotel business, but William C. Burris renovated and reopened his place, which was presumably the Messinger Hotel, under a lease arrangement with the doctor's estate. Many visitors to the springs continued to sleep in "tents, wagons, and ambulances" under the shady trees. Occasionally an excursion train brought travelers to the "beautiful fairy like grove, dotted thickly with white tents of the health and pleasure seekers who are camping out there." Local residents maintained the springs as best they could. For example, Sutherland Springs women held a fund-raiser to raise money for cleaning the white sulfur pool in 1901.[26]

Community leaders in Sutherland Springs may have been tempted by the prospects of yet another development project in 1900, but fortunately for them it was never completed. Belle A. McCanna, who claimed to be a medical doctor, bought a town lot and announced plans to build a sanitarium. Instead, she apparently settled in El Paso by 1910, when she advertised that she had been "trained in the Lovewell hospital of Los Angeles" in the "French method of electricity" to cure "every known disease," including such maladies as tuberculosis. The next year she began serving as the superintendent of "medical temperance" for the Women's Christian Temperance Union in San Antonio, where in May 1912 she began posting advertisements in a newspaper for "electro-vapor bath massages." This brought the attention of the Bexar County authorities, who had launched a campaign to eliminate the medical quacks who had been attracted to their city by the high number of health resorts in the surrounding area. McCanna was arrested in June 1912 for "unlawfully practicing medicine," i.e. applying an electric battery, known as a French battery, to her patients. She posted bond and left town before her trial. In fact, the census in 1900, when she bought a lot in Sutherland Springs, reveals that she was a nurse for Dr. Samuel J. Lovewell in Los Angeles, California. A widow, she boarded with Lovewell and his wife along with three other ladies. While Lovewell may have operated a clinic, it was not a hospital, and McCanna was his nurse, not a student or even a doctor.[27]

Despite the steady trickle of tourists, Sutherland Springs in the early 1900s remained primarily an agricultural community offering the services needed by families on the surrounding farms. A cotton gin owned by Jesse L. Tiner was struck by lightning and "burned to the ground" in 1901, but apparently merchant Henry Tally and farmer Sanford Brown already had another gin in town. Charles N. Vezey still worked as a blacksmith, while Tally had two competitors as a merchant, Charles P. Warren (who also served as postmaster) and John W. McLoud. There was a doctor, John M. Weston, but he sold his practice in 1906 after his eyesight failed. Clyde F. Elkins, who attended Sam Houston Normal Institute (later Sam Houston State University) and studied law at the University of Texas, taught school in Sutherland Springs. David Griffin Gunn, an Episcopal minister who previously served churches in New York, Minnesota, and Oklahoma, may have been involved in plans to build two new churches, Methodist and "union," at this time. William L. Wright, Brown's son-in-law, was a Texas Ranger who was elected sheriff of Wilson County in 1902 and served for fifteen years. A telephone line was installed from San Antonio to Sutherland Springs in 1902, although it is not clear how many of the 131 residents of the latter community actually had this service.[28]

As the twentieth century began, Sutherland Springs remained outside the mainstream of resort development in Texas. There were few facilities to house visitors, and the springs on the Cibolo had not changed much since the first settlers built some cabins and placed a few boards across the pools to serve as rude seats. Railroads into the area brought promises of increased growth and prosperity, but there simply was not enough capital available within the community to support large-scale development and promotion efforts. Sutherland Springs relied mainly on its small income as a farm town, providing the economic and social services that men who still raised mostly livestock and cotton needed. A railroad depot had been built, however, and some stakes had been hammered into the ground to mark big plans for a new town and a park. Local leaders could believe that if the right developers could be brought to the banks of the Cibolo, where a variety of springs still flowed, that their community might yet have a bright future.

4

New Sutherland Springs

Sutherland Springs by 1900 remained primarily an agricultural community, but the components were present for resort development if money could be found. There was a railroad with a depot, park, and town lots, and the springs still flowed, to the delight of locals and visitors alike. The prospect of finding oil, on the heels of the Spindletop bonanza that transformed Texas in 1901, brought new investors to Sutherland Springs. When their dreams of oil riches failed to materialize, they looked more closely at the potential for developing a resort, as many had during the 1890s at other sites in Texas. That decade had proven to be the peak of resort construction in the Lone Star State, but dozens of businessmen also tried their luck during the first two decades of the twentieth century, including some of the disappointed oil tycoons at Sutherland Springs.[1] They platted another town across Cibolo Creek from the original community and named it New Sutherland Springs. By 1912, the future looked promising as the development rapidly expanded in sales and settlement, although the ever-changing kaleidoscope of financial arrangements that underlay this growth greatly undermined its potential for sustainability.

The eruption of Spindletop from a salt dome at Beaumont, Texas, in January 1901, which produced 100,000 barrels of oil a day, changed business in Texas forever. Within a few decades the Lone Star State became the leading producer in the United States, which dominated world oil production prior to World War II. This boom of course inspired investors who wanted to be part of this explosion of wealth to comb Texas looking for the next big bonanza, but it also enhanced many older businesses and spawned many new ones. Railroads expanded throughout the state, feeding enterprises that included community and resort development. There were plenty of new customers: the state's population grew by 53 percent from 1900 to 1920, when there were more than 4.6 million Texas residents. Such growth led to greater demands for housing, paved roads, education, better communications, public utilities, and of course recreation, all of which created attractive new opportunities for the right investor, or investors. The period would be labeled the Progressive Era by historians, but in Texas it was the era of the big oil boom, with businessmen aggressively pursuing profits as much as progress.

A writer for the *Orange Daily Tribune* quipped in 1903, "Where it is a question of oil it is no longer a question of health resort." What he or she meant was that in the aftermath of the big oil discovery at Spindletop, which produced millions of barrels of oil, developers in many Texas communities, such as Sutherland Springs, refocused their attention from resort development to oil prospecting. Apparently residents around Sutherland Springs had long known about oil under their land; the first oil found in the region interfered with the digging of local water wells before the Civil War. Joseph H. Polley at that time corresponded with relatives who were involved in drilling for oil in Ohio, but the war interrupted his inquiries. Oil appeared again when someone tried to bore yet another water well at Sutherland Springs in 1880. As before, given the state of technology, the driller would probably have preferred to find water rather than oil, but interests soon changed. In May 1901, four months after Spindletop erupted, the International Oil and Asphalt Company of San Antonio was chartered and subsequently leased thousands of acres of land with potential oil deposits near Sutherland Springs. By the time they announced their plans for drilling in September, there was already competition. The Sutherland Springs Oil Company, a Floresville outfit that had applied for a state charter that would not be issued until January 1902, was drilling in the same area, while the Bexar Oil Company, encouraged by reports of an oil strike, was prospecting for a lease of their own. Patillo Higgins, the self-taught geologist whose predictions and negotiations brought successful drillers to Spindletop, purchased land at Sutherland Springs in the late summer of 1902, hoping to find oil on property he owned rather than have to sue for a share of the profits, as he had in 1901.[2]

The first rush to find oil at Sutherland Springs faded when a quarantine was placed over the area in an attempt to contain an outbreak of yellow fever, but reports of natural gas deposits brought a rush of new prospectors in late 1903, increasing land prices tenfold. Of course, florid advertisements in the *San Antonio Express* that referred to Sutherland Springs as "The Coming Spindletop of Southwestern Texas" also helped to boost local property values. Among the new enterprises was the Sour Springs Oil Company, chartered in January 1904. Three months later, the same paper referred to Sutherland Springs as the "Mecca of Oil Magnates." When the San Antonio and Aransas Pass Railway offered a low-cost excursion to Sutherland Springs, three hundred potential millionaires rode the "Davy Crockett" train to inspect the oil fields. Not to be outdone, the Southern Pacific Railroad offered low rates to oil speculators from Houston and nine other depots in southeast Texas for excursions to Sutherland Springs. By June 1904 the Sam Houston Oil Company had filed for a charter, while the directors for the Sutherland Springs Oil Company included H.P.N. Gammel, who had already become well-known as a publisher and bookseller.[3]

Lack of success began to cool interest in oil at Sutherland Springs, and then a natural gas explosion wrecked a drilling rig, convincing most developers to quit. They returned after the discovery of oil in the Mission Field in adjacent Bexar County, near San Antonio. An interesting group of "enterprising men" bought the land formerly owned by Gideon Lee Jr., which contained the most popular springs, in June 1907. Their acquisition totaled 4,300 acres, which they bought for $45,000 from the United States Trust Company of New York, which had recovered the title to all of the Lee property five years earlier after the legal wrangles over a railroad in the 1890s. The new owners intended to prospect for oil, and in late 1908 they gathered to inspect the tract. The group included San Antonio real estate developers J. A. Clopton, John N. Groesbeck, James L. Kerr, and Howard A. Speer; Seguin law partners Joseph B. Dibrell (a former state senator) and Emil Mosheim (a former district attorney); Southern Pacific agent Thomas J. Anderson; Sempronius E. "Semp" Russ, a former quarterback for the University of Texas who played tennis in the 1904 Olympics and later made a fortune in oil; and Henry C. Carter, a prominent attorney from San Antonio who served as the president of the American Bar Association. Interestingly, Groesbeck had leased the rights to drill for oil on the Lee property in 1901, then subleased them a few years later. Now he returned with a new business plan that had the active support of the Southern Pacific, as evidenced by the presence of Anderson.[4]

After some negotiations, the New Sutherland Springs Oil and Gas Company organized in December 1908 and received a charter in March 1909. Four of the original investors served as directors of the company: Dibrell, Groesbeck, Kerr, and Speer. But there were five new faces as well: W. A. Stewart, who like Anderson was an employee of the Southern Pacific; J. H. Terrell, a San Antonio physician; Marcus H. Townsend, a lawyer and financier who had been a legislator; Nathaniel M. "Nat" Washer, a successful merchant who was prominent in both the Masons and the San Antonio Businessman's Club; and T. C. Worthington, an employee of the Galveston, Harrisburg, and San Antonio Railway who had once traveled to the Klondike to prospect for gold. Speer became the president of the new company, which was again joined in the field by others. Among those who returned was Gammel, who believed like his competitors that if he could just drill deep enough, he would find lots of oil. A November 1909 advertisement in a San Antonio newspaper declared that Sutherland Springs was once more the "storm center of the Oil and Gas excitement." But again nothing came of this activity, at least as far as oil production. Gammel during January 1910 listed his drilling rig as being for sale "cheap" in the classified advertisements of the same San Antonio paper.[5]

While developers excitedly searched for oil around Sutherland Springs, the idea of a resort did not disappear entirely. The 1904 advertisements for railroad excursions to assess oil prospects in Sutherland Springs also urged the travelers to "see alum, sulphur, and other acids oozing out of the earth. See the White Lake District, the Alligator Pool, the Jelly Ponds, the Sour Springs, the wonderful possibilities of the Sutherland Springs country and the drilling rigs in operation." Hundreds of people, many of them brought by train from San Antonio, gathered in the "Sour Springs Park" on the Fourth of July that year, although rain forced a delay of the "goat roping contest and tournament" until a later date. The Southern Pacific announced plans in 1905 for a dam on the Cibolo to create a lake, with a hotel, sanitarium, and bathhouse with an indoor swimming pool at the springs. Sutherland Springs was intended to be one of two resorts on an extension of the popular Sunset Route, with another at Port Lavaca to offer access to the Gulf of Mexico. Hotel operator James W. Parish asked in a 1906 advertisement: "Why don't you go to Sutherland Springs, thirty miles east of San Antonio, and take your sulphur baths where the gas boils the water like fire under a furnace, and drink iron and mineral waters of all kinds." That summer the trains ran daily from San Antonio for fifty cents each way. Abner H. "Hub" Polley bragged that the Fourth of July events in 1906, hosted by the Farmer's Union of Wilson County, attracted a crowd of 3,000 to 4,000. The next month,

Parish personally greeted the participants in a special "Businessman's Excursion" on their trip down the new rail extension.[6]

The potential of Sutherland Springs as a resort must have been obvious to the developers swarming into the area in search of oil, if they were interested at all in alternative ways to make money. The establishment of resorts in Texas had hit its peak in the 1890s, but there was still a substantial number of such operations being built during the first decade of the twentieth century, especially around San Antonio, which was the largest city in the state. The Hot Sulphur Wells bathhouse and hotel opened near there in 1900 and within six years was so popular that visitors had to be turned away. An opulent place with a huge natatorium as well as a zoo, ostrich farm, and even a casino, Hot Sulphur Wells catered to a well-heeled clientele. Simpler operations soon followed, including Terrell Hot Wells, Dullnig's Well, and Harlandale Hot Sulphur Well, all of which offered a lower-cost experience for visitors who did not require, or even want, a busy vacation experience. Taking advantage of the extended visiting season afforded by the warm climate, these resorts made San Antonio a potential "Carlsbad of America," according to a San Antonio newspaper writer, who thus invoked the name of a famous resort in far-away Bohemia.[7] Sutherland Springs, with its multiple sources of mineral waters and its idyllic location on the Cibolo near San Antonio, with easy access by railroad, could offer weary tourists yet another attractive alternative and thereby return a substantial profit for savvy investors.

Some of the developers who purchased the Lee property as a possible site for an oil well in 1907 did realize the possible value of the springs on the Cibolo. Soon after the original sale, a group bought 1,000 acres of the tract for $75,000 to be developed as a resort and park. Among these investors were Kerr, Russ, Speer, and Worthington, all of whom later served as directors of the New Sutherland Springs Oil and Gas Company. Joining them were Guilford M. Magill, a newspaperman and developer popularly known as the "Father of Bay City" (where he lived); E. G. Millikan, a San Antonio engineer; A. S. Morton, who had served as the official physician for Bay City; Henry Ruguley, a prominent Bay City banker; Andral Vann, a well-known Houston attorney; and N. King of Chicago. Edward W. Knox, the president of the State Horticultural Society, met with Russ, Kerr, and Millikan, together with representatives from the Southern Pacific, at Sutherland Springs in December 1907 to talk about plans for development. Within weeks a grand scheme was announced that included the development of a new town site across the Cibolo from John Sutherland's original community as well as the construction of a 6,000-square-foot natatorium, 5,400-square-foot pavilion, and 2,800-square-foot dining hall. Millikan would serve as the general manager for the ambitious project, while his company would provide all of the necessary engineering services.[8]

By the time the Sutherland Springs Development Corporation received its charter in March 1908, plans had already expanded for the proposed resort and town. The new company, which had $70,000 in capital, listed Magill as its president, Kerr as vice president, and Russ as secretary and treasurer. Morton, Ruguley, Speer, and Worthington served with these three men on the board of directors, as well as a new face: Harry Redan, a well-known Houston magician who was a partner with Vann in a novelty company. Millikan remained as onsite manager of the project. The members took care to make it clear that their "movement" was "not associated with the recent oil operations," and they declared that their "pleasure resort" would include multiple pavilions and improved streets. An anonymous doctor from Mineral Wells, the location of yet another successful Texas resort, had submitted a bid for land on which to build a sanitarium as part of their development, and tests were underway to ascertain whether the natural gas found locally could be used for lighting.[9]

The Corporation worked hard to sell the lots in the proposed town of New Sutherland Springs. Lee Avenue, the main street, was graded and paved, while lumber was delivered for a forty-room hotel to be built between the Cibolo and "Redan Park." Promises were issued again for a natatorium and pavilion, though astute readers might have noticed that the square footage for each had been greatly reduced. An auction of town lots was announced for May 5, 1908, and large advertisements were placed in San Antonio and Houston newspapers. These described the site as a "natural park of marvelous grandeur" that had the "most wonderful cluster of medicinal springs in the United States." The hotel, they claimed, was almost complete, while "one of the biggest natatoriums in the world" stood nearby with 1,500 gallons of the "purest sulphur water" flowing through it every minute. Potential buyers were assured that, since it had the support of wealthy experienced businessmen and the railroad, "this undertaking cannot fail." On the day of the so-called auction, two trains brought people from San Antonio at half the usual round-trip fare (fifty cents rather than one dollar). Free barbecue was served, and all buyers had the chance to buy a lot on "Easy Terms" for a down payment of $25.00. Allegedly 2,000 people came to the event, and the Corporation sold $75,000 in lots.[10]

Sales efforts continued through the summer of 1908. The Southern Pacific offered half-price fares on Sundays, while "elaborate plans'" were laid for a Fourth of July celebration that included a baseball game. J. A. Clopton, an original investor in the Lee property and Speer's partner in selling property in San Antonio, was hired in mid-July as an agent to sell 200 lots. He offered corner lots for $125.00 and inside lots for $100.00 on no-interest terms of 20 percent down and ten dollars per month. Speer promised that $10,000 would be spent on improvements, including an outdoor pool filled by the springs that would measure fifty by one hundred feet. Plans were also announced for paving a second road and building a spur line to the springs. An elaborate advertisement claimed the title of "Carlsbad of America" for New Sutherland Springs, described as a "mecca for stricken humanity for half a century," while another estimated that the flow of sulfur water into the existing pool was 2,000 gallons per minute, an increase of 500 gallons per minute over assertions published just a few months earlier. Of course, testimonial letters were published as well, including one from Joseph B. Polley. By late August, Clopton reported that he had sold 180 lots.

The San Antonio *Daily Express* happily declared that "the men behind the town are the kind of men who make cities."[11]

Efforts to promote New Sutherland Springs intensified as the summer of 1908 drew to a close. It was an election year, so somehow the investors convinced the incumbent congressman for their district, Democrat John Nance Garner, to debate Republican challenger T. W. Moore, a doctor from neighboring Guadalupe County, at their new town in September 1908. It was the first meeting of the two candidates for the campaign, and many other activities such as a picnic and a baseball game were planned, but only about 150 people attended the event. Allegedly before Garner spoke he entertained himself with a swim in the pool, impressing others by doing a backward somersault off the diving board. The debate itself "was held beneath great trees in an alluring grove," on a temporary wooden platform specially built for the show. Joseph B. Polley had the honor of introducing both candidates in turn. Garner used the opportunity to endorse a new proposal, federal insurance for bank deposits, for the first time. Moore opposed the idea, arguing that it would lead to greedy actions that would ruin the national banking system.[12]

Clopton in September 1908 asked for bids from contractors to build a fifty-room hotel. It was designed by Atlee B. Ayres, a San Antonio architect educated in New York City who later served as state architect and became famous for his Mexican-influenced designs as well as other popular styles. By September 20 contracts had been awarded for the hotel, a pavilion, and a bath house with thirty-four rooms. Eugene Davis and J. A. Berry of San Antonio, who received the contract for the hotel, broke ground in November. Clopton's promise of a completion by March 1909 must have weighed on them, but an announcement that the hotel was complete except for its "waterworks" and "electric lighting plant" appeared on April 4, 1909, in time for a delegation from the Southern Pacific to tour the property in search of a site for a new depot on the Victoria Division of the Sunset Route. A full-page advertisement in the San Antonio *Daily Express* on June 14, 1909, which again declared

New Sutherland Springs to be the "Carlsbad of America," reported that the hotel had cost $30,000. It stood just four blocks from the Cibolo and the same distance from the proposed site for a new depot, and its fifty rooms boasted running water and electric lights, provided by a gasoline-powered generator that recharged dry cell batteries stored in a barn. The hotel dining room was a "poem," with attentive waiters and magnificent views. Of course, the best feature was the cement-lined swimming pool, measuring fifty by one hundred feet and filled with sulfur water flowing at a rate of 2,000 gallons per minute. The proud new manager was Herman Michaels, a native of Holland who had managed the Alta Vista Hotel at Corpus Christi after operating the California Restaurant in San Antonio.[13]

The hotel at New Sutherland Springs actually opened on the Fourth of July in 1909, but that it ever opened at all was somewhat miraculous. Plans for further development had almost been derailed when a young woman nearly drowned in the pool in August 1908. Contractor Berry in March 1909 was stabbed in the stomach during a card game in the kitchen of the hotel, which was still under construction at the time. Michaels, the manager, was then injured by a fall into an elevator shaft at a San Antonio furniture factory in June 1909, but like Berry he survived. Most spectacular was the stabbing of Sheriff William L. Wright at Floresville that same month by a prisoner who was being hanged. Wright in July 1908 had arrested Refugio Jaureque, a Mexican construction worker accused of stabbing and raping a teenaged Polish girl, Albina Olenick, near Sutherland Springs. When the two men arrived at Sutherland Springs en route to the Wilson County jail, a crowd of thirty or so men and boys tried to take the prisoner and lynch him. Wright "eluded" his attackers by a "ruse" and delivered his prisoner safely to Floresville, where Jaureque was tried and sentenced to death. He was hanged in June 1909 at Floresville but managed to stab Wright on the gallows inside the county jail with a knife he made from a spoon. Wright lived and served many more years as a sheriff and Texas Ranger. To add a fittingly grim end to a year of disruption and bad news, former hotel proprietor James W. Parish, who had begun selling real estate at Sutherland Springs, fell between two train cars at San Antonio in December 1909 and had his right arm crushed so badly that it had to be amputated.[14]

Presumably elated by the opening of the Hotel Sutherland, as it was called, Clopton and Speer in August 1909 announced plans for $50,000 in further improvements, including a golf course, tennis courts, sports field, and bath house, all to be completed within just a few months. Since the Sutherland Springs Development Corporation apparently did not have the money for such ambitious projects, it sold its 1,000 acres, including the town site, to the Sutherland Springs Development Company, which had $500,000 in capital. Speer, Kerr, and Russ were the primary stockholders in the new organization, while their manager was W. E. Nelson, the most successful agent in selling lots for the development of Aransas Pass earlier that year. Nelson claimed that he had sold 1,792 of the 6,000 town lots platted at Aransas Pass, and he had big plans for New Sutherland Springs. His proposals included paving the roads to San Antonio, Stockdale, and Floresville to facilitate automobile travel. He envisioned multiple large pools to accommodate even more people, a dam on the Cibolo to generate electricity, a "scenic electric railway," a large dance pavilion, a bottling plant to sell mineral water nationwide, and the belated completion of a long awaited spur line from the main railroad to the springs.[15]

Once again a call was issued for contractors to submit bids for a bath house, pavilion, and an enlarged pool, which was to be expanded from its original size of fifty by one hundred feet to new measurements of one hundred by two hundred and seventy five feet, allegedly the largest in the South. A handsome drawing of the proposed combination bathhouse and pavilion, with the adjacent pool, was produced by Frederick B. Gaenslen, a San Antonio architect who graduated from the Massachusetts Institute of Technology. A. B. Clark of the same city won the contract to create this centerpiece for the new "Saratoga of the South," as the resort community was being advertised. The plans also included a scaled-down version of the lake that had originally been discussed by Southern Pacific developers in 1905. They had declared that a five-mile-long lake would be created by a dam on the Cibolo, but discussions in the fall of 1909 apparently focused on a lake that would be a mile in length. Of course, new landscaping for the property around the springs, which was now being referred to as "Santa Claus Park," would ensure that the primary focus for visitors remained an attractive destination.[16]

Other improvements were planned at the same time, but clever arrangements were made for another organization to bear the cost of construction and operation. Texas Baptists had held their first camp meeting at Sutherland Springs in the summer of 1908. After another revival on the Cibolo a year later, the newly created Southwest Texas Baptist Workers Conference received a donation of twenty-five acres from the resort developers. In return, Baptist leaders promised to build a Chautauqua site that would include a $300,000 sanitarium, three stories high and clad in brick, and an auditorium. The site would be operated as an annex to a Baptist-run sanitarium to be built in San Antonio, linked to New Sutherland Springs through hourly trains operated by the Southern Pacific by the summer of 1910. Ultimately Baptist leaders hoped to have cottages, a commissary, meeting houses, and a pavilion at New Sutherland Springs. There they planned to host revivals, summer camps for children, and education programs for adults. A correspondent to the San Antonio *Daily Express* in November 1909 grumbled that New Sutherland Springs had won the contest for the Baptist Chautauqua over San Antonio "not by her chalybeate water and her Santa Claus trees, but by her cash and her terra firma." No matter how the deal was made, it appeared to be a great coup for the developers.[17]

The rapid development of New Sutherland Springs, coupled with brisk installment sales and bold plans for further growth, attracted a lot of positive attention. Gammel, back to look for oil in November 1909, bought several lots and enthusiastically endorsed the resort in a talk with a newspaper reporter. Developers of a residential farm project at nearby

Stockdale in December 1909 boasted in their advertisements about their proximity to New Sutherland Springs, which they claimed would "soon be the greatest place of its kind in the South." They explained, "Here you can fish in the Cibolo river, enjoy a swim in the largest concrete pool in the world, go to the theater, eat in a hotel that cannot be beaten for cuisine anywhere, and hobnob with the best of people from all over the world." They helpfully added in a later notice that the drive to "the greatest resort in southern Texas today" was only an hour in duration. As the new year began, the Sunset Route provided return trips to New Sutherland Springs for just fifty cents on both Thursdays and Sundays.[18]

Accolades from outside promoters generated some attention for Sutherland Springs, but if the town was truly to prosper, it needed a newspaper, which it had lacked since about 1880 when the *Western Chronicle* was relocated to Floresville. Thomas C. Richardson provided a solution during the fall of 1909 when he established the *Health Resort* at New Sutherland Springs. He later recalled the community as a "long-famed mineral water resort which was being reborn with railroad connections." He added that "the site was one of sub-tropical beauty, with giant pecan trees and moss-draped live oaks in a fertile valley of the Cibolo river." The Sutherland Springs Development Company promised that they would support him by buying advertisements and hiring him to do all of their commercial printing, which he did for them in large quantities. He bought his initial equipment from the "defunct San Antonio *Gazette*" and powered it with a small gasoline engine. Success allowed him to buy a larger, more complicated press and print a larger format newspaper, and he actually bought a Floresville newspaper, the *Advertiser*, in September 1911 and merged it with his own publication. As he prospered, he bought three lots and built a "handsome home." He noted that while carpenters for his project were "plentiful" in Sutherland Springs, he could find "no brick layers" so he had to build a chimney himself.[19]

Powerful investors were soon attracted by the success of New Sutherland Springs. Harry D. Barnitz, a former United States Army doctor and physician for the Southern Pacific who chaired the Board of

Health in San Antonio, established the Kendall Hotel Company in early 1910. He and his fellow developers intended to create a chain of rural inns within a 150-mile radius of the city. The first one was Ye Kendall Inn, an 1859 home in Boerne that had since been expanded into a hotel. At the same time, "in direct conjunction and co-operation with the scheme of hotels," a $200,000 development plan was announced for New Sutherland Springs. Apparently this was the brainchild of a "syndicate" led by former United States Senator Joseph R. Burton of Kansas. Burton had resigned from the Senate and served five months in jail in 1906, but he resumed his law practice and investments. He helped others to develop Aransas Pass and acquire Terrell Hot Wells, then he bought an orchard at New Sutherland Springs and there became directly involved in creating his own syndicate to become part of Barnitz's hotel scheme. During February 1910 Burton and his partners paid $303,000 for a land package that included the 1,000 acres owned by the Sutherland Springs Development Company, an adjacent plot that belonged to Russ and Kerr (2,400 acres), a section of land (640 acres) known as "Cibolo Gardens" owned by Sutherland Springs Realty Company (Speer's firm), and 5,500 acres held by "various persons." Brothers W. E. and H. P. Nelson were announced as the managers of the new project, while former Texas state senator Avery L. Matlock, who had served as an attorney for the syndicate that built the Capitol at Austin and created the XIT Ranch, provided legal services. Another newcomer, A. D. Powers of Chicago, supervised sales.[20]

Powers later claimed that before joining the organization at New Sutherland Springs he had sold lots in forty-four town developments, most recently at Aransas Pass, where he directed sales of 6,000 lots (and presumably had W. E. Nelson working for him). He and Matlock had devised the "UNIT" plan for selling Aransas Pass lots on installment plans for Burton, and they intended to use it again in New Sutherland Springs. The Nelsons quickly arranged a March 1910 excursion on the Southern Pacific and advertised it in the *San Antonio Express*: "Never in the history of San Antonio has such a list of high-class real estate men and experienced agents been secured for one proposition as is now lined up for the opening sale next Thursday, the 10th." Additional notices promised that everyone who bought a lot would get one hundred dollars in stock for the not-yet-created Sutherland Springs Improvement Company. This firm would own the springs, Santa Claus Park, and "all the amusement features connected herewith," including a "full complement of boats on the river" as well as electric and water plants and "scenic railroad." All this would be completed soon along with paved streets and sidewalks, and a larger Southern Pacific depot, with daily service provided by railroad motor car along a spur line to the pool. The price for a lot remained two hundred dollars, with a down payment of just ten dollars and payments of only ten dollars per month. The Nelsons continued to sponsor train trips to bring potential buyers from San Antonio, and they hosted an Easter egg hunt that allegedly attracted thousands of visitors. They reported $20,000 in sales by late April, but this actually indicated the purchase of only one hundred lots. Since the down payment was ten dollars, they made a profit of just one thousand dollars for two months of hard selling.[21]

After several more months of work, the Sutherland Springs Town and Land Company was chartered by the state in July 1910 with $100,000 in capital. Organized at Matlock's office in San Antonio, the firm contained a lot of familiar faces along with some newcomers. Among the directors were Burton, Matlock, and Powers, together with Kerr, Russ, and Townsend from other companies formed to prospect for oil or sell land in the area since 1907. Speer, another original investor, served as president of the new company, with Kerr as first vice president and Matlock as secretary. One newcomer was Isaac T. Pryor, a wealthy cattleman and banker who previously had invested with Burton in developing the town of La Pryor through the Zavala Land and Water Development Company. Pryor, who was also the president of the Trans-Mississippi Commercial Congress and the Texas Industrial League, became the new company's second vice president, while N. S. Graham, president of American Bank and Trust Company in San Antonio, served as treasurer.

4.1 Oil Well near Sutherland Springs. Courtesy of Elizabeth Lester

4.2 Advertisement from *San Antonio Express*, July 18, 1908.

4.3 Flyer for Sutherland Springs. Courtesy of Author's Collection

4.4 Advertisement from *San Antonio Express*, Sept. 12, 1909.

4.5 Sunset Depot. Courtesy of Sutherland Springs Historical Museum

4.6 Bathing Pool and Bathhouse. Courtesy of Author's Collection

4.7 Robbie Weston Herndon (on foot, in front) in front of her drugstore with her sister Louise (on horseback). Courtesy of Elizabeth Lester

4.8 Busby House Under Construction. Courtesy of Sutherland Springs Historical Museum

4.9 First State Bank (Charles E. Ford is second from left, while Charles F. Goodenough is fifth from the left). COURTESY OF WILSON COUNTY (TX) HISTORICAL SOCIETY

4.10 Map of New Sutherland Springs. From Plat Records, Volume 1, page 32, County Clerk's Office, Wilson County Courthouse, Floresville, TX

Powers assumed the additional title of “Managing Director,” while he also served in the same role at Terrell Hot Wells, where he later boasted that he sold more than one thousand lots for Burton while also directing the New Sutherland Springs project. To help him, Jack Powers, presumably a relative, was retained as the “General Sales Manager.”[22]

Powers and his associates continued selling lots for two hundred dollars, at ten dollars down and ten dollars per month, through the summer of 1910. Visitors enjoyed half-price train fares on Thursdays and Sundays, with special excursions that reportedly brought as many as five hundred people in a single day. The flood of potential customers may have been what led to the employment of Lillian Karsner as a “General Agent” for the company in August. The roads and sidewalks were completed, as well as a smaller pool completely lined in concrete, into which the larger pool overflowed. Powers worked hard to boost sales. Tourists who came on Sundays got bathing suits and towels if they did not bring their own. By the late summer buyers could choose a town lot or a five-acre mini farm for the same price of two hundred dollars. When that did not seem to work, Powers offered packages that combined a “least desirable” lot with a mini-farm, again at the same low price. He announced an interesting scheme on September 1: each buyer of a contract for a lot or farm or lot/farm combination would be allowed to bid in an “opening sale” on all of the property, including the hotel. All money derived from the sale, except for the two hundred dollars that the company got for each property, would be divided among the contract holders according to the number of contracts each one held. It was a confusing idea, and such a sale never seems to have occurred. Powers admitted in October 1910 that he had sold only 383 lots during his first three months at New Sutherland Springs, less than one-tenth the number that were actually available for sale and far less than he had sold elsewhere in Texas.[23]

The promoters of New Sutherland Springs claimed that twenty thousand visitors came in the summer of 1910, and that might have been true. Because the community lay on the Southern Pacific’s popular

Sunset Route, guests arrived regularly from all over the United States as well as the western world. Newspaper writers continued to compare the town favorably with venerable resorts such as Saratoga Springs in the United States and Carlsbad in Europe. The promoters of course were even more exuberant in describing New Sutherland Springs: "It is to San Antonio what Excelsior Springs is to Kansas City, Mineral Wells to Fort Worth, Hot Springs to Little Rock, [and] Saratoga, Coney Island, Long Branch and Atlantic City are to New York[:] health and pleasure." Such assertions may stretch the limits of credibility, but visitors from twenty-two states in the Union, along with a few from Mexico, Canada, and Britain, signed the ledgers of the Hotel Sutherland in 1910. San Antonio remained the best source of customers, serving as an initial destination for travelers to whom the Southern Pacific frequently offered discounts and special opportunities for short day trips to the springs on the west bank of Cibolo Creek. At the same time, the site remained a favorite place for visitors from all over Texas. The iron bridge across the Cibolo accommodated a steady stream of road-borne travelers. After all, "since there was no other entertainment in the area, this was the place to be." At least one descendant later recalled how her mother and father used to ride from Stockdale to Sutherland Springs in a buggy, an hour each way, just to spend the day courting in the park by the pools. The couple married in 1913 and settled near the site of their courtship.[24]

This flurry of activity transformed Sutherland Springs, both old and new. Probably three hundred people lived by 1910 in New Sutherland Springs, where the hotel had been built close to the springs. Two of these springs reportedly fed 2.8 million gallons of water each day into the concrete-lined swimming pool through its sandy bottom. The older community across Cibolo Creek had about two hundred residents. Most of those who had settled in the two towns were Texas-born whites, but there were two dozen from northern states, a dozen from Europe, and another dozen from Mexico. The first manager of the Hotel Sutherland, Herman Michaels, was Dutch, while his desk clerk was Irish and his two cooks were Mexican. One of two restaurateurs was a German.

There were only eight black residents. Development had brought trade diversity as well. There were three real estate brokers, twenty-one carpenters, seven laborers for "concrete work," two painters, and two electricians. A sign painter was kept busy working for two barbers, four druggists, three blacksmiths, two draymen, and ten merchants, as well as a baker, butcher, cabinetmaker, iceman, laundryman, liveryman, photographer, and pool room operator. The growth of public works was evident in the presence of a civil engineer, two "poolmen," four laborers for street maintenance, and three telephone operators. Of course, there was an oil prospector with a crew of three well drillers. There were four doctors including retiree John M. Weston (whose daughter Robbie Weston Herndon was one of the four druggists in town), a postmaster (George C. Everts, whose office was in the Southern Pacific depot in the new town), and four teachers to instruct 123 white children listed as attending school.[25]

In addition to the relocation of the post office, there were many indications that New Sutherland Springs was quickly surpassing the older community. As early as 1908 a new two-story building to house a store with $10,000 in inventory had been built on the new site. The 1910 census reported that an Apostolic minister, James W. Scott, lived in the new town, and the next year the First Street Presbyterian Church opened its doors in New Sutherland Springs. The older town still attracted summer religious encampments, but it apparently had no established church. In the new community, too, there was a 200-seat Star Theater, with a projector powered by a gasoline generator, and the Hotel Sutherland. Michaels was replaced as manager in the fall of 1910 by C. M. Rebou, who in turn was succeeded by Harry J. Hatch, formerly of the Alta Vista Hotel in Corpus Christi (which Michaels had previously managed). Under all three men the Hotel Sutherland continued to serve as a centerpiece for the new town. Among the several rooming houses in New Sutherland Springs was the Busby House, which had an interesting origin. Sarah Perdum "Perdie" Busby came with her mother, Margaret H. Gibson Busby, to New Sutherland Springs from Goliad in the summer of 1910. Margaret was apparently so crippled that she had to be carried from the train to a waiting carriage, but after several weeks of soaking in black sulfur water she could walk as much as one hundred yards. Impressed, she had her husband, Robert Brown Busby, join her and Sarah, and together they decided to construct a rooming house with ten rooms for rent. Margaret died in September 1910, but the Busby House began taking visitors in early 1911. Sarah in 1915 briefly tried to sell the operation, but she and her father apparently managed the place until his death in 1918, when he was buried in Goliad alongside his wife.[26]

Among the more interesting businesses in New Sutherland Springs was a bank, which organized during the early fall of 1909, just five years after the Texas constitution was amended to allow state-chartered banks. The New Sutherland Springs facility received a charter as the First State Bank in October and opened its doors in a rented building with Tom Morgan, the former city marshal of Ennis, as its president. Construction of a concrete building with proper bars began in December 1909 and was completed early the following year. The company only had $10,000 in capital, but its deposits, under a law adopted in 1909, were originally secured by both the West Texas Bank and Trust Company of San Antonio and Chase National Bank of New York. The Houston National Exchange Bank was added to that list as well by the end of October 1909, and in July 1910 the American Bank and Trust Company, whose president N. S. Graham also served as treasurer for the Sutherland Springs Town and Land Company, became a "reserve agent" for the First State Bank. At that time the president of the First State Bank was Charles F. Goodenough, a native of Britain. Finance was a difficult business in this period; the West Texas Bank and Trust Company became the largest state bank in Texas by early 1916, then within just a few months was shut down and its assets liquidated. Somehow the First State Bank survived into the 1920s, when it became one of many rural banks in Texas to close its doors after many failures ruined the state deposit security system.[27]

The directors of the Sutherland Springs Town and Land Company, while selling lots, also hunted for well-heeled partners to join their enterprise. J. C. Nelson, presumably a relative of W. E. and H. P. Nelson, escorted John H. Kellogg of the well-known Battle Creek Sanitarium to New Sutherland Springs during the fall of 1910 to assess the prospects for constructing a branch of his facility there. Kellogg praised the site and the quality of the water, but he did not build. It may have been some consolation that Kellogg's rival in Battle Creek, Charles W. Post, visited Mineral Wells that same year and also declined to invest. A. W. Withers bought part of the old Polley ranch property, 214 acres, and planned to subdivide it into lots for resale, but that also did not happen. Rumors surfaced in the late summer of 1910 of yet another development group that would construct a $250,000 resort. The Sutherland Springs Town and Land Company signed a contract in September with the Rest Cure Home Company of Kansas City; the Texas developers would provide one hundred acres for their Kansas counterparts to build a hotel and sanitarium. Some reported that the development was being funded in part by the family of the late August Belmont of New York, who had made a fortune in banking; Helen V. Gould, niece of railroad financier Jay Gould; and Olivia S. S. Sage, the widow of Russell Sage, New York financier and erstwhile partner of Gould. The Rest Cure Home Company claimed to have as much as one million dollars in capital and announced plans to begin construction in November 1910, but nothing happened.[28]

Efforts redoubled in early 1911 to sell land to visitors, most of whom obviously enjoyed their day trips to the springs but showed little interest in buying lots. The Sutherland Springs Town and Land Company hired yet another new sales manager, J. D. Cameron, who had previously sold lots in Sulphur, Oklahoma, which then lay adjacent to a national park. Among the innovations that appeared soon after his arrival was the screening of "Moving Pictures" of Sutherland Springs and activities in the resort community every evening except Sunday at the company office in the Gibbs Building, which stood at the corner of Alamo Plaza and Houston Street in San Antonio. Reportedly a film of people enjoying the big pool at Sutherland Springs drew a crowd of "several thousand" when it debuted. Within the community, new machinery was installed for pumping black sulfur water out of the ground, heating it, and then piping it into bathtubs for soaking. These waters remained the focus of much interest for alleged medical qualities; the *Health Resort* in 1910 published a letter from a man who claimed that he had long suffered so much from sciatica that he could not dress himself, but bathing in the black sulfur pool eliminated all of his pain.[29]

Businesses continued to expand and diversify in New Sutherland Springs throughout 1911. After three years of discussion, planning, and construction, a spur track was laid by the Southern Pacific from the main rail line to the pools. Its completion prompted the scheduling of a second train on Sundays to bring visitors from San Antonio. Kerr, Sam H. Burris (an original investor in the First State Bank), and H. M. Hastings incorporated as the Sutherland Springs Mercantile Company. During March 1911 it was announced that "Hume Sour Water" had been "discovered." It had "blood-making powers" that made it effective in treating "constitutional diseases" such as gout, rheumatism, and diabetes. Within one month the Sutherland Springs Hygeia Mineral Water Company received a state charter with Judson Hume and the Nelson brothers (W. E. and H. P.) as directors. Their avowed purpose was to bottle and market Hume Sour Water and "Hygeia splits." Investors for ten dollars would get one share in the company and forty-eight bottles of water, each of which held a half-gallon. Another spur line was laid to a local sand and gravel pit operated by the Calloway Coal and Sand Company, owned by W. P. Calloway, who had already tried similar operations at La Grange, Temple, and Houston. The manager of the Hotel Sutherland, Harry J. Hatch, served as Calloway's secretary and treasurer at New Sutherland Springs and claimed that they had orders for 3,600 railroad carloads of material. Coal had been reported in the Sutherland Springs area in early 1911, but Calloway did not find it. Within a year his operation was defunct and he had partnered with two other men to establish another sand and coal company at Poteet, Texas.[30]

Some racial conflict surfaced in Sutherland Springs in the summer of 1911, but it seems to have had little impact. Swayne C. Box, a barber who owned a house in the original town of Sutherland Springs that he rented to blacks, received a threatening letter saying that if he did not evict his tenants, the home would be burned with them in it. At about the same time, Leonidis Polk "Lon" Tatum, a rancher who rented a place to Mexicans in the same community, received a similar letter demanding their removal. The response of both men is unknown, but blacks as well as whites continued to take advantage of the low train rates from San Antonio and visit the Sutherland Springs area, though their exact destinations may have differed. The Farmers Home Improvement Society, a cooperative organization for black farmers that focused on combating the negative effects of share cropping and tenant farming, hosted a barbecue at the Sour Springs park just south of town in late July 1911. The principal speaker that day was Rev. R. J. Carnes, who had organized the Society in Texas. A second celebration for blacks at the same location in September lasted three days and featured an "orchestra" from San Antonio, dancing, barbecue, and baseball. Blacks celebrated Juneteenth in 1912 at Morgan Park, which had been presumably named in honor of Cato Morgan, in Doseido, but plans were announced the following month for a return to the Sour Springs grove during August 1912 for a two-day gathering that would again include dancing and baseball.[31]

By the summer of 1912, a little more than a decade after the first oil prospectors had come to Sutherland Springs, developers seemed to have made a success of the community as a resort and real estate venture. The high point of the season was on St. John's Day, June 24, 1912, when an estimated 3,000 people gathered for an outdoor installation service for the officers of eleven blue lodges and seven Royal Arch chapters of Texas Masons. In addition, officers were installed for seven Texas chapters of the Order of the Eastern Star. Three trains had to be used to bring all of the Masonic visitors from San Antonio. The members of a new lodge, Sutherland Springs Lodge No. 1073, served as the hosts for the event. Sutherland Springs also remained popular for visiting groups of Episcopalians, Methodists, and Baptists, although the latter did hire a promoter to boost attendance at their ten-day revival in July due to fears that attendance might be lagging. A rodeo in August attracted more visitors to watch riders test their skills on bucking horses, mules, and bulls. Apparently encouraged by all of this activity, Speer in July purchased the assets of the Sutherland Springs Town and Land Company from the Sutherland Springs Development Company, which had just recently re-acquired the property. Two months later he bought the Baptist meeting facilities, promising to lease it to them as needed but also announcing that anyone else could use the site as well. By the end of the year, newspaper writers declared that the 125-acre park at Sutherland Springs was the fifth largest of 298 public parks in Texas, indicating that Speer was already at work promoting his investment and trying to bring larger crowds to the popular springs by Cibolo Creek.[32]

Prosperity finally seemed to arrive in Sutherland Springs with the construction of New Sutherland Springs with its hotel and other amenities. Certainly the number of visitors who came was impressive, and they spoke well of the place. John W. Gray in January 1913 wrote to his cousin in Illinois that the community was "beautiful" and so "warm" that the "Natives go in swimming every week in the year."[33] The flow of tourists attracted a variety of new businesses, mostly to the new town site across the Cibolo from the older community. But a serious flaw in the business plans of the various developers appeared early: many people came to enjoy the springs, but relatively few of them bought lots, and even fewer built homes. This troubling lack of investment must be the explanation for the revolving cast of companies that sought to develop New Sutherland Springs—as costs mounted faster than profits, each gave way to the other in a series of somewhat incestuous deals. The innovative installment sales plans were effective in generating cash initially, but the fact that very few individuals protested many years later when farmers and road crews plowed through the town site indicates that most of them never paid in full for their lots. The companies thus retained ownership of the land and had to look for new buyers. Unless some way was found to convince more people to settle by the springs along the Cibolo, or at least build a vacation home, prosperity might ultimately prove to be very fleeting for New Sutherland Springs, as well as the older community that preceded it and still lingered nearby.

5

Century of Decline

The tourist season for New Sutherland Springs began with great promise in 1913, but that year also marked the departure of the developers who had promised so much for the community. By the summer of 1914, the resort property had been acquired by Thomas J. Williams, a Houston lumberman interested in finding a venue to sell his kits for building affordable homes. Despite his hard work, Sutherland Springs failed as a resort. The region briefly became a hunting ground for oil prospectors again, including Williams, before the community began fading into obscurity during the second half of the twentieth century. Any dreams of reviving Sutherland Springs as a resort ended when the springs stopped flowing as local groundwater levels fell after World War II. It survived only as a small agricultural community and a wayside stop on a highway, which was exactly what those who wanted more for Sutherland Springs had tried to avoid since its establishment during the early days of Texas statehood.

The special Sunday trains began running from San Antonio to New Sutherland Springs in April 1913, and by the end of May a second run had been added on Thursdays. Some travelers rode in a "motor car" manufactured by the McKeen Motor Car Company of Omaha, Nebraska. Seventy feet in length and fitted with seats for passengers, its gasoline engine could push it as fast as eighty miles an hour down the tracks during its twice-daily runs. Its distinctive double-ended aerodynamic styling, which included porthole-shaped windows, led some to say that it looked like a "torpedo boat." All of those arriving at the pools in Sutherland Springs debarked onto a new earth platform that was more than twice its previous size, measuring five hundred feet in length. Developer Howard A. Speer, who had assumed the duties of proprietor for the Hotel Sutherland, organized day trips for groups as the summer approached. In May, he laid plans for three hundred employees of Joske's Department Store in San Antonio to come aboard five chartered trains to Sutherland Springs for a picnic and a baseball game between their team and the town's players. The next month, 1,500 Masons and their guests, representing thirteen chapters and lodges, arrived by special train to conduct open-air installations of their officers on St. John's Day, as they had done the previous summer. The members of Sutherland Springs Lodge No. 1073, which included Speer, again served as hosts for the event.[1]

June 1913 marked a watershed in the history of New Sutherland Springs. That month more than 2,000 potential buyers attended an auction of the remaining lots in the community. Much had been spent to advertise in newspapers and provide both entertainment and barbecue, but the result was overshadowed by the filing of a lawsuit against the Sutherland Springs Town and Land Company. It was not the first legal dispute in the resort's history—Melissa Polley in February 1911 had sued E. G. Millikan for the property of the local telephone company after he failed to pay the rent on its facility—but it was the first to focus on the developers. Charles E. Ford, a Detroit doctor who had retired to Sutherland Springs, joined with others in complaining that long-promised improvements had not been provided. The lawsuit named all of the directors of the Sutherland Springs Town and Land Company: Joseph R. Burton, James L. Kerr,

Avery L. Matlock, H. P. Nelson, J. C. Nelson, W. E. Nelson, A. D. Powers, Isaac T. Pryor, Sempronius E. Russ, Howard A. Speer, and Marcus H. Townsend. Ford and his associates charged that the sale of land from the Sutherland Springs Development Company and other organizations to W. E. and H. P. Nelson in February 1910 was a "fictitious" transaction designed to emancipate the sellers from their financial obligations and provide the buyers with a convenient alternative in case their marketing scheme failed. When they did falter, the Nelsons sold their property to the Sutherland Springs Town and Land Company, which had the very same directors as the Sutherland Springs Development Company. In July 1912 all of the unsold lots, and the obligation to provide many advertised improvements, passed again to the Sutherland Springs Development Company, who in turn quickly sold the property to Speer.[2]

It appeared to be a complicated legal mess, but to Ford and his allies it was really quite simple. At no time, they alleged, did any money change hands. The boards of directors of the various companies were almost identical, and the sales transactions were exchanges of promises for future payments. The last person in the chain was Speer, who once more signed a note in July 1912 rather than spend money. Only the people who bought lots paid any real money, and they never saw many improvements that were repeatedly promised as sales inducements. At the same time, none of those who bought stock ever received dividends. Despite such arguments, Ford, who had purchased many lots from the Nelsons in 1910, and the other plaintiffs apparently failed to secure either legal redress or compensation from the state court. Nonetheless, they did block any further schemes for marketing New Sutherland Springs as a grand resort. Editor Thomas C. Richardson of the Sutherland Springs *Health Resort* later wrote that the "dissatisfied parties" who "sued the townsite company" had effectively "delayed the issuance of titles to lots that had been sold, [and] interfered with financing for further development." In a final transaction that seemed to confirm Richardson's interpretations, as well as the complaints in the lawsuit, Speer offered the entire Sutherland Springs resort property (park, hotel, pools, and unsold lots) for sale at a bargain price of $78,000 in October 1913, and one of his fellow former directors, Townsend, bought it in early November.[3]

One factor that contributed to the low price of the resort property was that it had been slightly damaged in a flood. As early as June 1913, reports appeared of heavy rains causing tremendous floods on the Nueces, Leona, and Frio rivers, some of which were so strong that bridges were washed away. The deluge resumed in September and more South Texas rivers overflowed; when the San Antonio River flooded on October 2, it killed four people in the city and damaged a shocking amount of property. At Sutherland Springs, Cibolo Creek rose forty-two feet, to the bed of the iron truss road bridge. Yet when losses were assessed, it was found that the damage was much less there than it had been on other streams. The bathhouse had been partially swept from its foundations, the railroad line had been damaged, and the approach to the iron road bridge had been undermined. There were no human casualties, at least until October 8. That day a false report that the creek was rising again prompted many residents to crowd onto the road bridge to watch the anticipated flood. It did not come, but in the excitement a boy fell off the span and broke his arm. The Cibolo did surge twenty-four feet again in early December, alarming those who lived along its banks, but again there was little damage, unlike the horrific losses on other Texas rivers. In Sutherland Springs, the approach to the bridge by that time had already been repaired, as had the rail line.[4]

The lawsuit, subsequent sale, and flood in 1913 changed but did not ruin New Sutherland Springs. The movie theater was actually offered for rent in April; after apparently receiving no good offers, L. C. Houk, the president of First State Bank, converted the building into a “modern garage.” He offered the theater seats for sale through a newspaper advertisement, perhaps in an effort to raise the money for renovations. “Legal complications” led Richardson to “temporarily suspend” publication of the Sutherland Springs *Health Resort* in October 1913. He mysteriously promised to resume printing the newspaper soon, but in the meantime he declared was going to engage "in commercial club work, having been appointed as missionary to the cannibals of the Atlantic Coast." In fact, he restarted his paper for a short time in 1914 but again left town, this time for good. But New Sutherland Springs was not defunct yet. The big white sulfur pool was cleaned and reopened in January 1914, after the dirt roads were graded and more sidewalks were installed. Earnest E. Perry opened a store that boasted 25,000 square feet of space that spring, while a Civic League of women organized to aid the Commercial Club in promoting the community.[5]

A different future for Sutherland Springs loomed in March 1914 with the purchase of the resort property—hotel, unsold lots, park, and pools—by Thomas J. Williams. He had moved to East Texas from Alabama in 1865, then as a teenager went to work in the lumber industry. He came to New Sutherland Springs as the owner of the Williams Lumber Company of Houston and the president of the Texas Lumber Manufacturing Company, although he claimed to be "retired." Within a few weeks he razed the damaged bathhouse to replace it, while construction began on an improved rail line to the park, where he planned to refurbish the smaller pool. The new bathhouse that he built provided sixty dressing rooms, while more such facilities were available in a nearby structure that had a dancing pavilion on the second floor. A new well was dug to supply fresh water to the Hotel Sutherland, while plans were laid for a baseball stadium that would seat five hundred spectators and a dam on the Cibolo to create a lake one mile in length. Ultimately Williams envisioned New Sutherland Springs as the perfect place to market his "ready-to-be-put houses," which could be delivered in sections on railroad cars and erected on lots at a fraction of the cost of stick-built homes. One of his models, a bungalow, was even named the "Sutherland." To prove the value of his methods, he had the dancing pavilion constructed with prefabricated parts.[6] It became clear that while Williams expended much time and effort on his property at New Sutherland Springs, he was more interested in the venture as a marketing forum to sell lumber and housing kits than as a grand resort.

Williams opened his park to visitors in early May 1914, with trains coming from San Antonio twice a day. The new bath house, dancing pavilion, and baseball stadium welcomed patrons lured by newspaper advertisements that claimed "There are few places in the country where nature has given more of her bounty and beauty to the pleasure and health of mankind than at Sutherland Springs." Rain forced the cancellation of the first baseball game on May 3, 1914, but the next day two hundred people visited the park, with one hundred attending a dinner at the Hotel Sutherland hosted by its new manager, Mrs. H. L. Roark. Continued rains damaged the railroad and interfered with construction projects, but Williams pressed ahead. He hosted many church groups and the annual installation of local Masonic officers in June, when three lodges participated in a ceremony in the dance pavilion, and he also sponsored the annual picnic of the Woodmen of the World for the area. That organization had been active in the community since April 1911, when the "Southern Moss Grove" of the Woodmen Circle, a women's auxiliary for the Woodmen of the World, had been established at Anderson Hall in Sutherland Springs with Perdie Busby as secretary. One thousand allegedly attended the Masonic event, hosted by the Sutherland Springs lodge in late June 1914, while several thousand came to the Woodmen gathering that same month.[7]

Richardson in the *Health Resort* congratulated Williams on the fifth anniversary of the opening of the Hotel Sutherland in July 1914, grandly declaring that "the time has arrived when Sutherland Springs is due to take a long step forward in her destined career as a health resort." While the community had been "woefully handicapped for the past two years," the "gates of opportunity" were once again opening, "not with a flourish of trumpets, it is true, but opening nevertheless." Hoping to attract even larger crowds, Williams continued to build through the summer of 1914 and into the spring of 1915. The smaller pool, which was fed by the black sulfur springs, was refurbished and made available only to female patrons, an interesting shift from the practices of previous years. He opened a sanitarium, again built with his prefabricated parts, in September 1914 and welcomed 300 customers on its first day. Two months later, Dr. Hal J. Palmer of Navasota announced his intention to acquire an old hotel in Sutherland Springs and remodel it as another sanitarium, but there is no record that it ever opened. Meanwhile, Williams expanded the dancing pavilion, installed two large decorative fountains, and opened an ice cream parlor. He also had the main street, Lee Avenue, resurfaced along with the driveway to the pools and the walkway around them. His investments seemed to yield a great return as hundreds of church members from San Antonio came in large groups to Sutherland Springs in the late spring of 1915, although one Methodist outing led to tragedy when a thirteen-year-old boy died after falling from a tree and hitting his head on the concrete wall of a pool.[8]

The death of the boy at New Sutherland Springs allegedly became a primary reason that Williams continued to support a longtime ban on the sale of alcoholic beverages in Sutherland Springs. Residents had voted on local prohibition several times prior to his arrival, but the town had remained dry. As the prohibition debate became more heated, those who spoke in favor of it, such as the Rev. John L. Andrews of Dallas on a tour of central Texas in 1911, found New Sutherland Springs to be a welcoming venue. With his 1914 purchase, Williams had acquired a family-style resort where drinking and gambling were forbidden, and he retained that focus, if only because it fit well with his efforts to sell homes. He refused overtures from bookmakers in San Antonio who offered to pay the cost of having a direct telephone line installed to the hotel so guests could place bets, and he was equally adamant against those who wanted to have saloons. Yet another referendum on prohibition at Sutherland Springs in 1916 failed to change its status, and the imposition of statewide prohibition in 1918, two years before national prohibition, made the argument moot.[9]

Williams was not the only businessman working hard to take advantage of the springs. The Sutherland Springs Hygeia Mineral Water Company filed for bankruptcy in the fall of 1914, with local Masons

Charles E. Ford and George C. Everts as the apparently unlucky president and secretary respectively. Undaunted, Ford and Everts secured a third partner, M. F. Grenier, and incorporated as the Dove Mineral Water Company in February 1915. Ford was "elected" as the president of the new organization one month later, with Everts as secretary-treasurer and Earnest E. Perry, the pharmacist and merchant, as vice-president. Soon "SUTHERLAND SPRINGS SOUR WATER" and "SUTHERLAND SPRINGS IRON TONIC WATER" were again being sold in local drug stores, with advertisements in newspapers assuring customers that both were "Excellent for Stomach Trouble, Catarrh, Rheumatism, Gout, or Diabetes." It seemed to be a good time to launch such a venture. Texas by 1912 ranked fourth in the nation in bottled water sales, and by 1920 the Lone Star State produced almost ten percent of all medical water sold in the United States each year. After that peak, bottled water sales plummeted, but by that time the Dove Mineral Water Company was no long extant.[10]

Transportation remained one of the hindrances to the development of Sutherland Springs as a resort, which of course reduced possible buyers for lots and houses marketed by Williams. Within the San Antonio area, Williams had rival operations that were accessible by streetcars, while tourists who wanted to visit him had to travel by train or automobile. The more opulent Hot Wells Hotel stood within the city limits on South Presa Street, Terrell Hot Wells, which had a sanitarium, was five miles south of town on Pleasanton Road, and the Harlandale Bath House, with an exotic variety of bathing experiences, was located three miles outside of the city on Corpus Christi Road. High-speed rail motorcar service to New Sutherland Springs apparently ended after 1914. President Ed Kennedy of the Houston, Richmond, & San Antonio Interurban spoke to a crowd at Sutherland Springs in September 1915 about building an electric rail line through their town from Houston to San Antonio, but nothing occurred beyond more discussions. By 1920, when the company reorganized, Kennedy was no longer its president, and Sutherland Springs was not on its proposed route.[11]

5.1 McKeen Motor Car. FROM *SAN ANTONIO EXPRESS*, SEPT. 28, 1913

5.2 Advertisement in *San Antonio Express,* June 8, 1913.

5.3 Advertisement in *San Antonio Express*, Oct. 24, 1913.

5.4 Bath House after October 1913 flood. Courtesy of Elizabeth Lester

5.5 Advertisement in *San Antonio Express*, June 27, 1914.

5.6 Earnest E. Perry's drug store. Courtesy of Wilson County (TX) Historical Society

5.7 John A McPhail's general store, ca. 1914-1915. Courtesy of Tennessee State Library and Archives

5.8 Sutherland Springs Sanitarium, 1940. Courtesy of Tambria L. Read

5.9 Buffel Grass Flyer featuring Patricia Ann Higgins [Read], Patillo Higgins Jr.'s Daughter who Earned a Doctoral Degree in Cytogenetics and Agronomy. Courtesy of Tambria L. Read

5.10 Artesian well at Sutherland Springs about 1912. Courtesy of Author's Collection

5.11 Ruins of First State Bank, January 2005. Courtesy of Wilson County (TX) Historical Society

Williams and Sutherland Springs had more success with the completion of an improved road for automobiles, which had been long delayed. As early as 1907, plans had been laid for a roadway that could be more easily traversed by cars. In 1911, when "sandy stretches" on the unpaved road between Sutherland Springs and San Antonio still made it "almost impassible," local supporters of the national "Good Roads" movement gathered for a rally at the Hotel Sutherland. When the legislature continued to leave the matter of improvements in the hands of county officials, another meeting was held at the Sutherland Springs Opera House in April 1912 to demand the sale of local bonds. These would fund a paved road to link the town to highways that would be built from San Antonio to the coast. Ford called the meeting to order, and Thomas C. Richardson was elected as chair. A week later, Ford and Richardson became vice president and secretary, respectively, of the new Wilson County Good Roads League. Another year passed without results, so in 1913 volunteers from Sutherland Springs and La Vernia, a total of 168 men, shoveled sand, clay, and gravel to resurface the 8.8-mile roadway between their towns. Richardson chaired a local committee organized in April 1914 to ask state, not county, officials to pay for road improvements. That initiative must have failed because in December 1914 voters in Sutherland Springs returned a margin of more than three to one in favor of a bond issue to upgrade the road from San Antonio to Sutherland Springs by way of La Vernia.[12]

Years of discussion and hard work finally bore fruit in 1916. Residents of Sutherland Springs welcomed a delegation from the Texas Good Roads Association during their tour of the state in September 1915. Women from the Civic League, led by Perdie Busby, hosted a banquet inside the Hotel Sutherland and then a meeting on the lawn after all of the travelers inspected the local roads and enjoyed a brief swim. A writer for the *San Antonio Express* reported that the "meeting was snappy and filled with enthusiasm and applause." He added that the locals had a motto, "If energy counts, we've got it," and were interested in having a highway built to their town. Specifically, they wanted a "southern route" to be chosen for a proposed San Antonio to Houston highway. The residents of Sutherland Springs did not get a highway, but they held a big celebration in May 1916 for the opening of an improved road for automobiles from their community to San Antonio. Invitations were sent to many local motoring clubs, and a special train was scheduled to bring more visitors for barbecue, speeches, baseball games, footraces, swimming contests, horse races, music, and dancing (including a Maypole dance). Everything was arranged by Williams, who also had the entire affair filmed. Anticipating a huge crowd, Williams proudly told a newspaper reporter that his "home" was at San Antonio, his "business" was in Houston, and his "playground" was in "Sutherland Springs, of whose franchise he [was] the owner."[13]

Williams continued to work hard to promote New Sutherland Springs, as did others in the community. He arranged for special trains to come every Sunday from San Antonio, as they had for several years. His Fourth of July celebration in 1916 was attended by "thousands," who came for barbecue, baseball, music, dancing, "riding wild mules," and a speech by Thomas P. Morris, a prominent local attorney who later served in the Texas legislature. Williams later offered his property to the YWCA that same year to be used free of charge for a summer Red Cross training camp, explaining that he would install all necessary water lines for camp sites and bath houses. He advertised his hotel in early 1917 as being located in a "beautiful park" with a "fine bathing pool" and "all kinds of mineral waters for stomach, kidney, and nervous troubles." He declared that his town had "all modern conveniences," and that he did not welcome "tuberculars." The entry of the United States into World War I in April 1917 offered new opportunities. Among the enterprising businessmen promoting New Sutherland Springs was W. C. Duncker, who came from Kansas in 1913, bought a local lumberyard, and by 1918 became the president of the First State Bank. Under his direction, sales of Liberty Bonds in the community exceeded the federal quota, which Duncker celebrated with a rally. Allegedly that same year the United States Army sent wounded soldiers to Sutherland Springs to recuperate at a sanitarium built by Williams. In 1919, the drive to sell

Victory Bonds began with an all-day celebration that featured speeches, dancing, swimming, music from the Fourteenth United States Cavalry band, exhibitions by stunt pilots from Kelly Field in San Antonio, and a baseball game.[14]

But all was not well for New Sutherland Springs. Earnest E. Perry, the secretary of the Commercial Club, advertised in January 1917 that there was a great opportunity for a doctor in his town as there was not one for eight miles in any direction. Six months later, he placed an advertisement to sell his drug store, the only one in town, after burglars used nitroglycerine to blow open his safe late one night and escaped on a railroad hand car. It was not the first such incident; in November 1915 someone used explosives to wreck the safe in the post office and then emptied it of money and stamps. Williams sold his Houston house manufacturing company in 1917, and then during the summer of 1918 offered his Sutherland Springs property for sale. The package included the hotel with a plant for generating electricity, a fifteen-room bathhouse, the sanitarium, the concrete-lined pools, a 150-acre park with concession buildings, and 2,500 town lots, although Williams's agents in San Antonio made it clear that the lots could be bought separately. Recalling the recent past for Sutherland Springs, Williams's realtors declared that the property provided a "wonderful opportunity" for the right investor because oil wells were being drilled in the area and someone was going to hit a "rich flow." While an amended advertisement in early 1919 did mention that there were eighteen springs on the property and claimed that they had medical value, again the listing agents noted that the Ray Oil Company and Alum Creek Oil Company (whose boards of directors were identical) were drilling near Sutherland Springs.[15]

Williams did not find a buyer for his resort, so he again hosted local visitors at his springs during the summer of 1920, albeit in smaller numbers. They came primarily to swim in the two concrete-lined pools filled with water laced with minerals, mostly sulfur. A summer camp was held in the sanitarium, dubbed "Camp Restawhile" and furnished with donations from Williams, the Sutherland Springs Commercial Club, and local Baptists. Children could stay free of charge and enjoy a wide range of activities, many of them water- and pool-related, while adults had to pay. The idea was that families could drive to Sutherland Springs, enjoy lunch on the grounds of the sanitarium building that overlooked the pools, and then either go home or pitch a tent nearby. Children could enroll in the camp for just a day or for as much as a week, and in the summer of 1920 more than 300 of them used the facility. Williams hosted a Fourth of July celebration that featured local speakers such as United States Representative Carlos Bee, the son of Confederate general Hamilton P. Bee, and music by the Sunset Jazz Band of San Antonio. Attendees enjoyed dancing at the pavilion and picnicking at the sanitarium. Two hundred boys and girls who were members of the agriculture and canning clubs in Bexar and Wilson counties stayed for two days of educational workshops and recreation later in July, with the boys boarding at the sanitarium and the girls in the Hotel Sutherland. In August a large tent housed a series of church meetings, with ministers from the Presbyterian, Methodist, Baptist, and Christian Church (Disciples of Christ) faiths presiding in turns during a three-week period.[16]

The 1920 season proved to be a last hurrah for Williams and the Hotel Sutherland. His wife, Jimmie Smith Williams, died at the age of fifty-six after a brief illness in May 1920, and there is no indication in the local newspapers that he welcomed guests on a regular basis after that. He officially closed the hotel in 1923 and reportedly sold his park's electric trolley to Brackenridge Park in San Antonio. Family members insist that acquiring the resort had been Jimmie's idea, and without her Williams lost interest. He moved into the sanitarium but kept the bathhouse and pools open, charging a small admission fee for those who still came to enjoy the springs on the Cibolo. Occasionally he unlocked the hotel for special events, such as meetings of the Parent-Teacher Association. Strangely, his place continued to be promoted as a resort for several years after he closed the hotel. William E. Fitch published a guidebook in 1927 in which he praised the site as being "pleasantly situated with pleasing scenic views," creating an atmosphere that was "tranquil in character, restful and serene." The Hotel Sutherland, which he said was open, was described as a "large commodious resort hostelry" that boasted a "large concrete swimming pool." Fitch included an analysis of eleven springs, all of which he reported as having medical value. Finally, he reported that the flow of two springs was still being marketed as Hume Sour Well Water and Scott's Laxatone Water. Perhaps Fitch visited years before Williams closed the hotel, when most of this was still true.[17]

In fact, while efforts to promote New Sutherland Springs as a resort dominated reports on the community for about a decade, efforts to find oil had never entirely ceased. The *San Antonio Express* noted that a "wild cat well" was being dug in May 1912. The Bear-Hunter Oil Company of San Antonio (founded by San Antonio dentist H. M. Hunter, Henderson doctor J. H. Spivey, and Boerne businessman August G. Vogt) bought land and started drilling at that time. The *Texas Almanac* reported that they discovered "traces of oil and gas," which of course attracted more drillers by 1913. Some of the newcomers leased property from Howard A. Speer, who in 1914 got a charter for his own Sutherland Springs Investment Company under the new "Blue Sky Law." This ironically regulated the selling of business stock in Texas in response to previous shady practices such as those that had led to the lawsuit against Speer and his former colleagues. William J. Wyatt, one of those drilling on Speer's land, placed an interesting advertisement in the *San Antonio Express* in 1916: "Mr. Oil Speculator, it will pay you to see me today at the Bexar Hotel or 503 West Travis Street. I am just like Lucus [*sic*] was just before the famous gusher came in at Spindletop. I need a little money. Oil is showing fine; only ninety feet to drill. I will give you the deal of a lifetime." Such offers once more attracted a wide variety of investors to Sutherland Springs. The president of Alum Creek Oil Company in 1919 was a cattleman, D. W. Light, while his vice president was a furniture merchant, James Kapp. Only their secretary, B. L. Raborn, was a "practical oil man." The Sour Springs Oil Company joined them in 1920, while Williams, who had originally come to Wilson County prospecting for oil and had tried drilling at Sutherland Springs in 1914 and 1917, established a company named for himself in January 1921 and started drilling again. Like many others, he found little or nothing.[18]

While the resort faltered and prospectors failed to find oil, Sutherland Springs continued to serve as a commercial center for local farmers. Cotton dominated market agriculture in the area. John W. Wiseman operated a cotton gin at Sutherland Springs in 1910, while in June of that same year three investors who were active in the Farmer's Union (R. A. Houck, William F. Cotter, and John C. Damron) secured a charter for the Farmer's Gin Company, as they had done in September 1909 at nearby Stockdale. The Sutherland Springs Gin Company incorporated in 1912 with erstwhile resort developers James L. Kerr, Marcus H. Townsend, and Sempronius E. Russ as investors. Kerr actually served as the president of the organization, which built a steam-powered gin. Local cotton growers were plagued with boll weevils but kept the gins busy until World War I, when conflict interrupted commerce, especially after the United States entered the fray in April 1917. The statewide "Buy-A-Bale" program, in which bales were displayed in local shop windows for sympathetic customers to bid upon, provided enough relief that area farmers continued producing through the war and afterward. Williams in 1921, at the same time that he invested in oil prospecting, also secured a charter for the Farmer's Supply Company, with Sam H. Burris and his daughter Bessie as his co-investors.[19]

The disruption of cotton production by pests and later war forced farmers to diversify, adding peanuts, watermelons, hay, and many other crops to their repertoire. Speer developed a model farm in his efforts to promote Sutherland Springs, and he raised 1,500 bushels of corn on his property there in 1910. Baptist minister William A. Clark took a break from being a pastor and managed the Experimental Fruit Farm at Sutherland Springs from 1909 to 1912. During the same period, J. D. Cameron, acting as an agent for some unnamed New York investors, bought 445 acres for $25,000 adjacent to the town. The land was to be developed as five- and ten-acre mini-farms, and it was advertised as being great for growing figs and grapes. Herbert Holmes bought 1,500 acres near Sutherland Springs in 1918 with the intention of planting peanuts on two-thirds of it. Of course, some farmers continued to invest in livestock, experimenting with different varieties of beef and dairy cattle as well as hogs and horses. In sum, while Sutherland Springs did not succeed as a resort development or as a source of oil and natural gas during the first half of the twentieth century, when many other Texas towns were transformed by similar commercial efforts, the community persisted as an agricultural center.[20]

The 1920 census clearly revealed the decline of Sutherland Springs, both old and new. The population, instead of increasing since 1910, had fallen to 330, or about two-thirds of the combined number of residents living in the new and old communities ten years earlier. Most of those who remained were native-born whites; only eight Europeans and three dozen Mexicans remained, and nine of the latter were in town only temporarily as maintenance workers for the railroad. Four teachers were listed, but they had just 73 children in one school, instead of the 123 recorded in the 1910 census. The most common occupation was laborer, a vague label that described a wide variety of employment, from farms to railroads to oil wells. Eight merchants remained, but there was only one barber, one carpenter, and one house painter. There was a bakery but no restaurants. No doctor lived in or around Sutherland Springs. Perhaps what most clearly indicated the community's economic decline was the fact that almost two-thirds of the heads of households rented homes instead of owning. The post office still operated, however, as did the First State Bank and two churches, Baptist and Presbyterian. Along with the school, this provided some semblance of political, economic, and social persistence.[21]

Williams almost got an unexpected buyer for part of his property in 1924 when Texas officials considered acquiring it as a state park. The idea was prompted by the 1923 visit of W. W. McCrory, the state highway commissioner, with a committee that was surveying the route for a paved road from San Antonio to Cuero, which was projected to go through Sutherland Springs. This road had already been approved as part of the Texas link in the "Glacier-to-Gulf Highway," which was a series of roads stretching from Glacier National Park near Billings, Montana, to the Texas Gulf Coast at Galveston. The developers intended to have lots of national and state parks along the route, among which might be Sutherland Springs. Williams made it clear that he was ready to donate his property, and it was the first site visited by the State Park Board in a March 1924 tour of potential sites for state parks in eighty-two Texas counties. An automobile caravan filled with Board members, accompanied by Gov. Pat M. Neff and his daughter Hallie Maud Neff, State Highway Commissioner George D. Armistead and others (including many reporters), rolled into New Sutherland Springs and feasted on fried chicken. Twenty-five acres were later offered to the Board and allegedly a deed was forwarded to Neff, but nothing ever came of the proposal. Neff became famous for sponsoring state parks in Texas, but Sutherland Springs did not become one of them.[22]

A run of bad luck ravaged Sutherland Springs during the 1920s. Farm prices remained low in Texas and the United States throughout the decade. In 1927, the same year that Fitch's glowing review appeared, a fire from an exploding oil stove on the back porch of a home once owned by Jack Sutherland burned several blocks in the original community. Six homes and the Baptist church were destroyed, for a loss of $25,000 in property, while a dozen other structures were badly damaged, including the Presbyterian church. Hundreds of men fought the blaze with buckets because they had no fire-fighting equipment. The First State Bank in New Sutherland Springs folded, recovered, was robbed, and then collapsed entirely in early 1929, when the La Vernia State Bank took over its accounts and assets. After Williams died in 1928, his pavilion closed permanently. His son, Brown C. Williams, moved his large family into the hotel, which had been repeatedly vandalized and stripped of its furniture, in 1930. He and his wife supported their seven children during the Great Depression by renting hotel rooms to other impoverished families, hosting dances in the hotel, and operating a grocery store in the old bank building until 1940.[23]

Old Sutherland Springs outlasted the resort community across the Cibolo, but just barely. In 1900, the original town site had three or four stores, a post office and telephone office, one hotel, a lumberyard, a school, and a church. Thirty years later the place was almost deserted; most of the businesses and population had settled on the new town site. The two communities combined had between 300 and 400 people, as they did in 1920, with most heads of households working as farmers (including dairymen), farm laborers, or truck drivers. Apparently many had purchased empty lots on both sides of the Cibolo to plant crops. A few worked as salesmen, carpenters, blacksmiths, mechanics, and clerks. The post office and telephone office remained, albeit on the far side of the Cibolo from where they operated in 1900. There was a cotton gin, but there were no hotels or restaurants on either town site. Three-fourths of the residents were Texas natives, with most of the others born in other Southern states. There were no blacks and only a dozen born outside of the United States, six of whom were from Mexico. A few familiar faces lingered from the past: Charles N. Vezey was seventy years of age, but he told the census taker that he still worked as a blacksmith. And Earnest E. Perry, who had tried to sell his drug store after burglars dynamited the safe, still operated a pharmacy at New Sutherland Springs until his death in January 1934.[24]

The Great Depression, during which all but one of the few remaining resorts around San Antonio closed for good, greatly reduced New Sutherland Springs. By 1933, the *Texas Almanac* estimated that the population of the town had fallen to 200. That same year, the Southern Pacific converted the railroad depot into a non-manned station except for the summer months of May, June, July, and August. This may have been in response to persistent seasonal tourist traffic. Thomas J. Williams had remarried on New Year's Day in 1923, and his second wife Elizabeth kept the pools open after he died. She charged a small admission fee, like he always did, but apparently her "Bathing Beach attendant," A. A. Parks, did not do a good job of maintaining the pools. They fell into disrepair and filled with silt. Few visitors came except on July 4 of each year, when a rodeo served as the highlight of a popular annual celebration. A doctor, D. T. Wood, rented the sanitarium and treated patients in the 1930s with the assistance of two nurses, one of whom was his wife Ethel. He used the hotel built by Daniel B. Messinger, which still stood on the far side of the Cibolo, for offices and examination rooms, and considered plans to renovate the springs to bring more visitors. He may have been put out of business by the railroad company's decision in 1935 to demolish the depot and replace it with a small shack for receiving mail for the post office, which moved from the depot back to the old town site across the Cibolo. As a further sign of decline, the Masonic lodge for Sutherland Springs stopped meeting and surrendered its charter in 1935.[25]

Writers who visited Sutherland Springs during this period recorded a much more dismal literary picture than Fitch's glowing report of 1927. A columnist for the *Dallas Morning News* referred to Sutherland Springs, old and new, as a "town of tragedy" in August 1930. The older community with its "tall plank hotel" had done well enough, the writer explained, but the coming of the railroad led to the growth of the new town. There under tall oak trees were "magnificent springs" that provided healing mineral waters. Some of these filled a "seductive swimming pool" with "soft waters, soft as silk, not too hot and not too cold, so clear a hat pin could be seen under twenty feet of water." People came, some built homes, and a "hotel grew like a big white mushroom under a nest of broad oaks." The writer included humorous stories, but sadly recalled that "someone sold the townsite to someone else, and so on. And so on." The result was that "a natural playground, a health resort that California would take and make a million a year from and let thousands enjoy, languished." But it was still beautiful, and the author added that perhaps the tragedy could be erased by creating a state park. A writer for the Works Progress Administration (WPA) visited New Sutherland Springs in the late 1930s and produced an even more depressing report.

He found "a large hotel, encircled by verandas, with hundreds of rooms and great gloomy halls" that "stands abandoned under the funereal oaks." He described how "cracked sidewalks wander off into the hogweeds, the whole reminiscent of an attraction that no longer appeals." He noted that swimmers still came but added, "On the whole, the region seems to wait for a time when the public will be as much interested in mineral waters as it once was."[26]

New Deal programs had some positive impacts on Sutherland Springs, both old and new. Wood had at least one sanitarium worker, Edgar Dragan, who was paid by the WPA according to the 1940 census. Other laborers listed in the same record also worked for the WPA in the region, as well as the National Youth Administration (NYA) and Civilian Conservation Corps. Some of them may have installed public water and electrical services in the community, which by 1940 had a resident city engineer. Others may have been among the workers employed by the NYA to construct a school gymnasium or those hired to build a shop for vocational training in agriculture at Sutherland Springs. Seventeen local women worked for the Public Works Administration as seamstresses. The development of the United States Highway system during the 1930s, with the designation of the roadway from Port Lavaca through Sutherland Springs and on to San Antonio as Highway 87, sparked a commercial migration. Businesses opened near the highway, almost a mile west of the older town site and three miles from New Sutherland Springs.[27]

By 1940 the focus of commercial life in Sutherland Springs was no longer the springs or the railroad, but the road to the coast, much like that which attracted John Sutherland Jr. in the 1840s. Farmer and farm laborer were still the most common occupations in 1940, but the stores and cotton gin were joined by a restaurant and two service stations to tend the stream of travelers in automobiles. Along with farming, this provided enough income to sustain a populace near the original town site of about 350 people, almost all of them white and born in Texas. The First Baptist Church, established in 1926, outlasted four other congregations as the Baptists became the largest denomination in

Texas and the only one in Sutherland Springs. They met in the school, a private home, and an old store before they built a sanctuary near the highway in 1949. As a sign of the changing times, the bell in their steeple came from the Methodists, who had gotten it from the Presbyterians. The latter may have left after the big fire in the 1920s, while Methodist records indicate that Sutherland Springs in the first half of the twentieth century was served by a minister assigned to La Vernia, which had more than twice as many parishioners. Like the Baptist church, the post office also endured near the highway, occupying two new buildings during the next fifty years.[28]

After Elizabeth, Thomas J. Williams's second wife, died in 1943, the pools in New Sutherland Springs closed for good. Brown C. Williams actually moved his family out of the Hotel Sutherland three years earlier, although Baptist minister Alfred M. Wister still used it as a parsonage. World War II greatly reduced the number of travelers, so Sutherland Springs during those years did not provide much support for residents who did not farm. The couple who had happily married in 1913 and settled in the community lost their home to a fire in 1942. In order to pay bills, the wife took a job away from Sutherland Springs. The expanding army bases of San Antonio, the primary location for military operations in Texas during the war, offered the best opportunities, so she boarded a train every morning at the mail shack where the depot once stood and rode to Kelly Field. Many of her neighbors were not so persistent. The community's population by 1945 fell to about 200, while the number of businesses declined to just six.[29]

Brown C. Williams died in 1944 after selling, together with his brother and sister, the Hotel Sutherland to Patillo Higgins Jr. This marked the end of New Sutherland Springs. The namesake of the pioneer in the Spindletop oil field and an oilman himself who had tried to herd cattle, Higgins had begun raising Buffel Grass. This potentially lucrative crop had been brought to the United States from Africa by the Soil Conservation Service, a New Deal agency concerned with erosion control. A San Antonio nursery of the Soil Conservation Service worked with the grass until 1950, when it was released for field trials. Higgins had one of the experimental farms from which interested parties could buy Buffel Grass, which proved to be effective for feeding cattle. After county commissioners converted abandoned town lots into acreage in 1925, 1937, and 1941, he bought much of what had been New Sutherland Springs, where some buildings had already fallen victim to either fires or vandals. He then razed houses, businesses, and the Hotel Sutherland to expand his grass production, and allowed the two pools to fill with dirt. A few remaining commercial buildings of New Sutherland Springs became ruins in his Buffel Grass fields, which expanded again after renovation of Farm to Market Road (FM) 539 during the late 1950s and early 1960s led state officials to acquire and sell more lots owned by long-absent landlords. Newspaperman Thomas C. Richardson remarked in his 1959 autobiography, "Pat Higgins is now irrigating grass where my proud handiwork once stood." On the edges of the grass fields, along Lee Avenue and several connecting roadways, a few of Williams's homes survived Higgins, who suddenly died at the age of 51 in October 1961. However, during the next decade other buildings that had not been taken down during Higgins's expansion, such as the Messinger Hotel, had to be demolished as well after neglect led to deterioration.[30]

The history of the schools in Sutherland Springs reflected the expansion and ultimately the decline of the community. As the twentieth century began, materials were bought to build a military school in town, but apparently locals continued to send their children to public schools, if they went at all. School administrators expected as many as one hundred children to attend at Sutherland Springs that fall, but only thirty came because there was a delay in harvesting cotton. Ten years later, as the resort developed, four teachers lived in the community, and 123 children attended school according to the census records. That year a new building was completed for the Sutherland Springs Independent School District that could hold 150, and it filled. In September 1912 New Sutherland Springs hosted a five-day institute for all of the teachers in Wilson County, and this was repeated for three additional years. Proud community leaders dedicated a new high school in 1916, but that marked a watershed in school development for the town. In 1938, after almost a decade of depression, the remaining two-room schoolhouse in New Sutherland Springs closed and the students merged with those attending classes in a new two-story building on the old town site. This provided enough high school students to field a six-man football team in a new statewide system and a basketball team as well. Sutherland Springs survived as a district through World War II, but the school burned in 1947. A consolidation of rural districts begun in 1949 under the Gilmer-Aiken Laws led to Sutherland Springs becoming a part of the Floresville Independent School District. The gymnasium built by the National Youth Administration, which had survived the 1947 fire, was remodeled as a community center in 1950 by the new Sutherland Springs Civic Club.[31]

Blacks in Sutherland Springs, of course, had a different school history. Under the Texas Constitution of 1876, educational facilities had to be segregated. In Sutherland Springs, the few Mexican children attended the white school, but blacks had their own place. In January 1899, local leaders asked the legislature for $5,000 to construct a high school at Sutherland Springs for the black children of Wilson County. Texas had the highest black literacy rate and the greatest number of black high schools in the New South in 1900, but much remained to be done. Black illiteracy was still 38.2 percent, and the state actually had only nineteen black high schools. One of the latter was at Sutherland Springs, and as completed it stood two stories high and provided 2,400 square feet of instructional space. Encased in brick, it was described by one writer as the "handsomest building in our town." The principal was Jesse Wilson, who also allowed his place to be used as a church. When the white two-room school closed at New Sutherland Springs in 1938 and its pupils joined other white students in the new two-story building at old Sutherland Springs, where five teachers worked under the direction of superintendent W. T. Donaho, there was no similar facility there for black students. While the town officially had an accredited four-year high school for blacks at that time, it appears to have been a building with just one or two rooms. When public education was desegregated in Wilson County in 1955, the black school at Floresville that served that district was closed and its pupils merged with the white students. Of the 84 black students who thereby integrated into the local white schools, only two came from Sutherland Springs.[32]

Sutherland Springs experienced a brief economic resurgence in the mid-1950s with the discovery of productive oil deposits, but this development did not prove to have a lasting impact on the town. Drillers had persisted in the area as late as 1930, but there is no record of profitable strikes. Maple C. Hughes of Louisiana drilled and found oil nearby in 1953, producing enough to attract the interest of several competitors. The L. H. and S. A. Drilling Company from Midland leased part of the former Joseph H. Polley estate from Oscar W. Linne, a San Antonio attorney who had purchased Whitehall and remodeled it as a residence. These drillers struck oil in April 1955 and within a year drilled thirty more wells in a field named in honor of Linne. Additional wells were drilled during the next sixty years in the Linne Field and other locations in the area, producing millions of barrels of oil. Profits were good for both investors and Wilson County, which benefitted from tax revenues. Unfortunately for Sutherland Springs, apparently the largest oil strike in its history brought little significant growth in the community. The nine businesses operating there in 1947 dwindled to three by 1957. The number remained at three through 1967, just after another local surge in oil production. That year the *Texas Almanac* reported that the community had 146 residents, or two-thirds of what it had at the end of World War II. The downward trend in population continued into the 1980s, but in 1989 the count suddenly rose to 362, where it remained into the new century. During this period the number of businesses varied from three up to seventeen and back down to eight, apparently depending mostly on who did the counting and their definition of a business. In any case, it was obvious that the belated discovery of oil did not bring the growth and prosperity that earlier developers had envisioned.[33]

Sutherland Springs thus did not profit greatly from oil prospecting, nor did agriculture bring great prosperity. This of course was the experience of many small communities in Texas. But it had a unique resource: the numerous springs by Cibolo Creek. Why did it not endure as a resort? First, it has to be admitted that those who invested substantially in developing the place as a resort did so as part of programs developed to sell real estate. Their ultimate goal was to make money through the creation of a town, not a vacation destination. Most of the visitors who came, however, were day-trippers, which explains why the Hotel Sutherland, with just fifty-two rooms, did not have serious competitors within the community. Many of those who did stay overnight were locals with little money, and they often camped under the shady oak trees along the Cibolo. If there ever was any significant potential for Sutherland Springs as a resort, it faded as spas went out of fashion by World War II. One report noted that the number of spring-based spas or resorts in the United States shrank from 425 in 1877, when Edward R. Tarver of the *Western Chronicle* celebrated "another start uphill" for his community, to 185 in 1927, when William E. Fitch's glowing but ill-timed description of the Hotel Sutherland appeared. By 1943, when Thomas J. Williams's widow closed the pools for good, there were only thirty-four spring-based spas or resorts in the country. The public and the medical profession had lost interest. There never had been much evidence of the effectiveness of mineral waters, so when modern medicine proved to be more effective in curing ailments, marginal resort operations that could not offer a dazzling variety of entertainments closed their doors.[34]

There was a more insidious factor that undermined the success of Sutherland Springs as a resort and precluded future development: the springs on the Cibolo quit flowing. Early reports concerning the site claimed there were more than one hundred springs; if one cuts that number in half, to mitigate the impact of understandable exaggeration, there still may have been dozens of flowing springs at one time. But Fitch in his 1927 publication wrote than only eleven were still productive, and this number is supported by a more systematic study that appeared in 1936. The surveyors then counted just five springs flowing on the Tarín grant, one of which was in the park owned by Elizabeth Williams. There were also six useable wells, of which three had windmills to pump water to the surface. Of the three that produced water without a pump, two were in the park owned by Williams. The surveyors found no flowing springs on the Treviño grant, where John Sutherland had long ago settled, although there were four usable wells, of which three used pumps to produce water. As far as mineral content, those in Williams's park had high levels of bicarbonate of soda, but no sulfur. A shallow test well drilled elsewhere on the old Tarín grant did produce water with very high levels of sulfur, indicating that the mineral waters that made the area famous were still present, but they no longer rose to the surface.[35]

The springs on the Cibolo were depleted by the settlement and development of Central Texas, a process that intensified after World War II. The principal source of groundwater in Wilson County, in which Sutherland Springs lies, is the Carrizo-Wilcox Aquifer. The region supported by this aquifer includes seventy-nine Texas counties, which more than doubled in population from 1950 to 2000. The number of residents then continued to grow rapidly during the new century. Wilson County followed suit, with the number of its residents increasing from 14,672 in 1950 to 32,408 in 2000. Water use of course increased sharply, and 90 percent of the water that is used in Wilson County comes from groundwater. For these reasons, the water level in the Carrizo-Wilcox Aquifer has fallen at least fifty feet during the period of its regular use, or since the nineteenth century. Near municipalities such as San Antonio, where population growth has been even more spectacular, the total decline has been several hundred feet. Violet Richardson Lowe, the daughter of newspaperman Thomas C. Richardson, described one spring in a 1972 article for the *New York Times* as "a red-stained trickle out of a crude iron pipe, now in somebody's cow pasture." Observers in 2005 found only nine identifiable springs at Sutherland Springs, where the Cibolo intersects a surface appearance of the Carrizo-Wilcox Aquifer, and none of them produced more than a mere trickle of water. The water level had fallen too far to produce the flowing springs that would support a resort.[36]

Travelers along Highway 87 by 2015 would see little in Sutherland Springs to attract their interest. Two self-service gas stations and a tire shop are the only signs of commercial life, apart from some rusty pumps and other oilfield equipment. The settlement never incorporated, so there is no city hall, but a community center, volunteer fire department, and modern post office serve local residents. There are six historical markers bearing the imprint of the Texas Historical Commission, but none of them mention the development companies that promised prosperity. Drivers who turn north across the new concrete bridge that spans the Cibolo may notice ruins standing in empty fields and remember that Sutherland Springs has been called a "ghost town," but these buildings have little other significance. The railroad depot was removed during the 1930s, and Southern Pacific officials dismantled their tracks in 1971, so train buffs do not stop.[37] Perhaps some who drive a few miles further north would find Whitehall, with the Polley family cemetery just across FM 539, to be of interest. Otherwise Sutherland Springs looks like many other fading farm towns in Texas, with a community park, baseball field, and Baptist church indicating the persistence of a social network.

What remains belies the potential of the place when the springs still flowed. That resource made this site unique on Cibolo Creek and attracted the attention of generations of travelers and settlers. The mineral waters provided hope to those who wanted more than just another farm town. Sadly, that vision failed in the hands of short-sighted developers, and the disappearance of the springs eliminated the opportunity for another resort development. In Texas, water is essential for success, and no one understands that more than those who tried to develop Sutherland Springs as a resort. Where mineral springs had once filled a "seductive swimming pool" with "soft waters, soft as silk, not too hot and not too cold," and a "hotel grew like a big white mushroom under a nest of broad oaks," now ruins stand near a weed-choked small pond, surrounded by the vestiges of a fading agricultural community.[38] Progressive-era developers hoped for population increases to feed their ambitious plans, but sadly that growth depleted the groundwater and made a ghost town of Sutherland Springs.

Endnotes

Introduction

1. David W. Meinig, *Imperial Texas: An Interpretive Essay in Cultural Geography* (Austin: University of Texas Press, 1969), 36, 38, 53 [quote]. For a thorough discussion of the development and decline of mineral water resorts in Texas, see Janet M. Valenza, "Places Lived, Places Lost: Taking the Waters in Texas" (Ph.D. Diss., The University of Texas at Austin, 1992); Janet M. Valenza, "'Taking the Waters' at Texas's Health Spas," *SHQ* 98 (Jan. 1995); and Janet M. Valenza, *Taking the Waters in Texas: Springs, Spas, and Fountains of Youth* (Austin: University of Texas Press, 2000). See also Jonathan P. DeVierville, "American Healing Waters ..." (Ph.D. Diss., The University of Texas at Austin, 1992).
2. Valenza, "Places Lived, Places Lost," 197 [first quote]; *New York Times*, Aug. 20, 1972 [second and third quotes]. Violet Richardson Lowe wrote the 1972 article published in the *New York Times*. Her father was Thomas C. Richardson, publisher of the New Sutherland Springs *Health Resort*, and she was born in the community.
3. Terry G. Jordan and Alyson L. Greiner, "The Texas Travel Diary of Henry H. Field, 1853," *SHQ* 99 (Jan. 1996), 354, 356; "The Writings of Fannie Amelia Dickson Darden," *Nesbitt Memorial Library Journal* 9 (Sept. 1999), 140. Darden's letter also appeared in the Columbia *Colorado Citizen*, Aug. 30, 1877, and the *Galveston Daily News*, Sept. 4, 1877.

Chpter 1

1. William R. Hutchison et al., eds., *Aquifers of the Upper Coastal Plains of Texas* (Texas Water Development Board Report 374, Oct. 2009), 1, 4, 6, 8, 9, 19, 23, 36–38 (http://www.twdb.texas.gov/publications/reports/numbered_reports/doc/R374_AquifersofUpperCoastalPlains.pdf) accessed Aug. 12, 2016; R. B. Anders, "Ground-Water Geology of Wilson County, Texas," *Texas Water Development Board Bulletin 5710* (July 1957), 2, 9–14, 16, plate 1 (http://www.twdb.texas.gov/publications/reports/bulletins/doc/B5710/B5710.pdf), accessed Aug. 12, 2016; Alexander Duessen, *Geology of the Coastal Plain of Texas West of Brazos River* (Washington: Government Printing Office, 1924), 60, 124; "Aquifers of Texas," *Texas Almanac* (http://texasalmanac.com/topics/environment/aquifers-texas), accessed Aug. 12, 2016; "CIBOLO CREEK (KENDALL COUNTY)," *Handbook of Texas Online* (http://www.tshaonline.org/handbook/online/articles/rbcee), accessed Nov. 8, 2015; William C. Pool, *A Historical Atlas of Texas* (Austin: Eakin Press, 1975), 7–12. For a great comparative discussion of the rise and fall of spring-based resorts in Texas, see Valenza, *Taking the Waters.*
2. Eleanor Claire Buckley, "The Aguayo Expedition into Texas and Louisiana, 1719–1722," *QTSHA* 15 (July 1911), 35–36; William C. Foster and Jack Jackson, eds., "The 1693 Expedition of Gregorio de Salina Varona to Sustain the Missionaries Among the Tejas Indians," *SHQ* 97 (Oct. 1993), 271, 290; Anna Muckleroy, "The Indian Policy of the Republic of Texas, I," *SHQ* 25 (Apr. 1922), 231; Leslie Pfeiffer, "Cibolo Creek Site," *Central States Archaeological Journal* 48 (Jan. 2001), 44, 46; William C. Foster, *Spanish Expeditions into Texas, 1689–1768* (Austin: University of Texas Press, 1995), 22; Donald E. Chipman, *Spanish Texas, 1519–1821* (Austin: University of Texas Press, 1992), 82, 94, 112, 121; Deed L. Vest, *A Century of Light* (Fort Worth: Masonic Home and School, 1959), 17; "Possibly the Most Prolific Paleo Site: Cibilo Creek," http://www.arrowheadology.com/forums/content/20-possibly-most-prolific-paleo-site-cibilo-creek.html (accessed Aug. 23, 2015); "CIBOLO CREEK (KENDALL COUNTY);" Donald E. Chipman, "DE LEON, ALONSO," *Handbook of Texas Online* (http://www.tshaonline.org/handbook/online/articles/fde06), accessed Nov. 8, 2015; Donald E. Chipman, "MASSANET, DAMIAN," *Handbook of Texas Online* (http://www.tshaonline.org/handbook/online/articles/fma71), accessed Nov. 8, 2015; Donald E. Chipman, "RAMON, DOMINGO," *Handbook of Texas Online* (http://www.tshaonline.org/handbook/online/articles/fra24), accessed Nov. 8, 2015; Robert Bruce Blake, "TERAN DE LOS RIOS, DOMINGO," *Handbook of Texas Online* (http://www.tshaonline.org/handbook/online/articles/fte13), accessed Nov. 8, 2015; Lewis W. Newton, "AGUAYO, MARQUES DE SAN

MIGUEL DE," *Handbook of Texas Online* (http://www.tshaonline.org/handbook/online/articles/fag02), accessed Nov. 8, 2015; Christopher Long, "WILSON COUNTY," *Handbook of Texas Online* (http://www.tshaonline.org/handbook/online/articles/hcw12), accessed Nov. 8, 2015.

3. *Floresville Chronicle- Journal*, Sept. 16, 1960; San Antonio *Daily Express*, Oct. 22, 1905; Sutherland Springs *Western Chronicle*, June 5, 1879; Clipping from *Pioneer Magazine*, n.d. (Joseph H. Polley Papers, CAH); Herbert E. Bolton, "The Spanish Abandonment and Reoccupation of East Texas, 1773–1779," *QTSHA 9* (Oct. 1905), 81, 82, 87, 88; Jack Jackson, "Father José María de Jesús Puelles and the Maps of Pichardo's Document," *SHQ* 91 (Jan. 1988), 336; Foster and Jackson, "1693 Expedition," 271; Chipman, *Spanish Texas*, 184, 290; Jack Jackson, *Los Mesteños: Spanish Ranching in Texas, 1721 to 1821* (College Station: Texas A&M University Press, 1986), 38, 40, 412, 413; Hubert H. Bancroft, *The Works of Hubert Howe Bancroft, Vol. 15: The History of the North Mexican States* (San Francisco: A. L. Bancroft & Company, 1884), 632; Vest, *Century of Light*, 17–18; Long, "WILSON COUNTY"; Claudia Hazlewood, "FLORESVILLE, TX," *Handbook of Texas Online* (http://www.tshaonline.org/handbook/online/articles/hgf03), accessed Nov. 8, 2015; Robert H. Thonhoff, "FUERTE DE SANTA CRUZ DEL CIBOLO," *Handbook of Texas Online* (http://www.tshaonline.org/handbook/online/articles/qcf14), accessed Nov. 8, 2015; Aníbal A. González, "NUESTRA SENORA DE LA PURISIMA CONCEPCION DE ACUNA MISSION," *Handbook of Texas Online* (http://www.tshaonline.org/handbook/online/articles/uqn09), accessed Nov. 8, 2015. A good map and discussion of the separate Hispanic and Anglo settlement patterns along the San Antonio River and Cibolo Creek can be found in "The Judgment of William B. Longworth," *Lost Texas Roads* (http://losttexasroads.com/people/271-the-judgment-of-william-b-longworth? showall =&start=3), accessed June 6, 2016.

4. El Paso *International Daily Times*, Aug. 11, 1891; *Fort Worth Gazette*, Aug. 13, 1891 [third and fourth quotes]; *Abilene Reporter*, Aug. 14, 1891; Jack Jackson, ed., *Almonte's Texas: Juan N. Almonte's 1834 Inspection, Secret Report, and Role in the Texas Revolution* (Austin: Texas State Historical Association, 2003), 237 [first and second quotes]; Texas General Land Office, Land Grants: Alexandro Treviño, http://www.glo.texas.gov/ncu/SCANDOCS/archives_webfiles/arcmaps/webfiles/landgrants/PDFs/1/0/3/4/1034815.pdf (accessed Nov. 9, 2015); Texas General Land Office, Map Collection, Map of Wilson County, June 1921, Portal to Texas History, http://texashistory.unt.edu/ark:/67531/metapth232135/m1/1/?q=wilson%20county (accessed Nov. 9, 2015); I. Waynne Cox, "Documentation of the San Pedro Acequia at Trevino Street, San Antonio, Texas" (Center for Archaeological Research, The University of Texas

at San Antonio, Archaeological Survey Report No. 230 [1995]), 2–3; Stephen L. Hardin, *Texian Iliad: A Military History of the Texas Revolution, 1835–1836* (Austin: University of Texas Press, 1994), 25; Stephen L. Moore, *Savage Frontier, 1835–1837: Rangers, Riflemen, and Indian Wars in Texas, Volume 1* (Denton: University of North Texas Press, 2007), 242; Jesús F. de la Teja, "SEGUIN, JUAN NEPOMUCENO," *Handbook of Texas Online* (http://www.tshaonline.org/handbook/online/articles/fse08), accessed Nov. 9, 2015.

5. George Bonnell, *Topographical Description of Texas* (Austin: Clark, Wing & Brown, 1840), 94, 95 [first-fourth quotes]; William Kennedy, *Texas: The Rise Prospects, and Progress of the Republic of Texas*, 2 vols. (London: R. Hastings, 1841), 1: 172 [fifth quote]; *Abstract of Titled and Patented Lands Compiled from the Records of the General Land Office, of the State of Texas* (Austin: General Land Office, 1860), 650 [sixth quote]; Valenza, *Taking the Waters*, 100; Texas General Land Office, Land Grants: Manuel Tarín, http://www.glo.texas.gov/ncu/SCANDOCS/archives_webfiles/arcmaps/webfiles/landgrants/PDFs/1/5/1/151196.pdf (accessed Nov. 9, 2015); Randell G. Tarín, "TARIN, MANUEL ANTONIO SANTIAGO," *Handbook of Texas Online* (http://www.tshaonline.org/handbook/online/articles/fta61), accessed Nov. 9, 2015; Thomas W. Cutrer, "COLQUHOUN, LUDOVIC," *Handbook of Texas Online* (http://www.tshaonline.org/handbook/online/articles/fco31), accessed Nov. 9, 2015;"Hispanic Texian Patriots in the Struggle for Independence," http://www.tamu.edu/faculty/ccbn/dewitt/tejanopatriots.htm (accessed Nov. 9, 2015).
6. Joseph M. Nance, ed., "Brigadier General Adrian Woll's Report on his Expedition into Texas in 1842," *SHQ* 98 (April 1955), 538, 539; John H. Brown, *History of Texas, from 1685 to 1892*, 2 vols. (St. Louis: L. E. Daniell, 1892), 2: 214; Bill Groneman, *Alamo Defenders* (Austin: Eakin Press, 1990), 104, 105; "Everything Seguin," http://johnwayne-thealamo.com/forum/viewtopic.php?f=9&t=131&start=430&st=0&sk=t&sd=a (accessed July 9, 2015); Bill Groneman, "SMITHER, LAUNCELOT," *Handbook of Texas Online* (http://www.tshaonline.org/handbook/online/articles/fsm87), accessed Nov. 9, 2015.
7. United States Department of War, Compiled Service Records of Volunteer Soldiers Who Served During the Mexican War in Organizations from the State of Texas (RG 94, NA), Chevallie's Battalion: Gideon Lee; Sutherland Springs *Western Chronicle*, May 4, 1877, June 5, 1879; "Abstract of Title Made for Sutherland Springs Development Company" (Thomas J. Williams Family Papers, in possession of Mittie Williams [Mrs. Fred] Anderson, Floresville), 10; Samuel A. Maverick, Jr., "Reminiscences" (TS, 1929, CAH), 43; Rena Maverick Green, ed., *Memoirs of Mary A. Maverick* (San Antonio: Alamo Printing Company, 1921), 105, 106; *Why Not Know*

Why? (Sutherland Springs: Sutherland Springs Development Corporation, 1909), 6; Pat I. Nixon, *The Medical Story of Early Texas* (San Antonio: Mollie Bennett Lupe Memorial Fund, 1946), 298, 299; Gail W. Shriber, "Sutherland Springs, Wilson County, Texas, 1848–1865" (TS, 1965, Historical Marker File, TSHC), 4; "Gideon Lee Jr.," *Lost Texas Roads* (http://losttexasroads.com/people/88-lee-gideon-cibolo-calhoun-springs?showall=1&limitstart=), accessed July 8, 2015; Thomas W. Cutrer, "BAYLOR, HENRY WEIDNER," *Handbook of Texas Online* (http://www.tshaonline.org/handbook/online/articles/fbaas), accessed Nov. 9, 2015; Harold J. Weiss Jr., "CHEVALLIE, MICHAEL H.," *Handbook of Texas Online* (http://www.tshaonline.org/handbook/online/articles/fch52), accessed Nov. 9, 2015.

8. Statement Filed Jan. 4, 1859, of Joseph Henry Polley's Service in the War of 1812, Jonathan Polley to Joseph H. Polley, Sept. 24, 1856, Polley Family Record, clipping from *Pioneer Magazine*, n.d. (Polley Papers, CAH); Joseph B. Polley to Lester G. Bugbee, July 28, 1899, Joseph B. Polley to Luther E. Widen, June 21, 1907 (Texas State Historical Association Records, CAH); Joseph H. Polley to Andrew Johnson, Apr. 20, 1866 (United States Department of War, Case Files of Applications from Former Confederates for Presidential Pardons, 1865–1867, RG 94, NA); Mary A. Polley Baylor, "Reminiscences of Mary A. Baylor" (TS, n.d., CAH), 1, 2; Jamie P. M. Frost, "Descendants and Ancestors of Joseph Henry Polley, 1625–1996" (TS, 1996, private collection), 2, 21; Austin *Texas State Gazette*, Aug. 7, 1852; Eugene C. Barker, ed., "Journal of Stephen F. Austin on His First Trip to Texas, 1821," *QTSHA* 7 (Apr. 1904), 288, 294, 304; J. P. Bryan, ed., *Mary Austin Holley: The Texas Diary, 1835–1838* (Austin: University of Texas Press, 1965), 47; D. W. C. Baker, comp., *A Texas Scrapbook* (New York: A. S. Barnes & Company, 1875), 88, 89; Josephine Polley Golson, *Bailey's Light: Saga of Brit Bailey and Other Hardy Texas Pioneers* (San Antonio: Naylor Press, 1950), 57; Clarence R. Wharton, *History of Fort Bend County* (San Antonio: Naylor Press, 1939), 4, 50; Mary Smith Fay, *War of 1812 Veterans in Texas* (New Orleans: Polyanthos, 1979), 245; *Biographical Souvenir of the State of Texas* (Chicago: P. A. Battey, 1889), 14; *Memorial and Genealogical Record of Southwest Texas* (Chicago: Goodspeed Brothers, 1894), 85, 334; John H. Brown, *The Indian Wars and Pioneers of Texas* (Austin: L. E. Daniell, 189-), 214; "J. B. Polley was a Texas Pioneer," *Frontier Times* 7 (Sept. 1928), 461; Myrtle Murray, "Home Life on Early Ranches of Southwest Texas," *Cattleman* 24 (May 1938), 9–12; Edward M. Golson, "The Polley Family in Texas," *Frontier Times* 22 (July 1945), 313; Bernice Strong, "JAMES, JOHN [1819–1877]," *Handbook of Texas Online* (http://www.tshaonline.org/handbook/online/articles/fja17), accessed

Nov. 9, 2015; Richard B. McCaslin, "POLLEY, JOSEPH HENRY," *Handbook of Texas Online* (http://www.tshaonline.org/handbook/online/articles/fpo11), accessed Nov. 9, 2015.

9. Polley Family Record, Marriage Certificate, July 21, 1831, Cash Book for 1825–1841, Accounts for 1833–1844, Charles D. Sayres to Joseph H. Polley, July 30, 1838, Summons for Heirs of Jonathan Polley, June 9, 1840 (Polley Papers, CAH); Will of James B. Bailey, Jan. 21, 1833 (James B. Bailey Papers, CAH); Vertical File: Joseph H. Polley (CAH); Baylor, "Reminiscences," 3; Frost, "Descendants and Ancestors," 2, 18, 87–89, 170; Eugene C. Barker, ed., *The Austin Papers*, 3 vols. (Washington: Government Publishing Office, 1924–1928), 3: 29; Marion D. Mullins, *The First Census of Texas, 1829–1836* (Washington: National Genealogical Society, 1959), 49; Golson, *Bailey's Light*, 2, 57–59, 62, 65; Vinton Lee James, *Frontier and Pioneer Recollections of Early Days in San Antonio and West Texas* (San Antonio: Privately published, 1938), 50, 51; *Wilson County Centennial, 1860–1960* (Floresville: Wilson County Centennial Association, 1960), n.p.; Lester H. Bugbee, "The Old Three Hundred: A List of Settlers in Austin's First Colony," *QTSHA* 1 (Oct. 1897), 111, 115; J. Villasana Haggard, "Epidemic Cholera in Texas, 1833–1834," *SHQ* 40 (Jan. 1937), 217, 218, 222–224; T. F. Harwell, comp., *Confederate Biography: Members, Camp Ben McCulloch, U.C.V., and Others* (Privately published, n.d. [1923]), 30; Wharton, *Fort Bend County*, 14, 50; Murray, "Early Ranches," 9; Golson, "Polley Family," 313; Ada Craighead, "Early Settlers of Texas" (B.A. Thesis, Incarnate Word College, San Antonio, 1936), 72, 73; Richard C. Randt, "Descendants of George Polly and Elizabeth Winn" (TS, Nov. 21, 1993, in possession of George B. Everts, Houston), 27, 28; Merle Weir, "BAILEY, JAMES BRITON," *Handbook of Texas Online* (http:// www.tshaonline.org/handbook/online/articles/fba08), accessed Nov. 27, 2015; Thomas W. Cutrer, "POLLEY, JOSEPH BENJAMIN," *Handbook of Texas Online* (http://www.tshaonline.org/handbook/online/articles/fpo10), accessed Nov. 27, 2015; "CHANCE, SAMUEL," *Handbook of Texas Online* (http://www.tshaonline.org/handbook/online/articles/fch13), accessed Nov. 27, 2015.

10. Cashbook for 1825–1841, Accounts for 1833–1844, Deed and Receipt for Sale of Land, Sept. 23, 1832, Sayres to Joseph H. Polley, July 10, 1838, Joseph H. Polley to Robert and David G. Mills, May 24, Aug. 20, Sept. 17, 1842, Robert Mills to Joseph H. Polley, Jan. 1, Apr. 9, 1844, Deed for Two Town Lots in Brazoria, Nov. 2, 1842, Tax Receipt, May 20, 1837 (Polley Papers, CAH); Baylor, "Reminiscences," 1, 4, 5, 11, 13–15, 17, 18; Columbia *Telegraph and Texas Register*, Dec. 6, 1837, Mar. 9, 1838; Frederick Law Olmsted, *A Journey Through Texas* (New York: Dix, Edwards & Company, 1857), 144; Ellen Garwood, "Early Texas Inns: A Study in Social

Relationships," *SHQ* 60 (Oct. 1956), 220, 221; Terry G. Jordan, *Trails to Texas: Southern Roots of Western Cattle Raising* (Lincoln: University of Nebraska Press, 1981), 77, 78; Marie Beth Jones, "MILLS, ROBERT," *Handbook of Texas Online* (http://www.tshaonline.org/handbook/online/articles/fmi39), accessed Nov. 27, 2015.

11. Joseph H. Polley to Johnson, Apr. 20, 1866 (Confederate Pardon Files); Cashbook for 1825–1841, Accounts for 1833–1844, Settlement of James B. Bailey Estate, July 29, 1833, Receipt for Taxes, May 20, 1837, Statement of Joseph H. Polley, 1839, Receipt for Hire of Negro Girl, June 2, 1842, Robert Mills to Joseph H. Polley, June 30, 1842, Tax Receipt, Oct. 3, 1848 (Polley Papers, CAH); Texas Comptroller, Republic of Texas Claim Files: Joseph H. Polley, 536, 2745, 7672, https://www.tsl.texas.gov/arc/repclaims/rephowto.html (accessed Nov. 24, 2015); United States Bureau of the Census, Seventh Census, 1850, Texas, Schedule One, Free Population: Guadalupe County (NA); Gifford White, ed., *The 1840 Census of the Republic of Texas* (Austin: Pemberton Press, 1966), 22; Mark Gretchen, *Slave Transactions of Guadalupe County, Texas* (Santa Maria, CA: Janaway Publishing, 2009), 106; Malcolm D. McLean, ed., *Papers Concerning Robertson's Colony in Texas, Volume 16: August 10, 1837, through November, 1838* (Arlington: University of Texas at Arlington Press, 1990), 384, 385, 428, 429; H. P. N. Gammel, comp., *The Laws of Texas, 1822–1897,* 10 vols. (Austin: Gammel Book Company, 1898–1902), 4: 244; Baylor, "Reminiscences," 13, 14; Golson, *Bailey's Light,* 5, 81; James, *Recollections,* 50, 51; Vest, *Century of Light,* 33; Jordan, *Trails to Texas,* 65, 66, 74–76; William R. Hogan, *The Texas Republic: A Social and Economic History* (1946; reprint, Austin: University of Texas Press, 1969), 20–22; Randolph B. Campbell, *An Empire for Slavery: The Peculiar Institution in Texas, 1821–1865* (Baton Rouge: Louisiana State University Press, 1989), 19, 32, 46–48, 97; Murray, "Early Ranches," 9–12.

12. Cash Book for 1825–1841 (Polley Papers, CAH); Joseph H. Polley to Johnson, Apr. 20, 1866 (Confederate Pardon Files); Bailey, "Reminiscences," 6–9, 11; Notes on Sutherland Springs (Historical Marker File, THC); Columbia *Telegraph and Texas Register,* Jan. 27, 1837; Houston *Telegraph and Texas Register,* Jan. 8, Apr. 30, 1845; Barker, *Austin Papers,* 1: 995, 996, 2: 1328, 1329, 1635; Gammel, *Laws of Texas,* 4: 244; E. W. Winkler, comp., *Manuscript Letters and Documents of Early Texians, 1821–1845* (Austin: Steck Company, 1937), 30; C. L. Patterson, "Wilson County," *Fletcher State Rights Farming* (Dec. 1, 1937), 1; Golson, *Bailey's Light,* 57 [quote], 80; Joseph B. Polley, *A Soldier's Letters to Charming Nellie,* ed. Richard B. McCaslin (New York, 1908; Knoxville: University of Tennessee, 2008), 156; Murray, "Early Ranches," 9–12; Roger A. Griffin, "PEASE, ELISHA MARSHALL," *Handbook of Texas Online* (http://www.tshaonline.org/handbook/online/articles/fpe08), accessed Nov. 27, 2015.

13. Thomas Robinson to Joseph H. Polley, July 7, 1849, Ben Milburn to Mary Bailey Polley, July 30, 1849, Mrs. Thomas Robinson to Joseph H. Polley, Mar. 12, 1850, John James to Joseph H. Polley, Dec. 29, 1847, Dec. 8, 1848 (Polley Papers, CAH); James to Johnson, Aug. 14, 1865 (Confederate Pardon Files); Benjamin F. Milburn to Joseph H. Polley, June 30, 1846 (Bailey Papers); Guadalupe County Deed Record (MF, TSLA); Guadalupe County Tax Rolls, 1860 (MF, TSLA); Map of Guadalupe County Grants, 1880 (Map Collection, TSLA); Charles D. Spurlin, *Texas Veterans in the Mexican War* (Privately published, 1984), 23; Sutherland Springs *Western Chronicle*, June 5, 1879; James, *Recollections*, 18–21, 28; Golson, *Bailey's Light*, 87, 88; Vest, *Century of Light*, 33; Jordan, *Trails to Texas*, 68–72; Randt, "Polly Descendants," 27. Polley apparently purchased half of the Luar league, then used headright certificates to acquire another 1,920 acres of it, which he sold to James in 1848 and in turn was allowed to use the property. See Bexar County Deed Records (MF, TSLA).
14. Accounts for 1833–1844, Receipt from Doctor D. L. Gilmore, Aug. 1, 1843, Polley Family Record, James to M. A. Dooley, Oct. 27, 1848, J. Coggswell to Joseph H. Polley, Sept. 30, 1859, clipping from *Pioneer Magazine*, n.d., clipping of Roger W. Fore, "Century of Service," San Antonio *Express Magazine*, n.d. (Polley Papers, CAH); Asa Brigham to Stephen Howe, Oct. 24, 1833 (Asa Brigham Papers, CAH); Sutherland Springs *Western Chronicle*, June 5, 1879; Olmsted, *Journey Through Texas*, 147, 148; Haggard, "Epidemic Cholera in Texas," 216–230; James, *Recollections*, 49, 50; Golson, *Bailey's Light*, 84, 88; C. L. Patterson, *Wilson County, Texas* (San Antonio: privately published, 1939), 7 [quote]; Pool, *Historical Atlas of Texas*, 7–12; Nixon, *Medical Story of Early Texas*, 295–299; Randt, "Polly Descendants," 27; Shriber, "Sutherland Springs," 4; Long, "WILSON COUNTY."
15. Polley Family Record (Joseph H. Polley Papers, DRT); newspaper clipping, n.d. (Wilson County Scrapbook, CAH); Texas Secretary of State, Confederate Pension Files: Joseph B. Polley (TSLA); Sutherland Springs *Western Chronicle*, June 5, 1879; James, *Recollections*, 49, 50; Randt, "Polly Descendants," 27, 43; Frost, "Descendants and Ancestors," 2, 41, 85–87, 89, 261–272. The grave marker at Whitehall for Emeline Elizabeth Polley James indicates that she died in 1849, but the Polley Family Record clearly records her death date as December 21, 1848. Her daughter and namesake died on August 28, 1850.
16. Vertical File: John Sutherland (CAH); Sutherland Family Bible (CAH); "Obituary of Doctor John Sutherland" (TS, n.d., CAH); Agreement Between George Sutherland et al. and Stephen F. Austin, Feb. 19, 1830 (Sutherland-Rogers Family Scrapbook, TSLA); Gail W. Shriber to Mrs. D. M. Parmelee, Feb. 18, 1966 (Historical Marker File, THC); John Sutherland, *The Fall of*

the Alamo, ed. Annie B. Sutherland (San Antonio: Naylor Company, 1936), 1, 2; John H. Jenkins, ed., *The Papers of the Texas Revolution, 1835–1836*, 10 vols. (Austin: Presidial Press, 1973), 3: 186; Worth S. Ray, *Austin Colony Pioneers* (Privately published, 1949), 298; Anne Sutherland, *We Cousins: The Robertsons, the Sutherlands, and the Making of Texas* (College Station: Texas A&M University Press, 2006), 57; Florence Sutherland Hudson, "We Cousins" (TS, 1957, CAH), 66, 67; Martha D. Freeman, "The Sutherland Plantation and the Alabama Settlement: A Study in Cluster Migration," *The Antebellum Period in the Stephen F. Austin Colony* (Research Report No. 70, Palmetto Bend Reservoir Series, The University of Texas at Austin, 1980), 2–33; Villamae Williams, ed., *Stephen F. Austin's Register of Families* (St. Louis: Ingmire Publications, 1984), n.p.; Gifford White, ed., *1830 Citizens of Texas* (Austin: Eakin Press, 1983), 4, 5; Fay, *War of 1812 Veterans*, 298; Nixon, *Medical Story of Early Texas*, 181; James T. DeShields, "Siege, Defense and Fall of the Alamo," *Alamo Magazine* (Dec. 1913), 4; Amelia Williams, "A Critical Study of the Siege of the Alamo and the Personnel of Its Defenders," *SHQ* 36 (Apr. 1933), 274; Richard B. McCaslin, "SUTHERLAND, JOHN, JR.," *Handbook of Texas Online* (http://www.tshaonline.org/handbook/online/articles/fsu07), accessed Nov. 27, 2015; Claudia Hazlewood, "SUTHERLAND, GEORGE," *Handbook of Texas Online* (http://www.tshaonline.org/handbook/online/articles/fsu06), accessed Nov. 27, 2015.

17. Texas Comptroller, Republic Claims: John Sutherland, 314 (1836), 1262, 1375, 1428, 4400, and Unnumbered 01, 08, 09; John Sutherland to "The Hon. Legislators of the State of Texas," Jan. 11, 1854, John Sutherland to "The Honourable the Congress of the Republic," n.d. (Texas Legislature, Memorial and Petition File, TSLA); David G. Burnet to John Sutherland, Apr. 3, 1836 (Historical Marker File); Vertical File: John Sutherland; John Sutherland, "The Alamo" (TS, n.d., CAH), 1–6; *San Antonio Express*, June 21, 1927; William F. Gray, *From Virginia to Texas,1835* (Houston: Gray, Dillaye and Company, 1909), 131, 142, 150; Jenkins, *Papers of the Texas Revolution*, 5: 304, 7: 26; *Memorial Record of Southwest Texas*, 138; George P. Red, *The Medicine Man in Texas* (Houston: Privately published, 1930), 37–41; Groneman, *Alamo Defenders*, 102, 108, 109; Jeff Long, *Duel of Eagles: The Mexican and U.S. Fight for the Alamo* (New York: William Morrow and Company, 1990), 158, 159, 161, 162; Walter Lord, *A Time to Stand* (New York: Harper & Brothers, 1961), 78, 94, 95, 97, 98; Sutherland, *We Cousins*, 97; Fay, *War of 1812 Veterans*, 298; DeShields, "Siege of the Alamo," 4–6; Hudson, "We Cousins," 66, 68; Thomas W. Cutrer, "PATTON, WILLIAM HESTER," *Handbook of Texas Online* (http://www.tshaonline.org/handbook/online/articles/fpa54), accessed Nov. 27, 2015; Bill Groneman,

"SUTHERLAND, WILLIAM DEPRIEST," *Handbook of Texas Online* (http://www.tshaonline.org/handbook/online/articles/fsu20), accessed Nov. 27, 2015; Cecil Collins Scanlan, "SMITH, JOHN WILLIAM," *Handbook of Texas Online* (http://www.tshaonline.org/handbook/online/articles/fsm30), accessed Nov. 27, 2015.

18. Shriber to Parmelee, Feb. 18, 1966 (Historical Marker File); Sutherland Family Bible; Vertical File: John Sutherland; Texas Secretary of State, Confederate Pension Files: Jack Sutherland; Sutherland, *Fall of the Alamo*, 3; Freeman, "Sutherland Plantation," 9, 10; Hudson, "We Cousins," 66; *Memorial and Genealogical Record of Texas (East)* (Chicago: Goodspeed Brothers, 1895), 287. John Sutherland to Joseph H. Polley, Aug. 22, 1849 (Polley Papers, CAH), mentions a stepson, Richard H. Dickson.
19. Bexar County Deed Records; John Sutherland to William E. Jones, Dec. 28, 1849 (Philip Dimmitt Papers, CAH); Notes on Arrest of Philip Dimmitt (Harbert Davenport Papers, TSLA); John Sutherland to "Legislators of the State of Texas," Jan. 11, 1854, John Sutherland to "Congress of the Republic," n.d. (Memorial and Petition File); Washington *National Register*, Feb. 22, 1845; Houston *Telegraph and Texas Register*, Feb. 5, 1845; Frances T. Ingmire and Robert L. Thompson, comps., *Bexar County Land Titles* (Privately published, 1980), 25; Kevin Ladd, comp., *Gone to Texas: Genealogical Abstracts from the Telegraph and Texas Register, 1835–1841* (Bowie, MD: Heritage Books, 1994), 261; Harriet Smither, ed., "Diary of Adolphus Sterne, IV," *SHQ* 31 (July 1927), 69; Charles A. Gulick et al., eds., *The Papers of Mirabeau Buonaparte Lamar*, 6 vols. (Austin: Texas State Library, 1923–1927), 3: 437; Gammel, *Laws of Texas*, 2: 1072; McLean, *Papers Concerning Robertson's Colony*, 16: 611; Pool, *Atlas*, 44, 45; Hogan, *Texas Republic*, 9–11; Long, *Duel of Eagles*, 159; *Record of Texas (East)*, 287; Joseph M. Nance, *After San Jacinto: The Texas-Mexican Frontier, 1836–1841* (Austin: University of Texas Press, 1963), 445–452, 456–469; Catherine George, "The Life of Philip Dimmitt" (M.A. Thesis, University of Texas at Austin, 1937), 69–78; Craig H. Roell, "DIMMITT, PHILIP," *Handbook of Texas Online* (http://www.tshaonline.org/handbook/ online/articles/fdi19), accessed Nov. 27, 2015.
20. John Sutherland to Sarah A. Sutherland, Oct. 14, 1842 [first quote], John Sutherland to James P. N. Craighead, Dec. 13, 1846 (John Sutherland Papers, CAH); John Sutherland to Sarah A. Sutherland, Aug. 6, 1842, Feb. 1, 1844 (John W. Lilly Papers, DRT); John Sutherland to Sarah A. Sutherland Craighead, Sept. 24, 1848, with postscript to Sarah from Ann Dickson Sutherland, Sept. 26, 1848, Ann Dickson Sutherland to Sarah A. Sutherland Craighead, Sept. 28, 1848 (Historical Marker File); Sutherland Family Bible; Frances Menefee [Mrs. George] Sutherland to "Sister," June 5, 1836, Agreement Signed Mar. 2, 1854, Between John Sutherland

and the Widow and Heirs of George Sutherland [second quote] (George Sutherland Papers, CAH); Bexar County Tax Rolls, 1850; Nixon, *Medical Story of Early Texas*, 181; Ray, *Austin Colony Pioneers*, 298; Smither, "Diary of Adolphus Stone," 69.

21. San Antonio *Daily Express*, Oct. 22, 1905; *Floresville Chronicle-Journal*, Jan. 19, 1989; Bonnell, *Topographical Description of Texas*, 95 [first quote]; Edward Stiff, *The Texian Emigrant* (Cincinnati, 1840; reprint, Waco: Texian Press, 1968), 125 [second quote]; Allen Johnson et al., eds., *Dictionary of American Biography*, 22 vols. (New York: Charles Scribner's Sons, 1922–1958), 18: 488, 489; Red, *Medicine Man*, 83; Nixon, *Medical Story of Early Texas*, 181; Sylvia V. V. Ferris and Eleanor S. Hoppe, *Scalpels and Sabers* (Austin: Eakin Press, 1985), 27–29. Susan J. Pickett to "My Dear Friend" [Elizabeth Mary Menefee Riddle Canterbury], Sept. 22, 1865 (Aline P. Carter Family Papers, Special Collections, University of Texas at San Antonio), reported that John Sutherland and others used blue mass and quinine, as well as mustard plasters, to treat Canterbury's ailing son.
22. John Sutherland to William S. Kennedy, Dec. 28, 1842 [first and second quotes], John Sutherland to Sarah A. Sutherland, Feb. 1, 1844, May 29, 1849 [third-sixth quotes] (Lilly Papers).
23. Deed for "Sulphur Spring League," Sept. 18, 1848, John Sutherland to James P. N. Craighead, July 29, 1854 (in private collection); Juan De Cordova, Map of Texas, 1856, United States Bureau of Topographical Engineers, Map of Texas and Part of New Mexico, 1857, and United States Military Division of the Gulf, Engineering Department, Map of Route From Indianola to San Antonio, 1865 (Map Collection, TSLA); Bureau of the Census, Seventh Census, 1850, Texas, Free Population: Bexar County; Bexar County Tax Rolls, 1848, 1850; Willie Mae Weinert to Mr. Hill, Aug. 6, 1962 (Historical Marker File); Sutherland, *Fall of the Alamo*, 4; Vest, *Century of Light*, 20, 38; Pool, *Atlas*, 139; Freeman, "Sutherland Plantation," 9, 10; Shriber, "Sutherland Springs," 1, 3. Cornelius C. Cox, in "Reminiscences of C. C. Cox," *QTSHA* 6 (Jan. 1903), 135, says that James Lansing owned the future site of Sutherland Springs before he left for California after 1849. There is nothing in the tax rolls to substantiate this claim.
24. Appointment of Claiborne Rector as Executor of James B. Bailey Estate, Nov. 27, 1844, James to Joseph H. Polley, Dec. 8, 24, 1848 (Polley Papers, CAH); Probate Records, James B. Bailey Estate (Bailey Papers); Houston *Telegraph and Texas Register*, Jan. 8, 1845, Apr. 30, 1845; San Antonio *Daily Express*, Oct. 22, 1905; *Dallas News*, Oct. 9, 1932; Bureau of the Seventh Census, 1850, Texas, Free Population: Bexar County; Ladd, *Gone to Texas*, 43; Homer S. Thrall, *History of Methodism in Texas* (Houston: E. H. Cushing, 1872), 35–36; Golson, *Bailey's Light*, 88, 90;

Freeman, "Sutherland Plantation," 11; J. L. Bryan, "RECTOR, CLAIBORNE," *Handbook of Texas Online* (http://www.tshaonline.org/handbook/online/articles/frebt), accessed Nov. 27, 2015.

25. Registration of Brands, July 24, 1847, James to Joseph H. Polley, Dec. 29, 1847, Dec. 8, 24, 1848, Sept. 14, 1849, C. G. Carver to Joseph H. Polley, Dec. 30, 1849, Walker K. Baylor to Joseph H. Polley, Feb. 6, 1851, Stock Branded of My Own [Walker K. Baylor], 1855–1863, Toll Calves from the JP Stock, 1855–1863, clipping of Fore, "Century of Service," from *San Antonio Light*, n.d. (Polley Papers, CAH); Bureau of the Census, Seventh Census, 1850, Texas, Free Population: Bexar County; Department of War, Compiled Service Records of Volunteer Soldiers in the Mexican War from Texas, Chevallie's Battalion: Walker K. Baylor; Guadalupe County Tax Rolls, 1860; *Floresville Chronicle-Journal*, Sept. 16, 1960; "Obituary of Mary Augusta Baylor" (TS, n.d., Wilson County Scrapbook); James, *Recollections*, 20, 21, 24, 28, 29, 49–51; Golson, *Bailey's Light*, 90, 91; Frost, "Descendants and Ancestors," 2, 85; Randt, "Polly Descendants," 27, 43; Orval W. and Henry B. Baylor, *Baylor's History of the Baylors* (LeRoy, IL: LeRoy Journal Printing Company, 1914), 26, 27, 34, 35; Cora M. Cross, "A. H. Polley Tells How He Turned the Western Trail," *Frontier Times* 6 (June 1929), 363; J. Evetts Haley, "A Log of the Texas-California Cattle Trail, I, II, and III," *SHQ* 35 and 36 (Jan.- July 1932), 208–237, 290–316, 47–66; Cutrer, "BAYLOR, HENRY WEIDNER."

26. John Sutherland to Joseph H. Polley, Aug. 22, Nov. 29, 1849, James to Joseph H. Polley, Sept. 14, 1849, Dec. 1, 1859, June 4, 1860, Agreement Signed by Joseph H. Polley, Nov. 6, 1851, Jonathan H. Rollins to Joseph H. Polley, Feb. 22, Mar. 4, 1854, William Milburn to Joseph H. Polley, Nov. 1, 1856, James Shaw to Joseph H. Polley, Oct. 22, 1856, Jan. 18, 1859, Walker K. Baylor to Joseph H. Polley, Dec. 10, 1857, A. Stafford to Joseph H. Polley, Feb. 19, Mar. 20, 1858, Receipt from R. M. Forbes and _____ McKee, Apr. 29, 30, 1858, Samuel Riggs to Joseph H. Polley, Dec. 28, 1858, Thomas E. Tullis to Joseph H. Polley, July 28, 1860, Joseph H. Polley to Tullis, July 28, 1860, Receipt from Jonathan Polley, Nov. 15, 1860, Tax Receipts, 1849–1860 (Polley Papers, CAH); John A. Rogers to Joseph H. Polley, Dec. 21, 1851, T. H. Duggan to Joseph H. Polley, June 23, 1856, A. Stafford to Joseph H. Polley, Mar. 19, 1858, Forbes McKee to Joseph H. Polley, July 25, 1859 (Joseph H. Polley Papers, Texas Collection, Baylor University, Waco); James to Joseph H. Polley, Sept. 28, Nov. 12, 1860, Mar. 22, 30, 1861 (Joseph H. Polley Papers, DRT); Guadalupe County Tax Rolls, 1848, 1860; United States Bureau of the Census, Eighth Census, 1860, Texas, Schedule Two, Slave Population: Guadalupe County (NA); Guadalupe County Deed Record; Gretchen, *Slave Transactions*, 106; *El Paso Times*, Sept. 13, 1908; James, *Recollections*, 52; Cornelius C. Cox, "Reminiscences of C. C. Cox, II,"

QTSHA 6 (Apr. 1903), 205 [quotes]; Ralph A. Wooster, "Wealthy Texans, 1860," *SHQ* 71 (Oct. 1967), 175. John James paid taxes on as many as ten slaves in Guadalupe County in the 1850s, but it is not clear if Joseph H. Polley's management of his land included control of those slaves. See Gretchen, *Slave Transactions*, 66–67.

27. Clarissa Polley to Mary B. Polley, July 31, 1851, Jonathan Polley to Joseph H. Polley, Apr. 30, July 2, Oct. 5 [quote], 1853, Sept. 24, 1856, Jan. 8, 31, 1857, Joseph H. Polley to Edward A. Kriegner, Sept. 23, Nov. 5, 1853, Mar. 19, Apr. 8, and May 29, 1854, Bills of Lading, R. M. Forbes, May 29, July 18, 1855, July 19, 1856, Aug. 25, 1856, James to Joseph H. Polley, Oct. 21, 1859, Clipping of Fore, "Century of Service," (Polley Papers, CAH); *San Antonio Express*, Dec. 30, 1928; *Floresville Chronicle-Journal*, Sept. 16, 1960; *Austin American*, Aug. 23, 1962; Vertical File: Joseph H. Polley (CAH); Weinert to Hill, Aug. 6, 1962 (Historical Marker File); "Gazetteer of the Streams of Texas" (TS, n.d., Works Progress Administration, Historical Records Survey, CAH); James, *Recollections*, 21; Golson, *Bailey's Light*, 93, 94; *Wilson County Centennial*; "The John Henry Polley Home Near Sutherland Springs," *Frontier Times* 22 (July 1945), 315.

28. Clipping from San Antonio *Express Magazine*, n.d., Frances A. Polley to Joseph H. Polley, Sept. 20, 1853, Receipt from T. C. Houghton, May 4, 1859, Receipt from _____ Smith and _____ Lounsberg, May 5, 1859, Jonathan Polley to Joseph H. Polley, Sept. 16, 1852, May 8, 1859, Bill of Lading from R. M. Forbes and _____ McKee, July 25, 1859 (Polley Papers, CAH); Golson, *Bailey's Light*, 97, 100, 102; Frost, "Descendants and Ancestors," 85. Jonathan Polley to Joseph H. Polley, Sept. 8, 1850, Sept. 16, 1852, Apr. 30, 1853, May 8, 1859, Frances A. Polley to Joseph B. Polley, Sept. 20, 1853, Receipt from T. C. Houghton, May 4, 1859, Receipt from _____ Smith and _____ Lounsberg, May 5, 1859, Bill of Lading from R. M. Forbes and _____ McKee, July 25, 1859, Clipping of Fore, "Century of Service" Clipping from San Antonio *Express Magazine*, n.d. (Polley Papers, CAH); Golson, *Bailey's Light*, 97, 100, 102; Frost, "Descendants and Ancestors," 85; San Antonio *Express Magazine*, Dec. 28, 1947; Myrtle Murray, "Early Ranches," 9, 10.

29. Joseph H. Polley to Johnson, Apr. 20, 1866 (Confederate Pardon Files) [quotes]; Emeline M. Kinner to Catherine S. Polley, Mar. 9, 1857; Receipt from R. M. Forbes, June 15, 1857, clipping of Fore, "Century of Service," (Polley Papers, CAH); *Floresville Chronicle-Journal*, Sept. 16, 1960; Bureau of the Census, Seventh Census, 1850, Texas, Schedules One and Two, Free and Slave Population: Guadalupe County; Bureau of the Census, Eighth Census, 1860, Texas, Free and Slave Population: Guadalupe County; Golson, *Bailey's Light*, 98, 99, 102; James, *Recollections*, 49, 50; Randt, "Polly Descendants," 27.

30. Harriet R. Polley to David H. Houston, July 19 [first quote], Aug. 18, 1859, Mary F. Sutherland to Harriet R. Polley, Oct. 9, 1858 [second quote] (in private collection); Harriet R. Polley to David H. Houston, Nov. 11, 1858 (Polley Family Papers, CAH)
31. Clipping from *San Antonio Light*, n.d., clipping from *Pioneer Magazine*, n.d., Connally F. Henderson to Joseph H. Polley, Apr. 19, 1859 (Polley Papers, CAH); Austin *Texas State Gazette*, Jan. 26, 1850; Sutherland Springs *Western Chronicle*, June 5, 1879; *Dallas Morning News*, Dec. 19, 1897, July 9, 1899; San Antonio *Daily Express*, Oct. 22, 1905, Dec. 16, 1906; *Cotulla Record*, Sept. 25, 1931; John W. Hunter, "John W. Hunter Literary Effort" (MS, n.d., TSLA), 31; Green, *Memoirs of Mary A. Maverick*, 115, 116; Golson, *Bailey's Light*, 80, 81, 91, 96, 97; Vest, *Century of Light*, 17, 21; "Chapter One—John S. McGee, Circuit Rider," http:// www.so-ky.com/books/mcgee/chapter-one.pdf (accessed Nov. 26, 2015).
32. John Sutherland to Joseph H. Polley, Aug. 22, 1849, P. W. Platt to Joseph H. Polley, Jan. 23, 1853, Kinner to Joseph H. Polley, Apr. 3, 1853 [second quote], Josephine Milby to Mary B. Polley, Sept. 15, 1856 (Polley Papers, CAH); John Sutherland to Sarah A. Sutherland, May 25, 1849, Ann Dickson Sutherland to Sarah A. Sutherland, Feb. 18, 1852 (Lilly Papers); William M. Hamilton to Louisa M. Hamilton, June 7, 1851, William Lucas to Ann Dickson Sutherland, July 15, 1851 (Dickson Family Papers, DRT); Notes on Sutherland Springs, Shriber to Parmelee, Feb. 18, 1966 (Historical Marker File); J. H. Colton, Map of Texas, 1855 (Map Collection, TSLA); Sutherland Springs Historical Display, Sutherland Springs Museum, Sutherland Springs, TX; Bexar County Tax Rolls, 1859; Wilson County Tax Rolls, 1860; Bureau of the Census, Eighth Census, 1860, Texas, Schedule One, Free Population: Bexar County; Austin *Texas State Gazette*, Nov. 23, 1850; San Antonio *Western Texan*, Dec. 30, 1852; Clarksville *Standard*, May 6, 1854; Sutherland Springs *Western Chronicle*, June 5, 1879 [first quote]; San Antonio *Daily Express*, July 10, 1904, Oct. 22, 1905; *Floresville Chronicle-Journal*, Sept. 19, 1960; Green, *Memoirs of Mary Maverick*, 102–106; Vest, *Century of Light*, 20; Jordan and Greiner, "Texas Travel Diary of Henry H. Field," 356; Nixon, *Medical Story of Early Texas*, 181, 295–299; Leavitt Corning, *Baronial Forts of the Big Bend* (San Antonio: Trinity University Press, 1967), 20, 86; Shriber, "Sutherland Springs," 1; Hudson, "We Cousins," 70; Jerry M. Sullivan, "The Ben Leaton Legend," tpwd.state.tx.us/news/magazine/leaton (accessed Nov. 26, 2015).
33. Ann Dickson Sutherland to Sarah A. Sutherland Craighead, Feb. 18, 1852 (Lilly Papers); Ann Dickson Sutherland to Sarah A. Sutherland Craighead, Mar. 11, 1853 (John Sutherland Papers); John Sutherland to James P. N. Craighead, July 2, 1854 (in private collection); Bureau of the Census,

Eighth Census, 1860, Texas, Free Population: Bexar, Guadalupe, and Wilson Counties; Bexar County Tax Rolls, 1853; Wilson County Tax Rolls, 1860; San Antonio *Daily Express*, Oct. 22, 1905; *Floresville Chronicle-Journal*, Sept. 16, 1960; Joseph B. Polley, "A Texas Reminiscence," *Frontier Times* 27 (Aug. 1950), 307 [quote]; Shriber, "Sutherland Springs," 1; *Wilson County Centennial*. In addition to John Sutherland and his wife Ann, who paid taxes on four and nine town lots respectively in 1860, others who were assessed for lots in Sutherland Springs in 1860 were Thomas Bannister, an English stonemason who lived in Panna Maria; Martin Butner, a blacksmith from New York who was a resident of Sutherland Springs; R. N. Cresap; Mary A. Highland, who resided in Sutherland Springs; John Irvin; John W. Lilly, a merchant in Sutherland Springs; R. T. Lyons; Andrew G. Pickett; Emanda C. Stevenson, the wife of Dr. R. Stevenson of Sutherland Springs; L. D. Stimson, a gunsmith from Georgia who lived in Sutherland Springs; and Creed Taylor. A copy of the original plat for Sutherland Springs can be found in the Bexar County Deed Records.

34. Ann Dickson Sutherland to "My Dear Sister," May 15, 1853 (Lilly Papers); Edward J. King to Joseph H. Polley, Jan. 4, 1857, List of Certification for Cibolo Institute by Thomas Pooley, Aug. 1, 1857, Quarterly Report, Nov. 15, 1858, Receipts to Joseph H. Polley from Cibolo Institute, Oct. 8, Nov. 5, Dec. 3, 1858, Jan. 1, Feb. 16, 1859, Joseph H. Polley to Pooley, February 28, 1858, Receipt to _____ Henderson and _____ Morgan, Dec. 4, 1858 (Polley Papers, CAH); Receipt from John Sutherland to William D. Mayes, Dec. 5, 1859 (in private collection); Bureau of the Census, Eighth Census, 1860, Texas, Free Population: Wilson County; *Floresville Chronicle-Journal*, Sept. 16, 1960; Gammel, *Laws of Texas*, 5: 86–88; Sutherland, *Fall of the Alamo*, 4; Sarah A. L. Hardinge, *Views of Texas, 1852–1856*, ed. Ron Tyler (Fort Worth: Amon Carter Museum, 1983), 10–15, 63; Olin W. Nail, ed., *Journal of the Rio Grande Mission Conference of the Methodist Episcopal Church, South* (Privately published, 1938), 6, 8, 14, 18, 19, 21, 25, 26, 28, 31, 32, 123; Mattie Jackson, comp., *The Rising and Setting of the Lone Star Republic* (Privately published, 1926), 15, 16; Golson, *Bailey's Light*, 98; Hudson, "We Cousins," 70; *Memorial Record of Texas (East)*, 287; Max Berger and Lee Wilborn, "EDUCATION," *Handbook of Texas Online* (http://www.tshaonline.org/handbook/online/articles/khe01), accessed Nov. 27, 2015. For more about William D. Mayes, see "Biographies of Wilson County, Texas," http://genealogytrails.com/tex/southtexas/wilson/bios1.html (accessed Nov. 26, 2015).

35. Mary F. Sutherland to Harriet R. Polley, Aug. 11, Oct. 9, 1858 [first and second quotes] (in private collection); Harriet R. Polley to David H. Houston, Nov. 11, 1858 (Polley Family Papers, CAH).

36. Bureau of the Census, Eighth Census, 1860, Texas, Free Population: Bexar County; Baylor, "Reminiscences," 16; Obituary for John Sutherland (MS, n.d., Wilson County Scrapbook); Houston *Telegraph and Texas Register*, Apr. 10, 1839; *San Antonio Ledger*, Apr. 20, 1867 [quote]; *Floresville Chronicle-Journal*, Sept. 16, 1960; Sutherland, *Fall of the Alamo*, 4; Rev. Herschel H. Homer, "The Site Location History of the Floresville United Methodist Church" (MS, n.d., in possession of Louise Stadler, Floresville, TX), n.p.; Thrall, *History of Methodism in Texas*, 35; Ada Craighead, "Early Settlers of Texas" (B.A. Thesis, Incarnate Word College, San Antonio, TX, 1936), 72, 73; Hardinge, *Views of Texas*, 63; Sutherland, *We Cousins*, 67, 68; Nail, *Journal of the Rio Grande Mission Conference*, 9, 22, 112, 113; Sterling Fisher, "The Rio Grande Conference," *Texas Methodist Historical Quarterly* 1 (Apr. 1910), 349; Norman W. Spellman, "METHODIST CHURCH," *Handbook of Texas Online* (http://www.tshaonline.org/handbook/online/articles/imm01), accessed Aug. 14, 2015.
37. Notes on Sutherland Springs (Historical Marker File); "Wilson County Commissioner's Court Minutes, Vol. A" (TS, n.d., Works Progress Administration, Historical Records Survey, CAH), 3; Bureau of the Census, Seventh Census, 1850, Texas, Free Population: Bexar County; Bureau of the Census, Eighth Census, 1860, Texas, Free and Slave Population: Wilson County; Wilson County Tax Rolls, 1860; Polley, "Texas Reminiscence," 308; Sutherland Springs *Western Chronicle*, June 5, 1879; *Floresville Chronicle-Journal*, Sept. 16, 1960; Patterson, "Wilson County," 2; Andrew J. Sowell, *Early Settlers and Indian Fighters of Southwest Texas* (Austin: B. C. Jones & Company, 1900), 805–810; Robert C. Sutton Jr., *The Sutton-Taylor Feud* (Quanah: Nortex Press, 1974), 12, 13; Maude T. Gilliland, *Wilson County Texas Rangers, 1837–1977* (Privately published, 1977), 15, 16, 99; "Hero of Texas Independence, " *Frontier Times* 5 (Sept. 1928), 492; Shriber, "Sutherland Springs," 4; J. T. Jaeggli Jr., *The Court House Story* (Privately published, 1971), 1; Dovie T. Hall, "TAYLOR, CREED," *Handbook of Texas Online* (http://www.tshaonline.org/handbook/online/articles/fta17), accessed Nov. 27, 2015.
38. David K. Sutherland to John Sutherland, Dec. 7, 1851 (Sutherland Family Papers in possession of Elise Kidd, Austin); Ann Dickson Sutherland to Sarah A. Sutherland, Feb. 18, 1852 (Lilly Papers); John Sutherland to James P. N. Craighead, July 29, 1854 (in private collection); Mary Sutherland to Eleanor J. R Dickson, Nov. 9, 1862 (Robert H. Dickson Papers, DRT); Texas Secretary of State, Confederate Pension Files: John S. Craighead; Shriber to Parmelee, Feb. 18, 1966 (Historical Marker File); Bureau of the Census, Seventh Census, 1850, Texas, Free and Slave Population: Bexar County; Bureau of the Census, Eighth Census, 1860,

Texas, Free and Slave Population: Wilson County; Bexar County Tax Rolls, 1859 and 1860; Wilson County Probate Minutes, Vol. B: 8 (MF, TSLA); *Floresville Chronicle-Journal*, Sept. 16, 1960; Freeman, "Sutherland Plantation," 9, 10. James P. N. Craighead died on August 5, 1854, just five months after his daughter, Diana K. Craighead.

39. John Sutherland to Sam Houston, Feb. 1860 [first and second quotes] (Texas Governor, Records, TSLA); Susan J. Pickett to "My Dear Friend" [Elizabeth Mary Menefee Riddle Canterbury], June 11, 1860 [third and fourth quotes] (Carter Family Papers); Texas Secretary of State, Election Register (MF, TSLA); Texas Adjutant General, Confederate Audited Civil Claims, 1861–1865 (TSLA); Muster Roll of Capt. W. R. Henry's Company of Texas Mounted Volunteers ... Sept. 15, 1855 (Texas Adjutant General, Militia Records, TSLA); "Wilson County Commissioners Court Minutes, Volume A," 3; Bureau of the Census, Eighth Census, 1860, Texas, Free Population: Wilson County; Gammel, *Laws of Texas*, 4: 1462; *San Antonio Ledger*, Aug. 18, Dec. 1, 1855; *Dallas Morning News*, Jan. 13, 1893; Olmsted, *Journey Through Texas*, 506, 507; J. Fred Rippy, "Border Troubles Along the Rio Grande, 1848–1860," *SHQ* 23 (Oct. 1919), 99–103; Ernest C. Shearer, "The Callahan Expedition, 1855," *SHQ* 54 (Apr. 1951), 430–451; Ronnie C. Tyler, "The Callahan Expedition of 1855: Indians or Negroes?" *SHQ* 70 (Apr. 1967), 574–585; Louise Stadler, comp., *Wilson County History* (Dallas: Taylor Publishing Company, 1990), 4, 129; *Wilson County Centennial*; Frost, "Descendants and Ancestors," 86; *Memorial Record of Southwest Texas*, 401, 402; Jaeggli, *Court House Story*, 1; Gilliland, *Wilson County Texas Rangers*, 99; *Memorial and Genealogical Record of Texas (East)*, 287; Russell Woodall, "CALLAHAN, JAMES HUGHES," *Handbook of Texas Online* (http://www.tshaonline.org/handbook/online/articles/fca16), accessed Nov. 27, 2015; Manuel Guerra, "HENRY, WILLIAM R.," *Handbook of Texas Online* (http://www.tshaonline.org/handbook/online/articles/fhehg), accessed Nov. 27, 2015.

Chapter 2

1. Bureau of the Census, Eighth Census, 1860, Texas, Free and Slave Populations: Guadalupe and Wilson Counties. Joseph H. Polley is listed in Guadalupe County, as is Ann C. Mayes, who was William D. Mayes's wife.
2. Joseph H. Polley to Johnson, Apr. 20, 1866 [first quote] (Confederate Pardon Files); Receipt for Subscription to *San Antonio Ledger*, Mar. 29, 1854, Jonathan Polley to Joseph H. Polley, June 29, Oct. 21, 1856, Mar. 9, Receipt for Subscription to Houston *Weekly Telegraph*, July 9, 1862 (Polley Papers, CAH); A. P. Hansen to Joseph H. Polley, Dec. 3, 1860 [second quote], Jonathan Polley to Joseph H. Polley, May 5, 1861 [third and fourth quotes] (Polley Papers, DRT); Walter L. Buenger, *Secession and the Union in Texas*

(Austin: University of Texas Press, 1984), 28–30, 43, 44; Marilyn M. Sibley, *Lone Stars and State Gazettes* (College Station: Texas A&M University Press, 1983), 260, 262–264, 273, 279, 283; James, *Recollections*, 27.

3. Joseph B. Polley to Mary B. Polley, Oct. 6, 1860, Joseph B. Polley to Joseph H. Polley, Nov. 21, 1860 [quote] (Polley Papers, CAH); W. Dean Burnham, *Presidentia1 Ballots, 1836–1892* (Baltimore: Johns Hopkins Press, 1955), 222, 812; Frank H. Smyrl, "Unionism in Texas, 1856–1861," *SHQ* 68 (Oct. 1964), 184.
4. "Obituary of Doctor John Sutherland;" Texas Secretary of State, Election Register; James, *Recollections*, 27; *San Antonio Ledger*, Apr. 20, 1867; Ernest W. Winkler, ed., *Journal of the Secession Convention of Texas, 1861* (Austin: Austin Printing Company, 1912), 22, 89, 90, 406, 407, 444, 452; James M. Day, comp., *The Texas Almanac, 1857–1873: A Compendium of Texas History* (Waco: Texian Press, 1967), 495; Burnham, *Presidential Ballots*, 782; Ralph A. Wooster, *The Secession Conventions of the South* (Princeton: Princeton University Press, 1962), 125–127, 130, 131, 133; Golson, *Bailey's Light*, 108; Bryan, "RECTOR, CLAIBORNE."
5. United States Department of War, Compiled Service Records of Confederate Soldiers Who Served in Organizations from Texas (RG 109, NA; hereafter cited as CSR), Fourth Texas Infantry: Joseph B. Polley and Jack Sutherland; Clipping from *Pioneer Magazine*, n.d. (Polley Papers, CAH); "J. B. Polley was a Texas Pioneer," 461; "Joseph B. Polley," *Bohemian* 1 (1900), 8; Joseph H. Crute Jr., *Units of the Confederate Army* (Midlothian, VA: Derwent Books, 1987), 341; Frank Wagner, "GRAY, MABRY B. [MUSTANG]," *Handbook of Texas Online* (http://www.tshaonline.org/handbook/online/articles/fgr24), accessed April 23, 2016. According to Texas historian Clarence R. Wharton, George Quinn Sutherland served in Hood's Texas Brigade, but he is not listed in the CSR. See *Texas Under Many Flags*, 5 vols. (Chicago: American Historical Society, 1930), 5: 90.
6. Russell Houston to Edward Clark, June 27, 1861 (Texas Governor, Records); Robert W. Brahan to Jefferson Davis, Aug. 15, 1861 (CSR, Fourth Texas Infantry: Haywood W. Brahan); Bureau of the Census, Eighth Census, 1860, Texas, Free Population: Guadalupe County; CSR, Fourth Texas Infantry and Eighth Texas Cavalry; Edward R. Crockett, Diary (CAH); Joseph B. Polley to Joseph H. Polley, Aug. 16, 1862, May 12, 1863 (Polley Papers, CAH); Robert N. Scott et al., comps., *The War of the Rebellion: A Compilation of the Official Records of the Union and Confederate Armies*, 128 vols. (Washington, DC: Government Printing Office, 1880–1901), Ser. I, Vol. 53, p. 746; Harold B. Simpson Jr., comp., *Hood's Texas Brigade: A Compendium* (Hillsboro: Hill Junior College Press, 1977), 130, 133–135; "The Texans at Sharpsburg," *Confederate Veteran* 22 (Dec. 1914), 555 [quote]; Ralph A. Wooster and Robert Wooster, "'Rarin' for a Fight': Texans in the

Confederate Army," *SHQ* 84 (Apr. 1981), 388; Vest, *Century of Light*, 78, 82, 83; James, *Recollections*, 49, 50; Randt, "Descendants," 27; Frost, "Descendants and Ancestors," 85, 88, 174; "Biographies of Wilson County." Ross Houston was from Tennessee, and his family's experience during the Civil War reflects the division among Upper Southerners. While his sons fought for the Confederacy, two of his brothers were Unionists: George S. Houston, a former Congressman and future governor and United States senator from Alabama, and Russell Houston, who was appointed to the Tennessee Supreme Court during the Civil War by Governor Andrew Johnson.

7. CSR, Fourth Texas Infantry; Scott et al., *War of the Rebellion*, IV, 1: 1,002; Polley, *Soldier's Letters*, 7, 10–12, 205; Joseph B. Polley, *Hood's Texas Brigade* (New York: Neale Publishing Company, 1910), 17; Mary Lasswell, ed., *Rags and Hope: The Recollections of Val C. Giles, Four Years with Hood's Brigade, Fourth Texas Infantry, 1861–1865* (New York: Coward-McCann, 1961), 43, 44; William A. Fletcher, *Rebel Private: Front and Rear* (1908; reprint, New York: Dutton, 1995), 7; Simpson, *Compendium*, viii, ix, 92, 93, 130–137; Wooster and Wooster, "'Rarin for a Fight,'" 423; Alvy L. King, *Louis T. Wigfall: Southern Fire-eater* (Baton Rouge: Louisiana State University Press, 1970), 126–135, 137, 138; Harold B. Simpson, *Hood's Texas Brigade: Lee's Grenadier Guard* (Waco: Texian Press, 1970), 80, 82, 83, 85; A. V. M. Winkler, *The Confederate Capital and Hood's Texas Brigade* (Austin: Eugene Von Boeckmann, 1894), 39, 40; B. L. Aycock, "Lone Star Guards," *Confederate Veteran* 31 (Feb. 1923), 61; Alvy L. King, "WIGFALL, LOUIS TREZEVANT," *Handbook of Texas Online* (http://www.tshaonline.org/handbook/online/articles/fwi04), accessed Nov. 27, 2015. Joseph B. Polley reported to his sister that he was one of 22 Mustang Grays who had to be hospitalized at Richmond in the fall of 1861. See Joseph B. Polley to Harriet R. Polley, Nov. 11, 1861 (Polley Papers, CAH).

8. James H. Manahan to "My Dear Friend," April 28, 1861 [1862] [first quote] (James H. Manahan Papers, CAH); Nicholas A. Davis, Diary (CAH); *Hood's Brigade Historical Papers* (Privately published, n.d.), 31; John Bell Hood, *Advance and Retreat* (New Orleans: G. T. Beauregard, 1880), 18–21, 22 [second quote], 23; Scott et al., *War of the Rebellion*, I, 11, pt. 1: 629–632; Fletcher, *Rebel Private*, 16, 17; Lasswell, *Rags and Hope*, 48, 97, 98; Polley, *Hood's Texas Brigade*, 15, 16, 23–28, 32, 33; Polley, *Soldier's Letters*, 23 [third quote], 29; Joseph B. Polley, "To Charming Nellie—Not So Funny," *Confederate Veteran* 4 (Feb. 1896), 44, 45; Joseph B. Polley, "Another 'Charming Nellie' Letter," *Confederate Veteran* 4 (Apr. 1896), 118; Joseph B. Polley, "Polley Off on Furlough," *Confederate Veteran* 5 (May 1897), 218; Don E. Henderson, "General Hood's Brigade," *Southern Historical Society Papers* 29 (1901), 300, 301, 304; Simpson, *Lee's Grenadier*

Guard, 78, 79, 95, 96, 99–101; Winkler, *Confederate Capital*, 51, 59–61; King, *Wigfall*, 126–135; Thomas W. Cutrer, "HOOD, JOHN BELL," *Handbook of Texas Online* (http://www.tshaonline.org/handbook/online/articles/fho49), accessed Nov. 27, 2015.

9. Davis, Diary; CSR, Fourth Texas Infantry; Nicholas Pomeroy, "Reminiscences of the American War, 1861–1865" (TS, n.d., CAH); *Hood's Brigade Historical Papers*, 31, 32; Scott et al., *War of the Rebellion*, I, 11, pt. 2: 503, 508, 556, 564, 565, 568, 569, 973, 990; Hood, *Advance and Retreat*, 25–29; Polley, *Soldier's Letters*, 35–39; Polley, *Hood's Texas Brigade*, 41–61, 70, 71, 323, 324; Henderson, "Hood's Brigade," 302–304; Aycock, "Lone Star Guards," 61; Joseph B. Polley, "Brave Texans in the Virginia Army," *Confederate Veteran* 4 (May 1896), 158, 159; William R. Hamby, "Fourth Texas in Battle of Gaines's Mill," *Confederate Veteran* 14 (Apr. 1906), 183, 184; Simpson, *Compendium*, 90, 93, 130–136; Lasswell, *Rags and Hope*, 43–47, 110; Evander M. Law, "On the Confederate Right at Gaines's Mill," *Battles and Leaders of the Civil War, Volume Two*, ed. Robert U. Johnson and Clarence C. Buel (New York: Thomas Yoseloff, 1956), 363 [second quote], 364, 365; Daniel H. Hill, "Lee's Attacks North of the Chickahominy," *Battles and Leaders, Volume Two*, 347–362; Clifford Dowdey and Louis H. Manarin, eds., *Wartime Papers of R. E. Lee* (New York: Bramhall House, 1961), 215 [third quote]; Sidney S. Johnson, *Texans Who Wore the Gray* (Tyler, TX: Privately published, 1907), 388–390 [first quote], 391–395; Simpson, *Lee's Grenadier Guard*, 114–122; Winkler, *Confederate Capital*, 79, 80; Clement A. Evans, ed., *Confederate Military History*, Extended ed., 17 vols. (Wilmington, NC: Broadfoot Publishing Company, 1989), 15: 586.
10. CSR, Fourth Texas Infantry; Polley, *Soldier's Letters*, 64–71; Dowdey and Manarin, *Lee Letters*, 277, 281–283; *Hood's Brigade Historical Papers*, 33; Scott et al., *War of the Rebellion*, I, 12, pt. 2: 605, 606, 609, 610, 614, 615, 650; Polley, *Soldier's Letters*, 41–45, 50–51 [quote]; Hood, *Advance and Retreat*, 34–37; Polley, *Hood's Texas Brigade*, 74, 75, 78–111, 325; Joseph B. Polley, "Battle Described to Charming Nellie," *Confederate Veteran* 4 (June 1896), 185, 186; Joseph B. Polley, "Second Manassas," *Confederate Veteran* 4 (July 1896), 218, 219; Fletcher, *Rebel Private*, 51–54; Henderson, "Hood's Brigade," 306; Simpson, *Lee's Grenadier Guard*, 131, 136, 137, 143, 144, 147–154; Winkler, *Confederate Capital*, 97–100.
11. CSR, Fourth Texas Infantry; O. T. Hanks, "Account of Civil War Experiences" [third quote] (TS, 1958, CAH); Dowdey and Manarin, *Lee Letters*, 316, 319 [first quote]; Hood, *Advance and Retreat*, 38–45; Polley, *Soldier's Letters*, 57 [fifth quote]; *Hood's Brigade Historical Papers*, 34; Scott et al., *War of the Rebellion*, I, 19, pt. 1: 811, 922, 923, 934–936; Polley, *Hood's Texas Brigade*, 48, 49, 114–135, 323–325;

"Texans at Sharpsburg," 555 [fourth quote]; Polley, "Brave Texans," 158; Henderson, "Hood's Brigade," 307, 308; William R. Hamby, "Hood's Texas Brigade at Sharpsburg," *Confederate Veteran* 16 (Jan. 1908), 19, 20; Val C. Giles, "The Flag of First Texas, A. N. Virginia," *Confederate Veteran* 15 (Sept. 1907), 417; Simpson, *Compendium*, 130, 131, 133–136; Wooster and Wooster, "'Rarin for a Fight,'" 401; Evans, *Confederate Military History*, 15: 214, 215; Simpson, *Lee's Grenadier Guard*, 161, 162, 165, 166, 169, 172–175, 187; Winkler, *Confederate Capital*, 101, 102, 107, 108 [second quote], 121.

12. CSR, Fourth Texas Infantry; Pomeroy, "Reminiscences," 51; Hood, *Advance and Retreat*, 51, 52, 57–59, 63, 64; Polley, *Soldier's Letters*, 100, 101, 113, 158, 161; Lasswell, *Rags and Hope*, 179, 181 [first quote], 182, 183, 186; Fletcher, *Rebel Private*, 78, 79 [second quote], 80, 82; Scott et al., *War of the Rebellion*, I, 27, pt. 2: 404–407, 411; "Official Reports of the Battle of Gettysburg," *Southern Historical Society Papers* 4 (1877), 162–164; "Official Reports of the Battle of Gettysburg," *Southern Historical Society Papers* 13 (1885), 190, 191; Polley, *Hood's Texas Brigade*, 148, 161–189, 225, 226; Joseph B. Polley, "Concernin' of a Hog," *Confederate Veteran* 5 (Feb. 1897), 58, 59; Simpson, *Compendium*, 90; Simpson, *Lee's Grenadier Guard*, 224–233, 251–261, 269–278, 280, 281, 283, 285.
13. CSR, Fourth Texas Infantry; Scott et al., *War of the Rebellion*, 1, 27, pt. 2: 330, 339, I, 30, pt. 2: 511, 512; "The Battle of Chickamauga, 19th and 20th of September, 1863," *Southern Historical Society Papers* 16 (1888), 380, 381; "Battle of Chickamauga," *Southern Historical Society Papers* 13 (1885), 384, 385; "Official Report of Gettysburg," 190; Polley, *Hood's Texas Brigade*, 198–208, 210, 211, 324, 325; Simpson, *Compendium*, 90, 131–137; Simpson, *Lee's Grenadier Guard*, 317–319, 321, 323, 324; "R. H. Skinner," *Confederate Veteran* 22 (Jan. 1914), 35; Evans, *Confederate Military History*, 15: 219. Joseph B. Polley, in *Hood's Texas Brigade* (New York: Neale Publishing Company, 1910), adds Pvt. James C. Murray to the list of Mustang Grays that are noted in the CSR, Fourth Texas Infantry as killed at Gettysburg (pp. 324, 325). He also explains how he was killed in an obituary of his brother, John D. Murray, which appeared in the *Floresville Chronicle-Journal* on March 3, 1916.
14. CSR, Fourth Texas Infantry; Jack Sutherland to "Sis," Mar. 3, 1864 (Historical Marker File); Pomeroy, "Reminiscences," 75; Hanks, "Experiences"; Thomas L. McCarty, Memoir (MS, n.d., Thomas L. McCarty Papers, CAH); Polley, *Soldier's Letters*, 145–150; Polley, *Hood's Texas Brigade*, 54, 55, 230–233, 323, 324; Simpson, *Compendium*, 93, 131, 132, 134–137; Simpson, *Lee's Grenadier Guard*, 320, 321, 326, 338–344, 351–357, 366, 376, 384–387, 393–402; Polley, "Furlough," 218; E. J. Parent, "General Lee to the Rear," *Confederate Veteran* 2 (Jan. 1894), 14; Joseph B. Polley,

"Simple Justice Asked," *Confederate Veteran* 3 (Oct. 1895), 317; Winkler, *Confederate Capital*, 164–170.

15. CSR, Fourth Texas Infantry; Joseph B. Polley to Joseph H. Polley, Nov. 13, 1864 (Polley Papers, CAH); McCarty, Memoir [first quote]; Crockett, Diary [second quote]; "Obituary for Jack Sutherland" (MS, n.d., Wilson County Scrapbook); Vertical File: John Sutherland; Scott et al., *War of the Rebellion*, I, 29, pt. 2: 869, 870; *Hood's Brigade Historical Papers*, 16, 25, 26; *San Antonio Express*, Oct. 21, 1936; Polley, *Soldier's Letters*, 151–156, 160, 163–169, 218, 219; Joseph B. Polley, "J. B. Polley About Texans in Virginia," *Confederate Veteran* 5 (Sept. 1897), 471; Joseph B. Polley, "Polley Lost a Foot—A Furlough," *Confederate Veteran* 5 (Nov. 1897), 570, 571; Polley, *Hood's Texas Brigade*, 245, 325; Simpson, *Compendium*, 8, 91, 93, 131, 132, 134–136; Simpson, *Lee's Grenadier Guard*, 419–422, 433–442; Winkler, *Confederate Capital*, 196; "Polley was a Texas Pioneer," 461; "Joseph B. Polley," 8; *Memorial Record of Southwest Texas*, 86; *Memorial Record of Texas (East)*, 287; Evans, *Confederate Military History*, 15: 586.
16. Robert W. Brahan to Jeremiah Y. Dashiell, Jan. 21, 1861, Muster Roll of the Cibolo Guards, Capt. Claiborne Rector, Nov. 1861, Muster Roll of the Wilson Guards, 30th Brigade, Capt. John W. Lilly, n.d., Orders No. 6, Headquarters, 30th Brigade, Texas State Troops, Apr. 2, 1862, James Duff to Dashiell, May 2, 1862, Andrew G. Pickett to Dashiell, May 15, 1862 [quote] (Texas Adjutant General, Militia Records); Texas Secretary of State, Election Register; CSR, Fourth Texas Infantry: Connally F. Henderson, Thirty-Third Texas Cavalry: James Duff, Joseph E. Polley; Bureau of the Census, Eighth Census, 1860, Free Population: Wilson County; Hunter, "Literary Effort"; Robert W. Shook, "DUFF, JAMES," *Handbook of Texas Online* (http://www.tshaonline.org/handbook/online/articles/fdu06), accessed Nov. 28, 2015; Hall, "TAYLOR, CREED."
17. Harriet R. Polley to David H. Houston, July 2, 1861 (Polley Family Papers, DRT Library); Hall, "TAYLOR, CREED."
18. Mary F. Sutherland to Harriet R. Polley, May 11, 1863 (in private collection); John Sutherland to John S. Ford, Jan. 18, 1864 (John S. Ford Papers, Nita Stewart Haley Memorial Museum, Midland); Bureau of the Census, Eighth Census, 1860, Texas, Free and Slave Population: Wilson County; Nannie E. Wyatt to Pendleton Murrah, Apr. 21, 1864 (Texas Governor, Records); CSR, Second Texas Cavalry, Arizona Brigade: Levin L. Sutherland, Thirty-Second Texas Cavalry: Telemachus S. Wyatt, Thirty-Third Texas Cavalry: Abner H. Polley, Joseph E. Polley, Border's Cavalry: J. Craighead, W. G. Southerland [*sic*], Texas Reserve: L. W. Stimpson [*sic*]; Texas Secretary of State, Confederate Pension Files: John S. Craighead, Joseph E. Polley, Abner H. Polley, William T. Sutherland, Telemachus S. Wyatt; Clipping from *Pioneer Magazine*, n.d. (Polley Papers, CAH);

Cross, "Polley Tells How He Turned the Western Trail," 363. John D. Wyatt owned 42 slaves in 1860, when Telemachus S. Wyatt had 24.

19. War Tax Receipts for Jack Sutherland, 1862 and 1865 (Sutherland Springs History Display, Sutherland Springs Museum, Sutherland Springs, TX); War Tax Receipts for John Sutherland, 1861, 1862, 1864, 1865 (in private collection); CSR, Thirty-Third Texas Cavalry: Samuel Ross Houston; Day, *Texas Almanac, 1857–1873: A Compendium*, 505.
20. Receipt for Wool, Nov. 15, 1860, Jonathan Polley to Joseph H. Polley, Dec. 8, 1860, James to Joseph H. Polley, Jan. 31, Apr. 18, May 15 and 17, 1862, Forbes and Ballard to Joseph H. Polley, Feb. 21, Apr. 27, June 4, 1861, _____ Hillman and _____ Hancock to Joseph H. Polley, Aug. 23, 1861, Walker K. Baylor to Joseph H. Polley, Feb. 8, 1862, J. Geibass to Joseph H. Polley, Jan. 9, 1861, Joseph H. Polley to Richard A. Howard, Oct. 2, 1864, Receipts for War Tax, Tithe Tax, and Specie Tax, 1861–1865, Receipt from Cotton Bureau, Trans-Mississippi Department, Confederate States of America, Receipt for United States Internal Revenue Tax, 1864–1866 (Polley Papers, CAH); James to Joseph H. Polley, Apr. 18, May 15, 17, 30, July 25, Aug. 11, 1862, Dec. 23, 1864 (Polley Papers, DRT); Susan J. Pickett to "My Dear Friend" [Elizabeth Mary Menefee Riddle Canterbury], June 11, 1860 (Carter Family Papers); Ann Dickson Sutherland to Richard H. Dickson, n.d. [1862] (Dickson Family Papers, DRT); Polley, "Texans in Virginia," 470, 471; Randolph B. Campbell, *A Southern Community in Crisis: Harrison County, Texas, 1850–1880* (Austin: Texas State Historical Association, 1983), 214, 215, 259, 260.
21. Joseph H. Polley to John Sutherland, Dec. 3, 1863 (Polley Papers, CAH); War Tax Receipts for John Sutherland, 1864, 1865 (in private collection); Wilson County Probate Minutes, Vol. B: 8 (MF, TSLA); Texas Secretary of State, Election Register; *Floresville Chronicle-Journal*, Sept. 16, 1960; Dorman H. Winfrey and James M. Day, eds. *The Indian Papers of Texas and the Southwest, 1825–1916*, 5 vols. (Austin: Pemberton Press, 1966), 4: 72, 73; Henry E. Dresser, "Notes on the Birds of Southern Texas," *Ibis* 6 (1865), 312, 314, 315; Polley, *Hood's Texas Brigade*, 210; Stanley D. Casto, "DRESSER, HENRY EELES," *Handbook of Texas Online* (https://www.tshaonline.org/handbook/online/articles/fdr12), accessed Apr. 23, 2016. According to the Wilson County probate records, Ann M. Sutherland had twelve slaves when she died. See "The Plantation Comes to Bexar County—Slavery in Bexar County," *Lost Texas Roads* (http://www.losttexasroads.com/events/107-the-plantation-comes-to-bexar-county?showall= &start=1), accessed Apr. 13, 2016.
22. Nail, *Journal of the Rio Grande Mission Conference*, 18, 21, 22, 26, 28–33, 36, 37, 39, 69, 112, 113; Spellman, "METHODIST CHURCH"; Olin W. Nail

et al., eds., *Texas Methodist Centennial Yearbook: The Story of Methodism During the Last One Hundred Years in Texas* (Elgin, TX: Privately published, 1934), 373.

23. Receipt from San Antonio Mutual Aid Association, Apr. 24, 1863 (Polley Papers, CAH); Gammel, *Laws of Texas,* 5: 645; Linda Mearse, comp., *Confederate Indigent Families Lists of Texas, 1863–1865* (Privately published, 1995), 406, 407.
24. CSR, Fourth Texas Infantry; Receipt from Robert W. Brahan, June 29, 1864, Resolutions of Texas Brigade, Jan. 24, 1865 [quote] (R. H. Porter Collection, Special Collections, University of Texas at San Antonio); Simpson, *Compendium,* 8, 91, 93, 95, 131, 133, 135; "Paroles of the Army of Northern Virginia," *Southern Historical Society Papers* 15 (1887), 160, 166, 167; Winkler, *Confederate Capital,* 288; Simpson, *Lee's Grenadier Guard,* 459–468; Polley, *Hood's Texas Brigade,* 298, 323.
25. R. H. Gilbert to Joseph H. Polley, Feb. 17, 1865, Parole of Abner H. Polley, Sept. 29, 1865 (Polley Papers, CAH); CSR, Second Texas Cavalry, Arizona Brigade: Levin L. Sutherland, Thirty-Third Texas Cavalry: Abner H. Polley, Joseph E. Polley; Texas Secretary of State, Confederate Pension Files: John S. Craighead, Abner H. Polley, William T. Sutherland; Polley, *Soldier's Letters,* xii, 177–183; *Memorial Record of Southwest Texas,* 86; Polley, "Polley Lost a Foot," 571; Joseph B. Polley, "The Gunboat Gen. Taylor Failed to Get," *Confederate Veteran* 15 (June 1907), 281.
26. James to Joseph H. Polley, Aug. 26, 1865, Executive Pardon for Joseph H. Polley, July 5, 1866 (Polley Papers, CAH); Joseph H. Polley to Johnson, Apr. 20, 1866, William P. Hughes to Johnson, Oct. 28, 1865, James to Johnson, Aug. 14, 1865 (Confederate Pardon Files); James to Elisha M. Pease, Sept. 30, 1865 (Pease-Graham-Niles Papers, Austin History Center, Austin, TX); James W. Throckmorton to William Sutherland, Mar. 12,1867 (Texas Secretary of State, Executive Record Book, TSLA); Frost, "Descendants and Ancestors," 165, 166; Griffin, "PEASE, ELISHA MARSHALL;" James A. Marten, "HAMILTON, ANDREW JACKSON," *Handbook of Texas Online* (http://www.tshaonline.org/handbook/online/articles/fha33), accessed Nov. 28, 2015.
27. Receipt for United States Internal Revenue Tax, 1864–1866, Cross T. Hensley to Joseph H. Polley, Feb 9, 1866, Receipt from William R. Wiseman, Apr. 3, 1866, Walker K. Baylor to Joseph H. Polley, Apr. 14, 1868, Joseph H. Polley to John R. Baylor, Oct. 7, 1867, Walker K. Baylor and Joseph H. Polley to James Barns, Dec. 9, 1867, Receipt from John H. Lawrence, William H. Bradley, and William B. Pardee, Apr. 24, 1868, Jonathan Polley to Joseph H. Polley, May 3, 1868 (Polley Papers, CAH); Susan J. Pickett to "My Dear Friend" [Elizabeth Mary Menefee Riddle Canterbury], Sept. 22, 1865 (Carter Family Papers); *Dallas Herald,*

May 25, 1867; Guadalupe and Wilson County Tax Rolls, 1865 and 1870; Golson, *Bailey's Light*, 117, 118, 122.

28. Joseph H. Polley to Johnson, Apr. 14, 1866 [first and second quotes] (Confederate Pardon Files); Will of Joseph H. Polley, Mar. 30, 1869, Theresa Moore to Mary B. Polley, Feb. 4, 1869 (3rd quote), Cato Morgan to Joseph H. Polley, Dec. 1865 (Polley Papers, CAH); Sutherland Springs *Western Chronicle*, Feb. 2, 1877 (fourth-eighth quotes); *Galveston Weekly News*, Feb. 19, 1877; *Galveston Daily News*, Feb. 7, 1877; *Texas Almanac, 1867* (Galveston: Richardson & Company, 1866), 172–176; United States Bureau of the Census, Ninth Census, 1870, Texas, Schedule One, Population: Wilson County; Frost, "Descendants and Ancestors," 160–164; Barry A. Crouch, *The Freedmen's Bureau and Black Texans* (Austin: University of Texas Press, 1992), 13; Alwyn Barr, *Black Texans*, 2nd ed. (Norman: University of Oklahoma Press, 1996), 41; Golson, *Bailey's Light*, 116, 117, 122–124. Josephine Polley Golson writes that Joseph H. Polley, her grandfather, deeded land to his former slaves, but there is no evidence of this in the Wilson County Index of Deeds, 1860–1899 (MF, TSLA), or Guadalupe County Deed Record. There is also no evidence there to support the report in the Sutherland Springs *Western Chronicle*, Feb. 2, 1877, that Gray Jones Houston sold land to his former slaves. The hamlet was known as Doisedo Colony because of a popular fiddler who lived there, Harry Doisedo, a black farmer born about 1832 in Tennessee. See United States Bureau of the Census, Tenth Census, 1880, Texas, Schedule One, Population: Wilson County; Shirley Grammer, "Doisedo Colony School and Doisedo Colony Cemetery" (TS, n.d., in possession of author).
29. John Sutherland to Emily E. Sutherland, Nov. 27, 1866, Sarah Sutherland Craighead to Emily E. Sutherland, May 9, 1869 [first quote] (Sutherland Family Papers); Bureau of the Census, Ninth Census, 1870, Texas, Population: Wilson County; Wilson County Tax Rolls, 1870 and 1871; Vertical File: John Sutherland; Notes on Sutherland Springs (Historical Marker File); *Texas Almanac, 1867*, 176 (second quote); Sutherland Springs *Western Chronicle*, Feb. 2, 1877; Carl H. Moneyhon, "RECONSTRUCTION," *Handbook of Texas Online* (http://www.tshaonline.org/handbook/online/articles/mzr01), accessed Nov. 29, 2015; Golson, *Bailey's Light*, 124, 125; Barr, *Black Texans*, 145, 146, 153, 154. Golson recalls how blacks who remained in the Sutherland Springs area by the early twentieth century avoided Whitehall at night, insisting in not very complimentary terms that the place was haunted.
30. Bureau of the Census, Ninth Census, 1870, Texas, Population: Wilson County; San Antonio *Daily Express*, Apr. 21, 1871; Charles L. Sonnichsen, *I'll Die Before I Run: The Story of the Great Feuds of Texas* (New York: Harper & Brothers, 1951), 31–87; Robert C. Sutton, Jr., *The Sutton-Taylor Feud*

(Quanah, TX: Nortex Press, 1974), 14–23; Hall, "TAYLOR, CREED." Joseph B. Polley provided some of the information on Creed Taylor recounted in both Sonnichsen's and Sutton's works. For a more accurate account of events, see Chuck Parsons, *The Sutton-Taylor Feud: The Deadliest Blood Feud in Texas* (Denton: University of North Texas Press, 2012).

31. Thomas H. Stribling to Andrew J. Hamilton, Aug. 27, 1865 [first and second quotes], William B. Longworth to Joseph Spence, Jan. 1, 1866 [third-seventh quotes], Susan J. Pickett to Hamilton, Jan. 13, 1866, James L. Dial to John Ireland, Feb. 27, 1866 (Texas Governor, Records); Texas Secretary of State, Election Register; Sutherland Springs *Western Chronicle*, June 5, 1879; Richard B. McCaslin, "William Longworth, Republican Villain," in *"Still the Arena of Civil War": Violence and Turmoil in Reconstruction Texas, 1865–1874*, ed. Kenneth Howell (Denton: University of North Texas, 2012), 135, 136, 146, 147; William L. Richter, *The Army in Texas During Reconstruction, 1865–1870* (College Station: Texas A&M University Press, 1987), 22, 23; Christopher B. Bean, "A Stranger Among Strangers: An Analysis of the Freedmen's Bureau Subassistant Commissioners in Texas, 1865–1868" (Ph.D. Diss., University of North Texas, 2008), 42, 43, 58. The best (but hardly unbiased) biography of William B. Longworth is "The Judgment of William B. Longworth," *Lost Texas Roads* (http://losttexasroads.com/people/271-the-judgment-of-william-b-longworth), accessed June 6, 2016.
32. Longworth to Hamilton, Oct. 10, 1865 [first-third quotes], Susan J. Pickett to Hamilton, Jan. 13, 1866 [fourth quote] (Texas Governor, Records); Longworth to Edgar M. Gregory, Oct. 28, 1865 (United States Department of War, Bureau of Refugees, Freedmen and Abandoned Lands, Records of the Assistant Commissioner for the State of Texas, 1865–1869, Letters Received, RG 105, NA); George Rawick, ed., *The American Slave: A Composite Autobiography, Supplement, Series 2*, 10 vols. (Westwood, CT: Greenwood Press, 1979) 10: 1596 [fifth quote]; William L. Richter, *Overreached on All Sides: The Freedmen's Bureau Administrators in Texas, 1865–1868* (College Station: Texas A&M University Press, 1991), 116, 119; Nora Estelle Owens, "Presidential Reconstruction in Texas: A Case Study" (Ph.D. Diss., Auburn University, 1983), 364, 365; McCaslin, "Republican Villain," 136, 137. Susan J. Pickett added that when the girl was asked by Longworth if "'she had not rather live at the Springs where she could see something,' ... like all children" she "said 'Yes.'" See Susan J. Pickett to Hamilton, Jan. 13, 1866 (Texas Governor, Records). White refugees could also get support from the Freedmen's Bureau, but very few did.
33. Longworth to William H. Sinclair, Mar. 28, 1866 [second and third quote], Lemuel P. Hughes et al. to Joseph B. Kiddoo, May 1866 [sixth-eighth

quotes], Statement of James L. Dial, May 7, 1866 [fifth quote], Statement of Robert W. Brahan, May 18, 1866 (BRFAL, Asst. Comm., TX, Lets. Recd.); Isaiah A. Paschal to Hamilton, Oct. 4, 1865 [fourth quote], Dial to Ireland, Feb. 27, 1866 (Texas Governor, Records); Gretchen, *Slave Transactions*, 31; Crouch, *Freedmen's Bureau*, 14; Richter, *Overreached on All Sides*, 117 [first quote], 118, 119; McCaslin, "Republican Villain," 137; Bean, "Stranger Among Strangers," 58. Companies of Federal infantry or cavalry were posted at San Antonio from August 1865 until March 1870. See Richter, *Army in Texas*, 18, 19, 28, 30, 55, 68, 149–153, 163, 185, 186.

34. Longworth to Sinclair, May 14 [first quote], 30 [second-fourth quotes], 1866 (BRFAL, Asst. Comm., TX, Lets. Recd.); Richter, *Army in Texas*, 39; Richter, *Overreached on All Sides*, 119–122; McCaslin, "Republican Villain," 137, 138; Bean, "Stranger Among Strangers," 118–122.
35. James B. Moore to Sinclair, July 29, 1866 (BRFAL, Asst. Comm., TX, Lets. Recd.); W. E. Goodrich to Throckmorton, Oct. 8, 1866 (Texas Governor, Records); James, *Recollections*, 49, 50; Nixon, *Medical Story of Early Texas*, 295–299; Crouch, *Freedmen's Bureau*, 21; Richter, *Army in Texas*, 40, 64, 65; Richter, *Overreached on All Sides*, 122–135, 162; McCaslin, "Republican Villain," 138, 139; Owens, "Presidential Reconstruction," 364, 365; Bean, "Stranger Among Strangers," 123–128; Cecil Harper Jr., "FREEDMEN'S BUREAU," *Handbook of Texas Online* (http://www.tshaonline.org/handbook/online/articles/NCF01), accessed Aug. 14, 2016. William H. Sinclair, sent by Maj. Gen. Joseph B. Kiddoo to investigate the allegations against Longworth after he was removed, generally confirmed the negative accusations against him. Vinton Lee James recalls that 293 people died in San Antonio during the cholera epidemic of 1866, the last to afflict that city in the nineteenth century, and that his father, John James, sent him to Whitehall for safekeeping.
36. Telemachus S. Wyatt to Texas Secretary of State, n.d. [July 1866], Nov. 3, 1866 (Texas Secretary of State, Election Returns); Texas Secretary of State, Election Register; Muster Roll of the Wilson Guards, 30th Brigade, Capt. John W. Lilly, n.d. (Texas Adjutant General, Militia Records); Agreement Between Walker K. Baylor and John W. Lilly, Sept. 1, 1866; Receipts Signed by Walker K. Baylor, Apr. 1, 1868 (Lilly Papers); *Journal of the Texas State Convention* (Austin: Southern Intelligencer Office, 1866), 372–375; Jaeggli, *Court House Story*, 5; Carl H. Moneyhon, *Republicanism in Reconstruction Texas* (Austin: University of Texas Press, 1980), 33, 34, 48; Carl H. Moneyhon, *Texas After the Civil War* (College Station: Texas A&M University Press, 2004), 43–51; McCaslin, "Republican Villain," 139; David Minor, "THROCKMORTON, JAMES WEBB," *Handbook of Texas Online* (http://www.tshaonline.org/handbook/online/articles/fth36), accessed Nov. 29, 2015; Moneyhon, "RECONSTRUCTION."

37. Wyatt to Texas Secretary of State, n.d. [July 1866] [quote] (Texas Secretary of State, Election Returns); Walker K. Baylor to Throckmorton, May 9, 1867 (Texas Governor, Records); Moneyhon, *Texas After the Civil War,* 69–70, 72, 75, 77; McCaslin, "Republican Villain," 139; Moneyhon, "RECONSTRUCTION." Longworth during this time apparently also served as "United States Commissioner for the Western District of Texas (at large)." This made him an officer of the federal district court for the area that included Sutherland Springs. See Galveston *Flake's Bulletin,* July 3, 1867.
38. Longworth to Joseph Spence, Aug. 19, 1867 [first and second quotes], Baylor and Daniel H. Bird to Pease, Aug. 19, 1867 [third and fourth quotes]; Baylor to Charles Griffin, Aug. 31, 1867, Pease to Griffin, Sept. 16, 1867, Longworth to Pease, Sept. 22, 1867 (Texas Governor, Records); Texas Secretary of State, Election Register; Longworth to J. P. Richardson, Dec. 9, 1867 (Texas Secretary of State, Election Returns); Moneyhon, *Republicanism,* 59–63, 67–69; Jaeggli, *Court House Story,* 6; McCaslin, "Republican Villain," 139, 140.
39. Notes on Sutherland Springs (Historical Marker File); "Wilson County Commissioners Court Minutes, Volume A," 97; Gammel, *Laws of Texas,* 4: 1462; Mattie Jackson, comp., *The Rising and Setting of the Lone Star Republic* (Privately published, 1926), 17, 18; Stadler, *Wilson County History,* 12; Patterson, *Wilson County,* 8; *Wilson County Centennial;* Jaeggli, *Court House Story,* 2, 5, 6; Patterson, "Wilson County," 1; McCaslin, "Republican Villain," 140, 141; Hazlewood, "FLORESVILLE;" Claudia Hazlewood, "LODI, TX (WILSON COUNTY)," *Handbook of Texas Online* (http://www.tshaonline.org/handbook/online/articles/hvl68), accessed Nov. 29, 2015.
40. Longworth to D. W. C. Phillips, Apr. 21, 1868 [quotes] (Texas Governor, Records); Texas Secretary of State, Voter Register, 1867–1869 (TSLA); Bureau of the Census, Ninth Census, 1870, Texas, Population: Wilson County; Dale Baum, *The Shattering of Texas Unionism* (Baton Rouge: Louisiana State University Press, 1998), 169; Moneyhon, *Republicanism,* 63–65, 10, 71, 72; Moneyhon, "RECONSTRUCTION"; McCaslin, "Republican Villain," 141.
41. Longworth to Pease, Dec. 12,1868 (first and second quotes), Longworth to Edmund J. Davis, Jan. 27, 1870 (third quote), Feb. 5, 1870 (fourth-sixth quotes), A. B. Chamberlain to Longworth, Feb. 3, 1870 (Texas Governor, Records); Longworth to James P. Newcomb, Aug. 27, 1869 (James P. Newcomb Papers, CAH); McCaslin, "Republican Villain," 141, 142.
42. Longworth to Davis, n.d. (Texas Governor, Records); Muster and Pay Roll of Captain A. McClung's Company of State Guards From the 15th Day of November 1870, to the 1st Day of March 1871 (Texas Adjutant General,

Muster Roll of County Special Policemen, TSLA); Gammel, *Laws of Texas*, 6: 185–190; San Antonio *Daily Express*, Sept. 23, 1870; Moneyhon, *Republicanism*, 135, 136, 139–142; McCaslin, "Republican Villain," 142; Bruce A. Olson, "TEXAS NATIONAL GUARD," *Handbook of Texas Online* (http://www.tshaonline.org/handbook/online/articles/qnt02), accessed Nov. 29, 2015. Barr in *Black Texans* (p. 48) reports that blacks comprised a majority of the Republican militia in Texas, and 40 percent of the State Guard, but this does not appear to be true of units in Sutherland Springs.

43. Longworth to Davis, Mar. 27, 1871 [with attachments], H. C. Burke to Davis, Aug. 28, 1872, Haywood W. Brahan to Davis, Sept. 14, 29, 1872, Andrew G. Pickett to Davis, Sept. 17, 1872, R. C. Houston to Davis, Oct. 31, 1872, Longworth to Davis, Nov. 18, Dec. 23, 1872 (Texas Governor, Records); Longworth to Newcomb, Oct. 8, 1871, Longworth to Board of Returning Officers of Election, Nov. 3, 1872, Affidavit of Nemacio de al Zerda, Jan. 11, 1873 [quote], Affidavit of Haywood W. Brahan, Jan. 21, 1873, Haywood W. Brahan to Ashley N. Denton, Jan. 21, 1873 (Texas Secretary of State, Election Returns); "Wilson County Commissioner's Court Minutes, Vol. A," 97, 134, 141; San Antonio *Daily Express*, Apr. 6, July 19, 1871; Austin *Weekly Democratic Statesman*, Sept. 21, 1871; Sutherland Springs *Western Chronicle*, Feb. 2, 1877; Moneyhon, *Republicanism*, 181, 182; Baum, *Texas Unionism*, 196; Jaeggli, *Court House Story*, 7; *Wilson County Centennial*; McCaslin, "Republican Villain," 143, 144, 150; Aragorn Storm Miller, "DENTON, ASHLEY NEWTON," *Handbook of Texas Online* (http://www.tshaonline.org/handbook/online/articles/fdeal), accessed Nov. 29, 2015. Registered voters in the Sutherland Springs area by 1871 included former Confederates Walker K. Baylor, Haywood P. Brahan, John S. Craighead, Andrew G. Pickett, Joseph B. Polley, Claiborne Rector, Jack Sutherland, and John W. Lilly. See Texas Secretary of State, Election Register. The petition signed by Dial, and taken to Austin by Joseph B. Polley, may be that from "Citizens of Wilson County" found in Memorials and Petitions (TSLA). Among the many signers are Joseph B. and Abner H. Polley, Walker K. Baylor, John W. Lilly, William T. Sutherland, John S. Craighead, and Telemachus S. Wyatt.

44. Longworth to Board of Returning Officers of Election, Nov. 1872, Longworth to Newcomb, Oct. 8, 1871 (Texas Secretary of State, Election Returns); *Galveston Daily News*, May 6, 1874; Gammel, *Laws of Texas*, 6: 87, 8: 23; Stadler, *Wilson County History*, 12; Patterson, *Wilson County*, 8; Jackson, *Lone Star Republic*, 17, 18; Patterson, "Wilson County," 1; Jaeggli, *Court House Story*, 7, 9; *Memorial Record of Southwest Texas*, 402; Long, "WILSON COUNTY;" Hazlewood, "FLORESVILLE"; Nancy Beck Young, "SAN ANTONIO AND ARANSAS PASS RAILWAY," *Handbook*

of *Texas Online* (http://www.tshaonline.org/handbook/online/articles/eqs06), accessed Nov. 28, 2015.

45. San Antonio *Daily Express*, Dec. 16, 1874 (first-third quotes); Austin *Weekly Democratic Statesman*, Jan. 21, 1875 (fourth quote).

Chapter 3

1. Susan J. Pickett to "My Dear Friend" [Elizabeth Mary Menefee Riddle Canterbury], June 11, 1860 [first quote], Dec. 11, 1868 [second quote], Sept. 20, 1870 [third and fourth quotes] (Carter Family Papers); Sutherland Springs *Western Chronicle*, Jan. 26, 1877.
2. Bureau of the Census, Ninth Census, 1870, Texas, Population: Wilson County; Wilson County Tax Rolls, 1871; Wilson County Probate Minutes, Vol. B: 52, 57, 65, 110, 113, 171; Sutherland Springs *Western Chronicle*, Jan. 26, 1877, May 3, 1878; Frost, "Descendants and Ancestors," 86; Stadler, *Wilson County History*, 4, 129; Miller, "DENTON, ASHLEY NEWTON;" Stanley D. Casto, "William A. Waugh: Pioneer La Salle County Rancher," http://www.historicdistrict.com/genealogy/lasalle/waugh.asp (accessed Dec. 18, 2015). Among the Polley family members who owned town lots in Sutherland Springs in 1871 were Walker K. Baylor (4), Josiah R. Brooks (6), Susan R. Henderson (5), Joseph E. Polley (8), and Walter W. Polley (2). The Sutherland family members who had town lots were John Sutherland's estate [Jack Sutherland, executor] (2), Heirs of Ann M. Sutherland (8), and E. T. Craighead (3). While many residents bought lots from John Sutherland while he was alive (Lilly purchased at least 18 lots in 1860 and 1865), 193 lots were sold at the temporary courthouse in Lodi in January 1869 to settle his estate. See deeds dated Aug. 27, 1860, and Nov. 11, 1865, Jack Sutherland's affidavit dated February 1, 1869, and a tax receipt dated Sept. 11, 1871 in the Lilly Papers at the Daughters of the Republic of Texas Library.
3. Wilson County Index to Deeds, 1860–1899; Benjamin Polley to Joseph H. Polley, Mar. 18, 1866, Registration of Brand for Mary B. Polley, Dec. 26, 1877, Registrations of Brands for Walter W. Polley, Feb. 16, Apr. 19, June 15, 1875, Walter W. Polley to Mary B. Polley, June 8, 1878, June 17, 1880, E. B. Polley to Mary B. Polley, Aug. 29, 1878, Abner H. Polley to Mary B. Polley, Jan. 19, June 19, 1880, Dec. 14, 1881, clipping from *San Antonio Light*, n.d. (Polley Papers, CAH); Registration of Brand for J. L. Tiner and Walter W. Polley, Wilson County, Feb. 16, 1875, Registration of Brand for Walter W. Polley, Goliad County, June 15, 1875, Abner H. Polley to Mary B. Polley, Mar. 1, 1877, July 2, 1879 (Polley Papers, Baylor); Sutherland Springs *Western Chronicle*, Feb. 9, 1877; Cross, "Polley Tells How He Turned the Western Trail," 363, 364; James, *Recollections*, 52–54; Frost, "Descendants and Ancestors," 85, 174; Pool, *Atlas*, 120, 121, 135, 136;

Randolph B. Campbell, *Gone to Texas: A History of the Lone Star State* (New York: Oxford University Press, 2003), 297–299; Moneyhon, *Texas After the Civil War*, 9, 10, 159, 160. Early settler William D. Mayes left Sutherland Springs after the Civil War, but his son E. D. Mayes later returned and drove cattle to Kansas for Walter W. Polley. See *Floresville Chronicle-Journal*, Oct. 7, 1932.

4. *Galveston Tri-Weekly News*, Dec. 3, 1873; *Galveston Daily News*, June 5, 1875, May 26, 1876 [second quote], Feb. 3, 1877, Oct. 4, 1878, Oct. 21, 1880; Sutherland Springs *Western Chronicle*, Jan. 26, Feb. 9, Mar. 16, 23, Apr. 27, Aug. 31, Sept. 21, 1877, Sept. 5, 12, 19, 1878 [first quote], Feb. 13, 1879; Bureau of the Census, Tenth Census, 1880, Texas, Population: Wilson County.
5. Sarah Sutherland Craighead to Emily E. Sutherland, May 9, 1869 (quote] (Sutherland Family Papers); Thomas T. Leach to "I P" [Isaiah A. Paschal], Apr. 11, 1870, William B. Ball to Juan N. Flores and J. W. Dickey, Nov. 22, 1870 (Texas Governor, Records); *San Antonio Ledger*, Apr. 20, 1867; *Galveston Daily News*, May 6, 1874; Sutherland Springs *Western Chronicle*, Mar. 9, 30, Apr. 20, 1877; Homer, "History of the Floresville United Methodist Church," n.p.; *Minutes of the Annual Conference of the Methodist Episcopal Church for the Year 1874* (New York: Nelson & Phillips, n.d. [1875]), 13; Nail, ed. *Journal of the Rio Grande Mission Conference*, 32, 33, 37, 39, 42, 43, 46, 52, 64, 75, 88, 83, 85, 88, 89, 94, 101, 105, 112, 113, 115, 117, 119, 124, 134, 146, 170, 178; Thrall, *Methodism in Texas*, 187, 202, 209, 210; Macum Phelan, *A History of the Expansion of Methodism in Texas, 1867–1902* (Dallas: Mathis, Van Nort & Company, 1937), 57, 58, 105, 443. Southern Methodist ministers who served the Sutherland Springs circuit from 1865 to 1876 were Eli Y. Seale, John S. McGee, H. A. Graves, Edward G. Duval, R. M. Leaton, C. R. Shepard, W. T. Thornberry, and Willard de L. Kingsbury. McGee's son was the boy killed by Indians near Sutherland Springs in 1855. See "Chapter One—John S. McGee, Circuit Rider." Beginning in 1866 for a few years there existed a separate "Colored Charge" for the district served initially by Preston W. Hobbs, who was murdered in 1872. See "Genealogy—Person Sheet: Preston Walter Hobbs," http://heathcock.org/genealogy/ps01/ps01_099.html (accessed Feb. 1, 2016).
6. Burke to Davis, Aug. 28, 1872 (Texas Governor, Records); *Galveston Tri-Weekly News*, Dec. 11, 1872; *Galveston Daily News*, Apr. 11, 1877; *Galveston Weekly News*, Apr. 16, 1877; Sutherland Springs *Western Chronicle*, Feb. 9, Mar. 30, Aug. 24 and 31, 1877, Jan. 11, 1878; *Floresville Chronicle-Journal*, July 15, 1971; Wilson County, Register of Deeds, Vol. C, p. 452 (Wilson County Courthouse, Floresville); Bureau of the Census, Ninth Census, 187, Texas, Population: Wilson County; *Memorial*

Record of Southwest Texas, 514, 515; *Annual Report of the Indiana University Including the Catalogue for the Academical Year 1881–1882* (Indianapolis: William B. Burford, 1882), 93, 95, 119; *Journal of Proceedings of the Forty-Fifth Annual Convention of the Protestant Episcopal Church in the Diocese of Indiana* (Madison, IN: M. C. Garber & Company, 1882), 6; "Capt. Edward Rex Tarver," http://www.findagrave.com/cgi-bin/fg.cgi?page=gr&GRid=25453501 (accessed Dec. 19, 2015); "TARVER-L Archives," http://archiver.rootsweb.ancestry.com/th/read/TARVER/2002-10/1034272229 (accessed Dec. 19, 2015). The Cibolo Hall school trustees included Joseph B. Polley, his brother-in-law Walker K. Baylor, Ashley N. Denton, Telemachus S. Wyatt, J. J. Hankinson, and Charles Harper.

7. Notes on Sutherland Springs, Gail W. Shriber, "Sutherland Springs, Wilson County, Texas, 1848–1965" (TS, n.d., Historical Marker File); Sutherland Springs *Western Chronicle*, Jan. 26 [third quote], Feb. 9, Mar. 2, 16, 23, Apr. 27, Aug. 31, Sept. 21, 1877, Sept. 5, 12, 19, 1878, Feb. 13, 1879; Columbia *Colorado Citizen*, Aug. 30, 1877; *Galveston Daily News*, July 31, Sept. 4, 1877; Austin *Weekly Democratic Statesman*, Jan. 31, 1878; San Antonio *Daily Express*, June 23, 1907; *Floresville Chronicle-Journal*, Sept. 16, 1960; "Writings of Fannie Amelia Dickson Darden," 140; *Pettengill's Newspaper Directory and Advertisers' Hand-Book for 1877* (New York: S. M. Pettengill & Company, 1877), 267; Ferdinand D. Baillio, *History of the Texas Press Association* (Dallas: Southwestern Publishing Company, 1916), 356; *Edward Alden & Brother's American Newspaper Catalogue, 1882* (Cincinnati: Edward Alden & Brothers, 1882), 599 [first and second quotes]; Donald E. Everett, "San Antonio Welcomes the 'Sunset'—1877," *SHQ* 65 (July 1961), 57; Patterson, "Wilson County," 3; Stadler, *Wilson County History*, 12; Charles P. Zlatkovich, *Texas Railroads: A Record of Construction and Abandonment* (Austin: Bureau of Business Research, University of Texas, 1981), 8.
8. *Galveston Tri-Weekly News*, Dec. 3, 1873; *Galveston Daily News*, May 6 [first and second quotes], Aug. 18 [third quote], 1874, June 5 [fourth quote], 1875, Feb. 3, 1877; San Antonio *Daily Express*, July 16, 1875; Sutherland Springs *Western Chronicle*, Jan. 26, Feb. 23 [fifth and sixth quotes], Apr. 27, June 15, Aug. 3, 24, Sept. 7, 1877; *Floresville Chronicle-Journal*, Sept. 16, 1960; Valenza, "Places Lost," 167,169. Shirley Grammer provided me with much information about Harry Doisedo including a paper entitled "Doisedo Colony School and Doisedo Colony Cemetery."
9. Receipts for purchases, 1873–1874, J. C. Hall to Mary B. Polley, May 23, June 6, 1877, "Jane" to "Auntie Polley" [Mary B. Polley], June 10, 1877, Jemina De Cordova to Mary B. Polley, June 24, 1877, Samuel D. De Cordova to Mary B. Polley, Sept. 10, 1877, Jonathan Polley to "Niece,"

Nov. 2, 1877, Emma V. Henderson to "Rolé" [Catherine S. Polley], Feb. 14, 1878, A. M. Young to Mary B. Polley, Apr. 3, 1878, Tom James to Mary B. Polley, Apr. 13, 1878, J. H. James to Mary B. Polley, May 5, 1878, E. B. Polley to Mary B. Polley, Aug. 29, 1878, Nellie Logan to "Teresa," May 24, 1879 (Polley Papers, CAH); *Galveston Tri-Weekly News*, Dec. 3, 1873; *Galveston Daily News*, May 6, Aug. 18, 1874; Sutherland Springs *Western Chronicle*, July 27, Aug. 3, 24, Nov. 9, 1877; *Dallas Daily Herald*, Oct. 25, 1877; Murray, "Early Ranches," 11, 12; *Wilson County Centennial*; Golson, *Bailey's Light*, 105, 116, 117.

10. Notes on Sutherland Springs, Shriber, "Sutherland Springs," 5 (Historical Marker File); *Galveston Daily News*, Apr. 15 [second quote], May 13, July 13, Aug. 15, 1876, May 22, 27, Aug. 9 [third quote], 13, 24, 25, 28, Sept. 4, Nov. 15, 1877, June 14, 15, 18, 22, 23, 25, July 9, 11, 12, 1878; Columbus *Colorado Citizen*, Aug. 30, Sept. 13, 1877; Sutherland Springs *Western Chronicle*, Jan. 26, 1877, Feb. 23, 1877 [first and fourth quotes], Mar. 16, May 11, June 8, Aug. 3, Sept. 14, Oct. 26, 1877, Mar. 1, 1878; Texas Secretary of State, *Biennial Report of the Secretary of State of the State of Texas, 1884* (Austin: State Printing Office, 1884), 141; "The Writings of Fannie Amelia Dickson Darden," 141; "Necrology," *Michigan Alumnus* 6 (Mar. 1900), 278.
11. Mathi Polley to Kate Polley, July 18, 1880 (Polley Papers, Baylor); Mary B. Polley to Catherine S. Polley, July 18, 1880 (Polley Papers, CAH); License #257, Nov. 4, 1874 [second quote] (Lilly Papers); Notes on Sutherland Springs, Shriber, "Sutherland Springs," 7 (Historical Marker File); Sutherland Springs *Western Chronicle*, Jan. 26, Feb. 9 [first quote], 16 [fourth quote], Mar. 16, 23, Apr. 6, 20, 27, May 4, June 22 [third quote], Aug. 3, 31, Sept. 21, 1877, Feb. 13, 1878, May 22, 1879; Gammel, *Laws of Texas*, 8: 657; Valenza, *Taking the Waters*, 111.
12. Mathi Polley to Kate Polley, July 18, 1880 (Polley Papers, Baylor); Notes on Sutherland Springs, Shriber, "Sutherland Springs," 7 (Historical Marker File); *Galveston Daily News*, May 6, 1874, Sept. 27, 1876, July 24, 1877, July 29, 1880; San Antonio *Daily Express*, Sept. 22, Oct. 13, 1875; *Galveston Weekly News*, July 30, 1877; Sutherland Springs *Western Chronicle*, Apr. 20, July 13, Aug. 3, Sept. 14, Nov. 16, 1877, June 21, 28, Aug. 8, 1878.
13. Bureau of the Census, Tenth Census, 1880, Texas, Population: Wilson County; Wilson County Tax Rolls, 1880; Sutherland Springs *Western Chronicle*, Feb. 2, Mar. 23, 1877; Dale L. Morgan, *Dale Morgan on the Mormons, Part 2: 1949–1970*, ed. Richard L. Saunders (Norman: University of Oklahoma Press, 2014), 270, 327; Texas State Medical Association, *Transactions of the Texas State Medical Association, 1875* (Columbus: Colorado Citizen, 1875), 8; Megan Seaholm and Chester R. Burns,

"TEXAS MEDICAL ASSOCIATION," *Handbook of Texas Online* (http://www.tshaonline.org/handbook/online/articles/sat05), accessed Jan. 28, 2016. No family link between Zadoc Brooks and Josiah D. Brooks has been found. The information on Jack Wilson and Nat Henderson having formerly been slaves owned by John D. Wyatt is from the Floresville *Chronicle-Journal*, Feb. 18, 1916.

14. Sutherland Springs *Western Chronicle*, Jan. 26, Apr. 20. 27, May 4, 1877, June 15, Aug. 3, 24, Sept. 7, 1877; *Galveston Weekly News*, June 18, 1877; *Galveston Daily News*, May 26 [third and fourth quotes], 1876, Feb. 3, June 20 [first and second quotes], Sept. 4, 1877; Columbia *Colorado Citizen*, Aug. 30, 1877; "The Writings of Fannie Amelia Dickson Darden," 140; Valenza, *Taking the Waters*, 118 [fifth quote], 119 [sixth quote], 120, 121; Valenza, "Places Lost," 167,169.
15. Sutherland Springs *Western Chronicle*, Apr. 20 [seventh quote], June 15, 1877; Columbia *Colorado Citizen* Aug. 30, 1877; *Galveston Daily News*, Sept. 4, 1877; "The Writings of Fannie Amelia Dickson Darden," 141; James Rock and W. I. Smith, *Southern and Western Texas Guide for 1878* (St. Louis: A. H. Pranger, 1878), 183 [first-fifth quotes]; Homer S. Thrall, *A Pictorial History of Texas* (St. Louis: N. D. Thompson and Company, 1879), 706 [sixth quote]; Gene Fowler, *Crazy Water: The Story of Mineral Wells and Other Texas Health Resorts* (Fort Worth: Texas Christian University Press, 1991), 228; Joseph B. Polley, *Wilson County, Texas: Its Description, Resources, Etc.* (Floresville: Privately published, 1888), n.p.; Valenza, "Places Lost," 42–45; 1; DeVierville, "American Healing Waters," 296–305, 351, 352.
16. Gulnare Garrison, "Southwestern Texas as a Health Resort," *The Medical and Surgical Reporter* 44 (Jan. 22, 1881), 91, 92.
17. Sutherland Springs *Western Chronicle*, Apr. 20, May 4, June 8, 15, Aug. 3, 1877; *Galveston Weekly News*, June 18, 1877; *Galveston Daily News*, June 20, 1877; *Why Not Know Why*, 6 [quote]; James, *Recollections*, 52–54; Valenza, *Taking the Waters*, 102, 111.
18. *San Antonio Light*, June 8, July 11, 21, Aug. 22, 1883; Jaeggli, *Court House Story*, 9, 11.
19. Sutherland Springs *Western Chronicle*, Mar. 23, 1877, May 3, 1878; *San Antonio Light*, June 8, 1883; *San Antonio Daily Express*, June 23, 1907; Sutherland Springs *Health Resort*, July 3, 1914; *Cotulla Record*, Sept. 25, 1931; *George P. Rowell & Company's American Newspaper Directory* (New York: George P. Rowell & Company, 1879), 328, 444; *Texas State Gazetteer and Business Directory for 1884* (Chicago: R. L. Polk & Company, 1884), n.p.; *Medical and Surgical Directory of the United States* (Detroit: R. L. Polk & Company, 1886), 895; "Necrology," *Michigan Alumnus* 6 (Mar. 1900), 278.

20. Sarah Sutherland Craighead to Emily E. Sutherland, May 9, 1869 [quote] (Sutherland Family Papers); Sutherland Family Bible (CAH); Obituary for Jack Sutherland (MS, n.d., Wilson County Scrapbook, CAH); clipping of obituary of Jack Sutherland, n.d., Notes on Sutherland Springs (Historical Marker File); Vertical File: John Sutherland; Jack Sutherland to Clement R. Johns, Sept. 12, 1876, probate petition of Jack Sutherland, July 21, 1883 (in private collection); *San Antonio Ledger*, Apr. 20, 1867; Catherine S. Polley to Mary B. Polley, Jan. 17, 1878 (Polley Papers, Baylor); Will of Joseph H. Polley, Mar. 30, 1869, L. B. Ewell to Joseph B. Polley, June 10, 1869, Walker K. Baylor to Joseph B. Polley, June 16, 1869, Edmund M. Ivens to Joseph B. Polley, May 1, 1869, Thomas B. Bodley to Joseph B. Polley, May 8, 1869, Joseph B. Polley to Mary B. Polley, Apr. 17, 1874, Jan. 15, 29, 1879, Abner H. Polley to Mary B. Polley, Mar. 1, 1877, Jan. 19, June 19, 1880, Dec. 14, 1881, E. B. Polley to Mary B. Polley, Aug. 29, 1878, Walter W. Polley to Mary B. Polley, June 8, 1878, June 17, 1880, Jonathan Polley to Walter W. Polley, June 22, 1878, Feb. 11, 1882, P. Hunter to Abner H. Polley, Mar. 19, 1884, Wilson County Tax Receipts, 1876–1879, Will of Mary B. Polley, Mar. 5, 1888, clipping of obituary of Walter W. Polley, n.d. (Polley Papers, CAH); Polley Family Record, David H. Houston to Harriet Polley Houston, June 6, 1875 (Polley Family Papers, DRT); Joseph B. Polley to Lester G. Bugbee, July 28, 1899, Joseph B. Polley to Luther E. Widen, June 21, 1907 (Texas State Historical Association Records, CAH); Bureau of the Census, Tenth Census, 1880, Texas, Population: Wilson; Wilson County Marriage Records (TSLA); Wilson County Probate Minutes, B: 117, 120, C: 70, 71, 151, 500, 501, 610, 611, 614–616, D: 378; Confederate Pension Files: Abner H. Polley, Joseph B. Polley, Jack Sutherland, Eunice S. Sutherland, John S. Craighead; Sutherland Springs *Western Chronicle*, Jan. 26, Feb. 9, 1877, Mar. 1, May 3, 1878, June 5, 1879; *San Antonio Express*, Feb. 3, 10, 1918, Apr. 6, 1939; *Floresville Chronicle-Journal*, Oct. 4, 1935, Sept. 16, 1960; Frost, "Descendants and Ancestors," 2, 85–89, 91, 174, 271, 272; Freeman, "Sutherland Plantation," 9, 10; Murray, "Early Ranches," 12; Cross, "A. H. Polley," 364–368; Randt, "Polly Descendants," 27, 43; Wharton, *Texas Under Many Flags*, 5: 90; Ernest E. Bailey, ed., *Texas Historical and Biographical Record* (Austin: Privately published, 1900), 442; "Eleanor Adelia Polley Pickett," http://image1.findagrave.com/cgi-bin/fg.cgi?page=gr&GRid=69244115 (accessed Jan. 28, 2016). It is interesting that both Abner H. and Walter W. Polley transferred their Masonic memberships from La Vernia to Floresville sometime after 1884. See Vest, *Century of Light*, 160, 168.
21. San Antonio *Daily Light*, Aug. 11, 1886; *San Marcos Free Press*, Nov. 17, 1887 [first quote]; *Galveston Daily News*, Aug. 10, 1888 [second quote], May 16, July 30, 1892, July 8, 1893, July 6, 1896; Dallas *Southern Mercury*,

Mar. 17, 24, 31, Apr. 7, 14, 21, 28, May 5, 1892, Apr. 7, 1898; *San Antonio Express*, May 30, 1912; Texas Agricultural Bureau, *Fourth Annual Report of the Agricultural Bureau of the Department of Agriculture, Insurance, Statistics, and History* (Austin: Hutchings Printing House, 1892), 303; Judith Berg-Sobré, *San Antonio on Parade: Six Historic Festivals* (College Station: Texas A&M University Press, 2003), 49, 50, 181, 182, 185, 202, 231, 241; David Minor, "KEARBY, JEROME CLAIBORNE," *Handbook of Texas Online* (http://www.tshaonline.org/handbook/online/articles/fke02), accessed Dec. 19, 2015; Rena Maverick Green, "BELKNAP RIFLES," *Handbook of Texas Online* (http://www.tshaonline.org/handbook/online/articles/qyb01), accessed Dec. 19, 2015.

22. Joseph H. Polley to Enoch Jones, Aug. 14, 1852 [second quote] (Polley Papers, Baylor); Jonathan Polley to Joseph H. Polley, Sept. 16, 1852, Promissory Note from Joseph H. Polley to Enoch Jones, Aug. 14, 1852, William J. Milburn to Joseph H. Polley, May 10, 1860 (Polley Papers, CAH); Bonds of San Antonio and Mexican Gulf Railroad (CAH); Charles de Silver, Map of Texas, 1858, J. H. Colton, New Map of Texas, 1861 (Map Collection, TSLA); "Abstract of Title Made for Sutherland Springs Development Company," 10; Sutherland Springs *Western Chronicle*, Feb. 9, Mar. 23, Apr. 20, 1877; *Galveston Daily News*, Apr. 4, 1877, Feb. 6, 1878 [first quote], Apr. 22, 1892; Everett, "San Antonio Welcomes the Sunset," 47, 48; *Wilson County Centennial*; Zlatkovich, *Texas Railroads*, 8; St. Clair Griffin Reed, *A History of the Texas Railroads* (Houston: St. Clair Publishing Company, 1941), 257–263; Charles S. Potts, *Railroad Transportation in Texas* (University of Texas Bulletin No. 119 [July 1909]), 32; Craig H. Roell, "SAN ANTONIO AND MEXICAN GULF RAILROAD," *Handbook of Texas Online* (http://www.tshaonline.org/handbook/online/articles/eqs08), accessed Feb. 03, 2016; Craig H. Roell, "GULF, WESTERN TEXAS AND PACIFIC RAILWAY," *Handbook of Texas Online* (http://www.tshaonline.org/handbook/online/articles/eqg28), accessed Feb. 03, 2016.
23. *Galveston Daily News*, June 6, July 8, 21, 1893; "Construction News," *Engineering News and American Railway Journal* 31 (Jan. 4, 1894), 17; "Nelson Mackey," *Lost Texas Roads* (http://losttexasroads.com/people/60-mackey-nelson), accessed Dec. 19, 2015; "Abstract of Title Made for Sutherland Springs Development Company," 16; Nancy Beck Young, "SAN ANTONIO AND GULF SHORE RAILWAY," *Handbook of Texas Online* (http://www.tshaonline.org/handbook/online/articles/eqs07), accessed Dec. 19, 2015. Apparently Nelson Mackey's real name was Nelson Mackey Laraway.
24. *Galveston Daily News*, Jan. 9, Feb. 18, Sept. 21, Nov. 1, 1894, July 8, 1896, Mar. 27, 1897; *Fort Worth Gazette*, Apr. 7, 1895; *Houston Daily Post*, Mar. 27, 1897; "Abstract of Title Made for Sutherland Springs Development

Company," 23–26; *The Southwestern Reporter, Volume 44* (St. Paul: West Publishing Company, 1898), 1012–1016; *Texas Court Reporter, Volume 8* (Austin: Ben C. Jones & Company, 1904), 495–499; Zlatkovich, *Texas Railroads,* 34, 85; Reed, *History of Texas Railroads,* 255, 256; Potts, *Railroad Transportation in Texas,* 47, 48; George C. Werner, "GALVESTON, HARRISBURG AND SAN ANTONIO RAILWAY," *Handbook of Texas Online* (http://www.tshaonline.org/handbook/online/articles/eqg06), accessed Jan. 28, 2016; Nancy Beck Young, "SAN ANTONIO AND GULF RAILROAD," *Handbook of Texas Online* (http://www.tshaonline.org/handbook/online/articles/eqsdp), accessed Jan. 28, 2016; Young, "SAN ANTONIO AND GULF SHORE RAILWAY;" "San Antonio and Gulf Shore Railroad," http://www.txtransportationmuseum.org/SAG.htm (accessed Nov. 10, 2015). The term "Sunset Route" originated with the Galveston, Harrisburg, and San Antonio Railway Company, but it is most popularly associated with the Southern Pacific Railroad.

25. "Jane" to "Auntie Polley" [Mary B. Polley], June 10, 1877 [quote] (Polley Papers, Baylor); "Abstract of Title for the Sutherland Springs Development Company," 16, 65–67, 94–95, 97–99; *Floresville Chronicle-Journal,* Sept. 16, 1960, Jan. 3, 1974; *Why Not Know Why,* 5, 10, 13; 23–26, 91, 92, 94, 95, 97–99; Billy M. Jones, *Health-Seekers in the Southwest, 1817–1900* (Norman: University of Oklahoma Press, 1967), 108, 109; Fowler, *Crazy Water,* 209–220; Conversation with Fred and Mittie Williams Anderson, Apr. 20, 1985.
26. *El Paso Daily Herald,* July 27, 1898 [second quote]; San Antonio *Daily Express,* Aug. 1, 1898 [first quote], Feb. 9, 1900, Sept. 2, 1901.
27. San Antonio *Daily Express,* Feb. 9, 1900; *El Paso Herald,* Mar. 23, 1910 [first-third quotes]; *San Antonio Express,* Sept. 8, 9, 1911, Jan. 12, 1912 [fourth quote], May 5, 6, 7, 8, 9, 10, 11, 12 [fifth quote], June 14, 1912; "Bexar County Medical Society Active in Exterminating Illegal Practitioners," *Texas State Journal of Medicine* 8 (Oct. 1912), 174 [sixth quote]; "The Propaganda for Reform," *Journal of the American Medical Association* 61 (Aug. 16, 1913), 504; Bureau of the Census, Twelfth Census, 1900, California, Schedule One, Population: Los Angeles County.
28. San Antonio *Daily Express,* Feb. 9, 1900, Oct. 12, 1902; *Shiner Gazette,* Aug. 21, 1901 [quote]; *McKinney Democrat,* Aug. 15, 1901; *Dallas Morning News,* Apr. 24, 1906; Bureau of the Census, Twelfth Census, 1900, Texas, Population: Wilson County; *Catalogue of the University of Texas, 1902–1903* (Bulletin of the University of Texas, No. 20, June 1, 1903), 298; *Texas Almanac and State Industrial Guide, 1904* (Dallas: Dallas Morning News, 1904), 43; Charles H. Harris and Louis R. Sadler, *The Texas Rangers and the Mexican Revolution: The Bloodiest Decade, 1910–1920* (Albuquerque: University of New Mexico Press, 2004), 340–341; Jim Wheat, *Postmasters*

and Post Offices of Texas, 1846–1930, http://www.rootsweb.ancestry.com/~txpost/postmasters.html (accessed Jan. 28, 2016); Maurine Liles, "Texas Ranger Captain Will Wright," http://wilsoncountyhistory.org/Moments/TEXAS%20RANGER%20CAPTAIN%20WILL%20WRIGHT%20doc%20(short).pdf (accessed Jan. 28, 2016).

Chapter 4

1. Valenza, *Taking the Waters,* 34, 35.
2. Jonathan Polley to Joseph H. Polley, July 29, Oct. 2, Dec. 8, 1860, Mar. 9, 1861 (Polley Papers, CAH); *Galveston Daily News,* May 6, 1880; *Dallas Morning News,* May 7, July 6, 1901, Sept. 4, 1902; *Houston Post,* July 6, 1901; San Antonio *Daily Express,* Sept. 2, 8, Dec. 29, 1901; Beaumont *Daily Enterprise,* Jan. 10, 1902; *Orange Daily Tribune,* Aug. 6, 1903; *San Antonio Express,* Sept. 24, 1916; William B. Phillips, *Texas Petroleum* (Bulletin of the University of Texas No. 5, July 1900), 50; Patterson, *Wilson County,* 10; Patterson, "Wilson County," 3.
3. San Antonio *Daily Express,* Mar. 15 [quote], Sept. 20, Oct. 11, Nov. 8, Dec. 27, 1903, Mar. 6 [quote], June 2, Dec. 7, 1904; *Dallas Morning News,* Nov. 13, 1903, Jan. 5, Mar. 19, 1904; *Houston Post,* Jan. 5, Mar. 11, 12, 17, 19, 1904; *Texas Almanac for 1904,* 149; Tracé Etienne-Gray, "HIGGINS, PATTILLO," *Handbook of Texas Online* (http://www.tshaonline.org/handbook/online/articles/fhi07), accessed Jan. 21, 2016; Robert Wooster and Christine Moor Sanders, "SPINDLETOP OILFIELD," *Handbook of Texas Online* (http://www.tshaonline.org/handbook/online/articles/dos03), accessed Jan. 21, 2016.
4. San Antonio *Daily Express,* Apr. 21 [quote], June 19, 1907, Jan. 4, Dec. 8, 1908; "Abstract of Title for the Sutherland Springs Development Company," 65–67, 94, 95, 97–99; *Giving Multiplied: The Semp Russ Foundation Fund,* http://www.saafdn.org/HowtoGive/ThePowerofEndowment/TheSempRussFoundationFund.aspx (accessed Jan. 21, 2016); Lauri Gray Eaton, "Carter House: Hidden Jewel of the Concrete Jungle," http://www.mysanantonio.com/community/northwest/news/article/Carter-House-Hidden-jewel-of-the-concrete-jungle-2270578.php (accessed Jan. 21, 2016); W. W. White, "DIBRELL, JOSEPH BURTON," *Handbook of Texas Online* (http://www.tshaonline.org/handbook/online/articles/fdi04), accessed Jan. 21, 2016.
5. *Dallas Morning News,* Dec. 28, 1908, Mar. 5, 1909; San Antonio *Daily Express,* Dec. 27, 1908, Mar. 5, Nov. 3 [first quote], 26, 1909, Jan. 2, 7 [second quote], 1910; Fort Worth *Star-Telegram,* Mar. 5, 1909; Lois Goldsmith Oppenheimer, "WASHER, NATHANIEL MOSES [NAT]," *Handbook of Texas Online* (http://www.tshaonline.org/handbook/online/articles/fwaav), accessed Jan. 21, 2016.

6. *Houston Post*, Mar. 17, 1904 [first quote]; San Antonio *Daily Express*, July 6, 1904 [second and third quotes], Oct. 17, Nov. 28, 1905 Apr. 1 [fourth quote], 4, May 29, Aug. 12, 14, 16, 1906, July 27, 1909; *Dallas Morning News*, Sept. 29, 1905; *Bastrop Advertiser*, Oct. 7, 1905; Dallas *Southern Mercury*, July 12, 1906. James W. Parish may have been operating the former Messinger hotel, which was still standing and was offered for sale to settle the doctor's estate in 1908 by Joseph B. Polley as attorney, along with other lots in Sutherland Springs and adjoining lands. See San Antonio *Daily Express*, Nov. 15, 1908.
7. San Antonio *Daily Express*, Mar. 4, 1908 [quote]; Valenza, *Taking the Waters*, 91–93, 108, 125, 132, 133, 197, 198.
8. San Antonio *Daily Express*, Aug. 15, Oct. 24, Dec. 15, 1907; Robert M. Magill, *Magill Family Record* (Richmond, VA: R. E. Magill, 1907), 109, 110; Dermot H. Hardy and Ingham S. Roberts, *Historical Review of Southeast Texas*, 2 vols. (Chicago: Lewis Publishing Company, 1910), 1: 618; *Industrial Development and Manufacturers Record* 53 (Jan. 16, 1908), 62. The father of Henry Ruguley, Henry L. Ruguley of Bay City, was a classmate of Simpson Russ at Chapel Hill in the Class of 1859, and both men became doctors. Perhaps there was a link there that played a part in the formation of this development team.
9. *Dallas Morning News*, Mar. 7, 1908; San Antonio *Daily Express*, Feb. 18, Mar. 6, 7 [first and second quotes], Apr. 19, 1908; "Miscellaneous Enterprises," *Industrial Development and Manufacturers Record* 52 (Jan. 2, 1908), 104 [third quote].
10. San Antonio *Daily Express*, Mar. 6 [quotes], Apr. 19, May 7, 1908; *Houston Post*, May 3, 1908.
11. San Antonio *Daily Express*, June 7, July 3, 12, 13, 19 [quotes], Aug. 2, 7, 29, 1908.
12. San Antonio *Daily Express*, Sept. 4, 6 [quote], 1908; *Houston Post*, Sept. 6, 1908; Bascom N. Timmons, *Garner of Texas: A Personal History* (New York: Harper & Brothers, 1948), 58.
13. San Antonio *Daily Express*, Aug. 19, Sept. 11, 13, 20, Nov. 15, 1908, Apr. 4 [first and second quotes], June 14, 25 [third and fourth quotes], 1909; *Houston Post*, June 27, 1909; *San Antonio Gazette*, Nov. 14, Dec. 5, 1908; [Terrell] Bartlett and [Willis] Ranney, Map of New Sutherland Springs, Aug. 1910 (Williams Family Papers); *Why Not Know Why*, 5, 6, 10, 13, 14, 21, 31; Stadler, *Wilson County History*, 12; Valenza, *Taking the Waters*, 102; "AYRES, ATLEE BERNARD," *Handbook of Texas Online* (http://www.tshaonline.org/handbook/online/articles/fay03), accessed Jan. 24, 2016; Conversation with Andersons, Apr. 20, 1985; Conversation with Lillian Williams Masters, Apr. 17, 1985. Mittie Williams Anderson and

Lillian Williams Masters are daughters of Brown C. Williams and thus granddaughters of Thomas J. Williams.

14. San Antonio *Daily Express*, July 4, 9 [quotes], Aug. 18, 1908, Feb. 4, Mar. 16, June 5, 11, 12, July 22, Dec. 11, 1909; *Palestine Daily Herald*, Dec. 18, 1908; *Houston Post*, Feb. 4, Mar. 16, June 12, 1909; *Dallas Morning News*, Feb. 4, 1909; *Abilene Daily Reporter*, Dec. 12, 1909; *San Antonio Express*, May 14, Aug. 14, 1914; John P. White, *Texas Criminal Reports, Volume 55* (Chicago: T. H. Flood & Company, 1909), 221–227.
15. San Antonio *Daily Express*, Aug. 1, 19, 30, 1909, Feb. 27, 1910; Keith Guthrie, "ARANSAS PASS, TX," *Handbook of Texas Online* (http://www.tshaonline.org/handbook/online/articles/hfa06), accessed Jan. 24, 2016; "History of Aransas Pass," http://www.aransaspass.org/about/history-of-aransas-pass/ (accessed Jan. 24, 2016).
16. San Antonio *Daily Express*, Aug. 30, 1909; *A Twentieth Century History of Southwest Texas*, 2 vols. (Chicago: Lewis Publishing Company, 1907), 1: 409–411.
17. "Texas," *American Architect* 96 (Sept. 29, 1909), 14; San Antonio *Daily Express*, July 27, 1908, May 8, Sept. 10, 11, Nov. 1 [quote], 1909, Jan. 15, 1910.
18. Fort Worth *Star-Telegram*, Dec. 7, 1909 [first and second quotes], Jan. 2, 1910 [third quote]; San Antonio *Daily Express*, Nov. 26, 1909, Jan. 5, 1910.
19. *San Antonio Express*, Sept. 25, 26, 1911; Thomas C. Richardson, *The Autobiography of the Rambling Longhorn* (Oklahoma City: Farmer Stockman Magazine, 1959), 58, 59 [quotes]; Patterson, "Wilson County," 2; Stadler, *Wilson County History*, 12.
20. San Antonio *Daily Express*, Jan. 2 [first quote], Feb. 27 [rest of quotes], Mar. 6, 1910; *Twentieth Century History of Southwest Texas*, 1: 347, 348; Carolyn Hyman, "MATLOCK, AVERY L.," *Handbook of Texas Online* (http://www.tshaonline.org/handbook/online/articles/fma76), accessed Jan. 24, 2016; "The Expulsion Case of Joseph R. Burton of Kansas (1906)," http://www.senate.gov/artandhistory/history/common/expulsion_cases/092JosephBurton_expulsion.htm (accessed Jan. 24, 2016).
21. San Antonio *Daily Express*, Jan. 13, Mar. 5 [first quote], 6 [second-fourth quotes], 16, 23, 24, 25, 26, 27, 28, Apr. 24, Oct. 14, 1910; Guthrie, "ARANSAS PASS, TX;" "History of Aransas Pass."
22. *Dallas Morning News*, July 15, 1910; San Antonio *Daily Express*, Feb. 15 July 15, 16, 26 [quotes], 28, Oct. 14, 1910; Jimmy M. Skaggs, "PRYOR, ISAAC THOMAS," *Handbook of Texas Online* (http://www.tshaonline.org/handbook/online/articles/fpr17), accessed Jan. 24, 2016. A. D. Powers cited two examples regarding his sales prowess—San Luis Valley Land Company in Colorado (developed Blanca in 1908) and the Oregon Valley Land Company (founded Lakeview in 1909). Neither company

established successful towns. See San Antonio *Daily Express*, Oct. 14, 1910.

23. San Antonio *Daily Express*, July 27, 28, 29, 30, Aug. 4 [first quote], 11, 16, 26, 29, Sept. 1 [second and third quote], 3, Oct. 14, 1910; Conversation with Andersons, Apr. 20, 1985.
24. San Antonio *Daily Express*, June 14, 1909; San Antonio *Express-News*, Aug. 22, 1971; Hotel Sutherland Ledger Books, Aug. 14, 1910, to Apr. 10, 1918 (in possession of Lillian Masters, Floresville); Bartlett and Ranney, Map of New Sutherland Springs, Aug. 1910; *Why Not Know Why*, 5 [quote], 10, 13, 24; Valenza, *Taking the Waters*, 102; Stadler, *Wilson County History*, 199.
25. San Antonio *Daily Express*, Apr. 4, 1910; Bureau of the Census, Thirteenth Census, 1910, Texas, Schedule One, Population: Wilson County; *Texas Almanac and State Industrial Guide for 1910* (Dallas: Galveston-Dallas News, 1910), 280; San Antonio *Daily Express*, June 14, 1909; Valenza, *Taking the Waters*, 102, 104. A "Program" for "Sutherland Springs School" for the 1907–1908 academic year lists a single teacher, J. L. Nance, and twenty white pupils. It is in the possession of Liz Lester of Lubbock, Texas, who has also provided some of the images used in this book.
26. San Antonio *Daily Express*, Sept. 20, 1908, June 14, 1909, Aug. 18, 24, Sept. 22, Nov. 17, 20, 21, Dec. 12, 1910; Feb. 6, 1911; *Dallas Morning News*, Jan. 28, 1910; *San Antonio Express*, May 6, 7, 13, 22, 1911, Apr. 10, Sept. 6, 1913, July 25, Aug. 1, Oct. 25, 1914, Jan. 3, 1915, Mar. 12, 1915, Nov. 20, 1917; Bureau of the Census, Thirteenth Census, 1910, Texas, Population: Wilson County; Valenza, *Taking the Waters*, 62, 104.
27. "Banking, Legislative, and Financial News," *The Commercial and Financial Chronicle* 102 (Apr. 22, 1916), 1515; "San Antonio Banks Consolidate," *The Texas Bankers Record* 5 (Jan. 1916), 37; San Antonio *Daily Express*, Oct. 1, 5, 14, 31, Dec. 13, 1909, July 30, 1910; *Houston Post*, Oct. 3, 14, 1909; *Dallas Morning News*, Sept. 1, Oct. 5, 9, 1909; Lawrence L. Crum, "BANKS AND BANKING," *Handbook of Texas Online* (http://www.tshaonline.org/handbook/online/articles/czb01), accessed Jan. 24, 2016.
28. San Antonio *Daily Express*, Aug. 24, 28, 30, Sept. 21, Oct. 18, 26, 1910; *Houston Post*, Dec. 12, 1910; Valenza, *Taking the Waters*, 11.
29. San Antonio *Daily Express*, Aug. 22, Dec. 9, 1910, Jan. 15, 17 [quote], 1911; *San Antonio Express*, Apr. 3, 1911; Valenza, *Taking the Waters*, 50. The question of whether or not Sutherland Springs had hot springs is still debated. A writer in the *Beaumont Enterprise*, Mar. 27, 1911, claimed that hot and cold springs could be found at Sutherland Springs, and surviving postcards from this same era advertise "Hot and cold sulphur baths." Barbara J. Wood, a local historian, agreed with this, but Fred and Mittie Williams Anderson, who were both raised in the community, said no.

Historian Janet Valenza declared that hot water could be found if drillers went deep enough. She wrote that the Carrizo-Wilcox Aquifer serves as the principal source of groundwater for Wilson County, and while Sutherland Springs's "natural springs" flow cold from this aquifer, you can get hot water from drilling deeper. See Valenza, *Taking the Waters*, 32, 33.

30. *Houston Post*, Apr. 26, 1908; San Antonio *Daily Express*, July 13, 1908, Oct. 24, 1909, May 1, 1910, Feb. 9, 1911; *San Antonio Express*, Mar. 22 [first four quotes], 30 [fifth quote], Apr. 7, 15, May 21, 27, 28, June 27, 29, Sept. 5, 8, 11, Oct. 11, 12, 1911; *Bryan Daily Eagle and Pilot*, Feb. 21, 1911; *Dallas Morning News*, Apr. 7, 1911; "General Mining News: Texas, Fayette County," *Engineering and Mining Journal* 65 (Jan. 15, 1898), 83; *Coal Mining Companies and Operators of the United States* (Chicago: Mining World, 1905), 63; "New Enterprises," *Fuel Magazine: The Coal Operators National Weekly* 9 (June 11, 1907), 193; "Construction Department: Texas," *Industrial Development and Manufacturers Record* 51 (June 6, 1907), 670; Texas Secretary of State, *Biennial Report of the Secretary of State of the State of Texas, 1910* (Austin: Austin Publishing Company, 1911), 122; "New Coal Trade Enterprises," *Fuel Magazine: The Coal Operators National Weekly* 19 (Aug. 13, 1912), 549; "The Machinery Markets: Texas," *Iron Age* 90 (Aug. 1, 1912), 284; Stadler, *Wilson County History*, 12; Valenza, "Places Lost," 223; Valenza, *Taking the Waters*, 34, 110, 111.
31. *Beaumont Journal*, June 21, 1911; Fort Worth *Star-Telegram*, June 21, 1911; *San Antonio Express*, June 21, July 22, Sept. 3, 21 [quote], 1911, June 20, July 30, 1912; *Houston Post*, June 22, 1911; *Abilene Daily Reporter*, June 22, 1911; Bureau of the Census, Thirteenth Census, 1910, Texas, Population: Wilson County; United States Bureau of the Census, Fourteenth Census, 1920, Texas, Schedule One, Population: Matagorda County; United States Bureau of the Census, Fifteenth Census, 1930, Texas, Schedule One, Population: Matagorda County; Lawrence D. Rice, "FARMERS' HOME IMPROVEMENT SOCIETY," *Handbook of Texas Online* (http://www.tshaonline.org/handbook/online/articles/aaf03), accessed Jan. 26, 2016; "Leonidis Polk 'Lon' Tatum," http://www.findagrave.com/cgi-bin/fg.cgi?page=gr&GRid=73583716 (accessed Jan. 26, 2016).
32. *San Antonio Express*, May 29, June 20, 25, 30, July 1, 27, 31, Sept. 21, 1912, Apr. 5, 1913; Corsicana *Morning Review*, Dec. 15, 1912; *Houston Post*, Dec. 15, 1912; Vest, *Century of Light*, 148, 160; *The Southwestern Reporter, Volume 159* (St. Paul: West Publishing Company, 1913), 876–879. The change in development companies was accompanied by a change in the bank that served as the reserve institution for the First State Bank in New Sutherland Springs. As of January 1, 1913, the Citizens Bank and Trust Company of San Antonio assumed that responsibility. See *Dallas Morning*

News, Jan. 19, 1913. The Masonic Lodge in Sutherland Springs formally organized during December 1912; its first Worshipful Master was Abner H. "Hub" Polley. See *Proceedings of the Grand Lodge of Texas, 1913* (Fort Worth: Texas Masonic Home, 1914), 438.

33. John W. Gray to Olive G. Thayer January 15, 1913 (postcard in author's collection).

Chapter 5

1. *San Antonio Express,* Apr. 5, 19, May 8, 20, 23, 27, June 19, 20, 24, 25, July 19, 1913, Jan. 20, 1914; "The Distinctive and Aerodynamic McKeen Rail Motor Car," http://theoldmotor. com/?p=134946 (accessed Nov. 10, 2015).
2. San Antonio *Daily Express,* Dec. 19, 1910, Feb. 10, 1911; *San Antonio Express,* June 7, 8, 10, 12, 13, 1913; *Houston Post,* June 19, 1913; *Southwestern Reporter, Volume 159,* 876–879.
3. *Houston Post,* June 19, 1913; *San Antonio Express,* Oct. 19, 24, Nov. 5, 1913; *Southwestern Reporter, Vol. 159,* 876–879; Richardson, *Autobiography,* 59 [quotes]; Valenza, *Taking the Waters,* 139. Marcus H. Townsend reportedly paid only $47,000 for the Sutherland Springs resort property. See Notes on Sutherland Springs and Shriber to Parmelee, Feb. 18, 1966 (Historical Marker File); Stadler, *Wilson County History,* 12; Conversation with Andersons, Apr. 20, 1985.
4. *San Antonio Express,* June 30, Sept. 11, 12, 18, 25, 28, Oct. 1, 3, 4, 9, 10, 18, Dec. 7, 8, 1913; *Dallas Morning News,* Oct. 3, 1913.
5. Texas Department of Insurance and Banking, *Fourth Annual Report ... of the Commissioner ... for the Year 1913–1914, Volume 2* (Austin: Von Boeckmann-Jones, 1915), 371; *San Antonio Express,* Apr. 10, Sept. 6 [quote], 1913, Jan. 11, 17, Feb. 8, 1914; *Dallas Morning News,* Nov. 2, 1913. Library records indicate that Thomas C. Richardson resumed publishing his newspaper at Sutherland Springs in 1914, then quit for good that same year.
6. Mrs. Thomas J. Williams to Thomas J. Williams, n.d. (Williams Family Papers); *San Antonio Express,* Mar. 7 [first quote], 21, 28, Apr. 11, 25, 1914; *Better Built Homes: What You Have Been Looking For, For Less Money* (Houston: Thomas J. Williams House Manufacturing Company, 1915), n. p. [second and third quotes]; Stadler, *Wilson County History,* 187, 188; Frank W. Johnson, *Texas and Texans,* 5 vols. (Chicago: American Historical Society, 1914), 4: 1882–1884; Margaret Culbertson, *Texas Houses Built by the Book: The Use of Published Designs, 1850–1925* (College Station: Texas A&M University Press, 1999), 83, 84; Conversation with Andersons, Apr. 20, 1985. By 1916 Williams was referring to himself as the "President of T. J. Williams House Manufacturing Company at Houston." See *San Antonio Express,* Apr. 24, 1916.

7. *San Antonio Express*, Apr. 7, 9, 1911, Apr. 30, May 2 [quote], 3, 5, 22, 23, 31, June 6, 21, 22, 24, 28, 1914; *Dallas Morning News*, June 25, 1914.
8. *San Antonio Express*, June 6, July 4 and 11, Aug. 1, Sept. 12, Nov. 7, 1914, Apr. 12, 22, 23, June 4 and 5, 1915; Sutherland Springs *Health Resort*, July 3, 1914 [first-fourth quotes]; *Floresville Chronicle-Journal*, July 27, 1928, Jan. 19, 1989; *Better Built Homes*, n. p.; "San Antonio and Gulf Shore Railroad," http://www.txtransportationmuseum.org/SAG.htm (accessed Nov. 10, 2015); Stadler, *Wilson County History*, 187, 188; Conversation with Masters, Apr. 17, 1985; Conversation with Katherine Berger, Apr. 17, 1985; Conversation with George B. Everts, Aug. 14, 1998.
9. *San Antonio Express*, Mar. 23, 1916, *Dallas Morning News*, May 19, 1894, June 28, 1911; Conversation with Berger, Apr. 17, 1985; Conversation with Mittie Williams (Mrs. Fred) Anderson, Apr. 20, 1985.
10. *San Antonio Express*, June 22, Oct. 17, 1914, Mar. 4, 1915, Mar. 18, 1916; *Dallas Morning News*, Feb. 13, 1915; George C. Matson, "Mineral Waters," *Mineral Resources of the United States, 1912, Part II* (Washington, DC: Government Printing Office, 1913), 1027; Arthur J. Ellis, "Mineral Waters," *Mineral Resources of the United States, 1918, Part II* (Washington, DC: Government Printing Office, 1921), 528; *The Texas Almanac and State Industrial Guide, 1926* (Dallas: A. H. Belo & Company, 1926), 169; Valenza, *Taking the Waters*,110, 111.
11. *San Antonio Express*, Sept. 29, 30, 1915; *Gonzales Reform*, Oct. 7, 1915; "Track and Roadway," *Electric Railway Journal* 54 (Nov. 8, 1919), 880; "Railway News," *Railway Review* 66 (Jan. 24, 1920), 158; Valenza, *Taking the Waters*, 91–93, 197, 198.
12. *San Antonio Daily Express*, Aug. 21, 1907; *San Antonio Express*, Aug. 13, 1911, Apr. 12, 21, 1912, July 2, 3, 1913, Apr. 12, Dec. 16, 1914.
13. *Houston Post*, Sept. 21, 1915; *San Antonio Express*, Sept. 21 [first-third quotes], 1915, Apr. 23, 24, May 4 [fourth-sixth quotes], 1916.
14. *San Antonio Express*, June 1, July 6 [quote] 1916, Feb. 24, 25, 26, 27, 28, Mar. 1, 2, 4, 5, 6, 7, 8, 9, 10, 11, 12, 13, 14, 15, 16, 17, 18, 20, 21, 22, 23, 1917, May 10, 1918, Apr. 12, 15, 22, 1919; "T. P. Morris," *Texas Legislators Past & Present*, http://www.lrl.state.tx.us/legeleaders/members/memberdisplay.cfm?memberID=2327 (accessed Nov. 16, 2015); Valenza, *Taking the Waters*, 140.
15. *San Antonio Express*, Dec. 1, 1915, Jan. 13, May 7, June 21, 1917, June 30, 1918 [first and second quotes], Mar. 3, 16, 1919; *Dallas Morning News*, Dec. 1, 1915; *Houston Post*, Dec. 1, 1915; "Southside Place: Incorporated City Preserves Small Town Culture," *Houston Business Journal*, http://www.bizjournals.com/houston/stories/2010/03/22/newscolumn2.html (accessed Nov. 16, 2015).

16. *San Antonio Express*, Jan. 30, June 15, 19, 30, July 2, 12, 14, 15, Aug. 12, 13, 28, Sept. 7, 1920.
17. *San Antonio Express*, May 2, 1920; San Antonio *Express-News*, Aug. 22, 1971; *Floresville Chronicle-Journal*, Jan. 19, 1989; Shriber to Parmelee, Feb. 18, 1966 (Historical Marker File); William E. Fitch, *Mineral Waters of the United States and American Spas* (Philadelphia: Lea and Febiger, 1927), 611 [quotes], 612, 613; *Wilson County Centennial*; Stadler, *Wilson County History*, 187, 188; Fowler, *Crazy Water*, 46–49; Valenza, *Taking the Waters*,140; Valenza, "Places Lost," 71, 72, 223, 232; DeVierville, "American Healing Waters," 168; Conversation with Andersons, Apr. 20, 1985; Conversation with Masters, Apr. 17, 1985.
18. *San Antonio Express*, May 26 [first quote], Jan. 6, 1912, Mar. 23, 26, 29, June 10, Oct. 9, 1913, Jan. 6, 1914 [third quote], Jan. 23, 1916 [fourth quote], Mar. 16, 1919 [fifth quote], Sept. 30, Nov. 6, 1920; Fort Worth *Star-Telegram*, Apr. 6, 1913; *Houston Post*, Jan. 6, 1914, Sept. 16, 1917; *Dallas Morning News*, Jan. 15, 1921; Lubbock *Morning Avalanche*, June 26, 1943; Bureau of the Census, Fourteenth Census, 1920, Texas, Population: Wilson County; *Texas Almanac and State Industrial Guide, 1912* (Dallas: Dallas Morning News, 1912), 367 [second quote]; *Texas Almanac and State Industrial Guide, 1914* (Dallas: Galveston-Dallas News, 1914), 243; "Wildcat Tests," *Fuel Oil Journal* 5 (Dec. 1914), 54; "August Gustav 'A. G.' Vogt," http://www.findagrave.com/cgi-bin/fg.cgi?page=pv&GRid=63889176 (accessed Nov. 16, 2015); Conversation with Mittie Williams (Mrs. Fred) Anderson, Apr. 20, 1985. William J. Wyatt refers to Anthony F. Lucas, the engineer who drilled the tremendously successful oil well at Spindletop in 1901.
19. *Galveston Weekly News*, Sept. 17, 1877; *San Antonio Express*, July 6, 1904, Aug. 5, 1904, Sept. 13, 1906, July 8, Sept. 21, 1909, June 9, Aug. 26, 1910, Nov. 21, 1911, July 9, Aug. 10, 1912, Oct. 24, 1913, Aug. 22, Sept. 19, 1914; Dallas *Southern Mercury*, July 12, Sept. 20, 1906 *Houston Post*, Sept. 21, 1909, June 9, 1910, July 9, 1912; *Dallas Morning News*, July 10, 1912, Jan. 27, 1921; Bureau of the Census, Thirteenth Census, 1910, Texas, Population: Wilson County (NA); "John C. Damron, Sr.," http://www.findagrave.com/cgi-bin/fg.cgi?page=gr&GRid=72109742 (accessed Nov. 16, 2015).
20. *San Antonio Express*, Jan. 4, 1911, Apr. 14, 1918, Jan. 30, 1920; *Houston Post*, Jan. 4, 1911; *San Antonio Light*, Sept. 27, 1941; "Field Copy," District 10 (Wilson County Scrapbook, CAH); *Why Not Know Why*, 24; *Wilson County Centennial*, n. p.; Patterson, *Wilson County*, 10, 11, 14; American Baptist Association History and Archives Committee, "Servants Among Us," http://www.bogardstore.org/images/Servantssample.pdf (accessed Nov. 16, 2015).

21. Bureau of the Census, Fourteenth Census, 1920, Texas, Population: Wilson County; Sutherland Springs *Health Resort,* July 3, 1914; *Why Not Know Why,* 24; *Wilson County Centennial;* Conversation with Andersons, Apr. 20, 1985. Among the heads of households listed for Sutherland Springs (Old and New) in 1920, 28 owned their homes, while 51 rented, including most of the Mexican families.
22. *Meridian Tribune,* Jan. 26, June 8, 1923; *Victoria Advocate,* Jan. 19, 1923; *Dallas Morning News,* Mar. 11, 1924, Jan. 19, 1925; Texas Senate, *Journal of the Senate, State of Texas, Regular Session, Thirty-Ninth Legislature* (Austin: A. C. Baldwin & Sons, 1925), 23; *Texas Almanac, 1926,* p. 327.
23. *Dallas Morning News,* Nov. 22, 1924, July 13, 1927, July 22, 1928, Feb. 4, 1929; *San Antonio Light,* May 10, 1939; *Floresville Chronicle-Journal,* July 27, 1928, Jan. 19, 1989; Valenza, *Taking the Waters,* 140; Stadler, *Wilson County History,* 12, 187, 188; Conversation with Ruth J. S. Smith, Mar. 28, 1985; Conversation with Masters, April 17, 1985; Conversation with Mittie Williams (Mrs. Fred) Anderson, Apr. 20, 1985; Conversation with Andersons, Apr. 20, 1985; Conversation with Everts, Aug. 14, 1998.
24. *Floresville Chronicle-Journal,* Jan. 12, 1934, Sept. 16, 1960; San Antonio *Express-News,* Aug. 22, 1971; United States Bureau of the Census, Fifteenth Census, 1930, Texas, Schedule One, Population: Wilson County; *Wilson County Centennial;* Stadler, *Wilson County History,* 12, 22, 23, 56, 62; *Texas Almanac and State Industrial Guide, 1931* (Dallas: Dallas Morning News, 1931), 149; Conversation with Barbara J. Wood, Apr. 17, 1985; Conversation with Andersons, Apr. 20, 1985;
25. *Dallas Morning News,* Jan. 31, 1933; Bureau of the Census, Fifteenth Census, 1930, Texas, Population: Wilson County [quote];*Texas Almanac and State Industrial Guide, 1933* (Dallas: Dallas Morning News, 1933), 66; *Texas Almanac and State Industrial Guide, 1936* (Dallas: Dallas Morning News, 1936), 159; *Texas Almanac and State Industrial Guide, 1941–42* (Dallas: Dallas Morning News, 1941), 130; Patterson, *Wilson County,* 26; Fowler, *Crazy Water,* 215, 216, 219–221; Conversation with Masters, Apr. 17, 1985; Conversation with Andersons, Apr. 20, 1985; Conversation with Everts, Aug. 14, 1998. The Sutherland Springs railroad depot according to at least one source was not demolished but relocated to Stockdale, where it survives today in a substantially remodeled format. See "San Antonio and Gulf Shore Railroad," http://www.txtransportationmuseum.org/SAG.htm (accessed Nov. 17, 2015). The information on the closing of the Sutherland Springs Masonic Lodge was provided by Richard Schlaudroff from the published proceedings of the Grand Lodge of Texas.

26. *Dallas Morning News,* Aug. 17, 1930 [first-eighth quotes]; "Field Copy," District 10 [ninth-twelfth quotes]; Valenza, *Taking the Waters,*140.
27. United States Bureau of the Census, Sixteenth Census, 1940, Texas, Population: Wilson County; Texas Department of Transportation, *Highway Designation File,* http://www.dot.state.tx.us/tpp/hwy/US/US0087.htm (accessed Nov. 17, 2015).
28. Bureau of the Census, Sixteenth Census, 1940, Texas, Population: Wilson County; *Dallas Morning News,* Nov. 6, 1900, Nov. 5, 1901, Nov. 9, 1903, May 26, 1940, June 2, 1947, May 2, 1948, May 3, 1949, May 28, 1951, June 2, 1952, May 31, 1954; *Mexia Weekly Herald,* Dec. 20, 1940; *Floresville Chronicle-Journal,* Sept. 16, 1960; Patterson, *Wilson County,* 26; Conversation with Woods, Apr. 17, 1985; Conversation with Mittie Williams (Mrs. Fred) Anderson, Apr. 20, 1985. Of the people who lived in Sutherland Springs in 1940, 86 percent were born in Texas. Of the rest, 29 came from other Southern states, twelve from the North, and five from outside of the United States (one each from Mexico, Germany, and England, and two from Canada).
29. Bureau of the Census, Sixteenth Census, 1940, Texas, Population: Wilson County; *Texas Almanac and State Industrial Guide, 1945–46* (Dallas: Dallas Morning News, 1945), 126; Conversation with Masters, Apr. 17, 1985; Conversation with Andersons, Apr. 20, 1985; Conversation with Everts, Aug. 14, 1998.
30. *Floresville Chronicle-Journal,* Sept. 16, 1960; *Dallas Morning News,* Oct. 31, 1961; *New York Times,* Aug. 20, 1972; San Antonio *Express-News,* Aug. 22, 1971; *Rio Grande Herald,* Oct. 19, 1978, Feb. 14, 1980; Shriber to Parmelee, Feb. 18, 1966 (Historical Marker File); Richardson, *Autobiography,* 59 [quote]; *Wilson County Centennial;* Stadler, *Wilson County History,* 187, 188; Valenza, *Taking the Waters,* 141; "Patillo 'Pat' Higgins Turns Grass into Gold," *Wilson County News,* http://www.wilsoncountynews.com/article.php?id=24931 (accessed Nov. 17, 2015); Conversation with Everts, Aug. 14, 1998; Conversation with Masters, Apr. 17, 1985; Conversation with Wood, Apr. 17, 1985; Conversation with Andersons, Apr. 20, 1985; Conversation with Devy Collins, Mar. 10, 2001. According to Sutherland Springs historian and teacher Tambria L. Read, who is a great-granddaughter of Patillo Higgins Sr., the elder Higgins bought the Hotel Sutherland from Thomas J. Williams and later sold it to his son and namesake about 1945. Michael Cavazos, in "Small Town History: Sutherland Springs," http://www.accd.edu/pac/history/rhines/StudentProjects/2002/SutherlandSprings/mvcfp.htm (accessed Nov. 21, 2015), reproduces a great map of the lots in Sutherland Springs with written comments by Higgins Jr. indicting when the lots were reverted to farm acreage by the county commissioners. Among the buildings demolished by Higgins was the Busby House. Perdie Busby had taken

work as a teacher by 1940 and lived in San Antonio, but when she was hospitalized in 1947 at Floresville, where she died, she declared her home address was Sutherland Springs. Apparently after Perdie left, her sister Lola moved into the Busby House with her husband, Chauncey S. Southern. In addition to the sources cited previously in this footnote, see Bureau of the Census, Sixteenth Census, 1940, Texas, Population: Bexar and Wilson Counties; Death Certificate for Perdie Busby, https://www.fold3.com/image/101014107/?terms=Busby (accessed Nov. 21, 2015); "Gravestone for Chauncey S. and Lola Busby Southern," http://www.usgwarchives.net/tx/wilson/photos/tombstones/sutherlandspring/southern17366gph.jpg (accessed Nov. 21, 2015).

31. San Antonio *Daily Express*, Feb. 9, Nov. 11, 1900, Aug. 29, Oct. 9, 1910; *San Antonio Express*, Sept. 11, 1912, Sept. 4, 6, 1913, Sept. 14, 1914, Sept. 6, 8, 1915, Apr. 23, 1916; *Dallas Morning News*, May 22, 1935, Sept. 23, Oct. 19, Nov. 18, 1938, Feb. 16, 1939, Apr. 6, 15, 1940; Bureau of the Census, Thirteenth Census, 1910, Texas, Population: Wilson County; *Texas Almanac, 1945–1946*, p. 372; *Wilson County Centennial*; Valenza, *Taking the Waters*, 140; Conversation with Masters, Apr. 17, 1985; Conversation with Everts, Aug. 14, 1998; Conversation with Andersons, Apr. 20, 1985; Oscar Mauzy, "GILMER-AIKIN LAWS," *Handbook of Texas Online* (http://www.tshaonline.org/handbook/online/articles/mlg01), accessed Jan. 27, 2016.

32. Petition from Town of Sutherland Springs, Jan. 19, 1899 (Texas Legislature Memorial and Petition File, TSL); San Antonio *Daily Express*, Mar. 19, Apr. 16 [quote], 1899; *Dallas Morning News*, June 24, 1939; *San Antonio Register*, Nov. 11, 1955; Conversation with Everts, Aug. 14, 1998; Patterson, *Wilson County*, 18; *Wilson County Centennial*; Barr, *Black Texans*, 100, 156–158; Campbell, *Southern Community in Crisis*, 321, 322. The Jesse Wilson who served as the principal of the black school in Sutherland Springs at the start of the twentieth century is probably the J. S. Wilson listed in the 1900 census at Floresville as a 37-year-old teacher from Mississippi. See Bureau of the Census, Twelfth Census, 1900, Texas, Population: Wilson County.

33. *Floresville Chronicle-Journal*, Sept. 16, 1960; Bureau of the Census, Fifteenth Census, 1930, Texas, Population: Wilson County; *Texas Almanac, 1958–1959* (Dallas: Dallas Morning News, 1957), 127; *Texas Almanac and State Industrial Guide, 1968–1969* (Dallas: Dallas Morning News, 1967), 189; *Texas Almanac and State Industrial Guide, 1976–1977* (Dallas: Dallas Morning News, 1975), 205; *Texas Almanac, 1980–1981* (Dallas: Dallas Morning News, 1979), 205; *The Texas Almanac, The Encyclopedia of Texas, 1984–1985* (Dallas: Dallas Morning News, 1983), 364; *Texas Almanac, 1990–1991* (Dallas: Dallas Morning News, 1989),

299; *Texas Almanac and State Industrial Guide, 1996–1997* (Dallas: Dallas Morning News, 1995), 308; *Texas Almanac, 2002–2003* (Dallas: Dallas Morning News, 2001), 312; *Texas Almanac, 2004–2005* (Dallas: Dallas Morning News, 2004), 368; "Sutherland Springs, Texas, United States," http://openplaques.org/places/us/areas/sutherland_springs_tx/plaques (accessed July 8, 2015).

34. Sutherland Springs *Western Chronicle*, Jan. 26, 1877 [quote]; Fitch, *Mineral Waters*, 611; Valenza, *Taking the Waters*, 12, 13, 27, 103.
35. Fitch, *Mineral Waters*, 611–613; E. L. Marck, "Works Progress Administration Ground Water Survey: Wilson County, Texas" (TS, Aug. 2, 1936, CAH), 3–6, 62–63. Albert C. Peale, in his 1886 report on mineral springs in the United States, declared there were "25 to 30" springs at Sutherland Springs, which is still far more than there are today. See Albert C. Peale, *Lists and Analyses of the Mineral Springs of the United States* (Bulletin Number 32 of the United States Geologic Survey, 1886), 127.
36. Hutchison, et al., eds., *Aquifers of the Upper Coastal Plains of Texas*, 1, 4, 6, 8, 9, 78–79; *New York Times*, Aug. 20, 1972; Valenza, *Taking the Waters*, 32, 33.
37. Historical Marker File; T. Lindsay Baker, *More Ghost Towns of Texas* (Norman: University of Oklahoma Press, 2003), 167–169; Zlatkovich, *Texas Railroads*, 87; "Western Ghost Towns: Sutherland Springs, Texas," http://www.ohio.edu/people/gulino/Ghosttownweb/Texas/Sutherland%20Springs/sutherland_springs_tx.html (accessed Jan. 27, 2016); "Deserted Texas: Sutherland Springs, Texas," http://desertedtexas.com/post/120039989558/sutherland-springs-texas (accessed Jan. 27, 2016). The six historical markers are for Whitehall, the Polley family cemetery, the Sutherland Springs Cemetery, Pat Higgins's grass farm, the Sutherland Springs school, and the Community Center [Building].
38. *Dallas Morning News*, Aug. 17, 1930 [quotes].

Bibliography

Primary

Unpublished

Bailey, James B. Papers. Dolph Briscoe Center for American History, The University of Texas at Austin.

Baylor, Mary A. Polley. "Reminiscences of Mary A. Baylor." Typescript, n.d. Dolph Briscoe Center for American History, The University of Texas at Austin.

Brigham, Asa. Papers. Dolph Briscoe Center for American History, The University of Texas at Austin.

Bryan, Guy M. Papers. Dolph Briscoe Center for American History, The University of Texas at Austin.

Carter, Aline P. Family Papers. Special Collections, University of Texas at San Antonio.

Crockett, Edward R. Diary. Dolph Briscoe Center for American History, The University of Texas at Austin.

Davenport, Harbert. Papers. Texas State Library and Archives, Austin.

Davis, Nicholas A. Diary. Dolph Briscoe Center for American History, The University of Texas at Austin.

Dickson, Robert H. Papers. Daughters of the Republic of Texas Library, San Antonio.

Dickson Family Papers. Daughters of the Republic of Texas Library, San Antonio.

Dimmitt, Philip. Papers. Dolph Briscoe Center for American History, The University of Texas at Austin.

Erskine, Andrew M. Papers. Dolph Briscoe Center for American History, The University of Texas at Austin.

Ford, John S. Papers. Nita Stewart Haley Memorial Museum, Midland.

Hanks, O. T. "Account of Civil War Experiences." Typescript, 1958. Dolph Briscoe Center for American History, The University of Texas at Austin.

Historical Marker File. Texas State Historical Commission, Austin.

Hotel Sutherland Ledger Books, August 14, 1910, to April 10, 1918. In possession of Lillian Williams Masters, Floresville.

Lilly, John W. Papers. Daughters of the Republic of Texas Library, San Antonio.

Manahan, James H. Papers. Dolph Briscoe Center for American History, The University of Texas at Austin.

Map Collection. Texas State Library and Archives, Austin.

Marck, E. L. "Works Progress Administration Ground Water Survey: Wilson County, Texas." Typescript, August 2, 1936. Dolph Briscoe Center for American History, The University of Texas at Austin.

Maverick, Samuel A., Jr. "Reminiscences." Typescript, 1929. Dolph Briscoe Center for American History, The University of Texas at Austin.

McCarty, Thomas L. Papers. Dolph Briscoe Center for American History, The University of Texas at Austin.

Newcomb, James P. Papers. Dolph Briscoe Center for American History, The University of Texas at Austin.

"Obituary of Doctor John Sutherland." Typescript, n.d. Dolph Briscoe Center for American History, The University of Texas at Austin.

Pease-Graham-Niles Papers. Austin History Center, Austin, TX.

Polley Family Papers. Dolph Briscoe Center for American History, The University of Texas at Austin.

Polley, Joseph H. Papers. Dolph Briscoe Center for American History, The University of Texas at Austin.

______. Papers. Daughters of the Republic of Texas Library, San Antonio.

______. Papers. Texas Collection, Baylor University, Waco.

Pomeroy, Nicholas. "Reminiscences of the American War, 1861–1865." Typescript, n.d. Dolph Briscoe Center for American History, The University of Texas at Austin.

Porter, R. H. Collection. Special Collections, University of Texas at San Antonio.

San Antonio and Mexican Gulf Railroad. Bonds. Dolph Briscoe Center for American History, The University of Texas at Austin.

Sutherland, George. Papers. Dolph Briscoe Center for American History, The University of Texas at Austin.

Sutherland, John Jr. Papers. Dolph Briscoe Center for American History, The University of Texas at Austin.

______. "The Alamo." Typescript, n.d. Dolph Briscoe Center for American History, The University of Texas at Austin.

Sutherland Family. Bible. Dolph Briscoe Center for American History, The University of Texas at Austin.

Sutherland Family. Papers. In possession of Elise Kidd, Austin.

Sutherland-Rogers Family. Scrapbook. Texas State Library and Archives, Austin.

Sutherland Springs. Historical Display. Sutherland Springs Museum, Sutherland Springs.

Texas. Adjutant General. Confederate Audited Civil Claims, 1861–1865. Texas State Library and Archives, Austin.

______. Militia Records. Texas State Library and Archives, Austin.

______. Muster Roll of County Special Policemen. Texas State Library and Archives, Austin.

______. Bexar County. Deed Records. Texas State Library and Archives, Austin.

______. Tax Rolls. Texas State Library and Archives, Austin.

______. Comptroller. Republic of Texas Claim Files. Texas State Library and Archives, Austin.

______. General Land Office. Land Grants. Texas General Land Office Archives and Records, Austin.

______. General Land Office. Map Collection. Texas General Land Office Archives and Records, Austin.

______. Governor. Records. Texas State Library and Archives, Austin.

______. Guadalupe County. Deed Records. Texas State Library and Archives, Austin.

______. Tax Rolls. Texas State Library and Archives, Austin.

______. Karnes County. Tax Rolls. Texas State Library and Archives, Austin.

______. Legislature. Memorial and Petition File. Texas State Library and Archives, Austin.

______. Secretary of State. Confederate Pension Files. Texas State Library and Archives, Austin.

______. Election Register. Texas State Library and Archives, Austin.

______. Election Returns. Texas State Library and Archives, Austin.

______. Executive Record Book. Texas State Library and Archives, Austin.

______. State Historical Association. Records. Dolph Briscoe Center for American History, The University of Texas at Austin.

______. Wilson County. Index to Deeds, 1860–1899. Texas State Library and Archives, Austin.

______. Marriage Records. Texas State Library and Archives, Austin.

______. Probate Minutes. Texas State Library and Archives, Austin.

______. Register of Deeds, Vol. C. Wilson County Courthouse, Floresville.

______. Scrapbook, Dolph Briscoe Center for American History, The University of Texas at Austin.

______. Tax Rolls. Texas State Library and Archives, Austin.

United States. Department of the Interior. Bureau of the Census. Seventh Census of the United States, 1850. Schedule 1 (Free Population) and Schedule 2 (Slave Population). Record Group 29. National Archives, Washington.

______. Eighth Census of the United States, 1860. Schedule 1 (Free Population) and Schedule 2 (Slave Population). Record Group 29. National Archives, Washington.

______. Ninth Census of the United States, 1870. Schedule 1 (Population). Record Group 29. National Archives, Washington.

______. Tenth Census of the United States, 1880. Schedule 1 (Population). Record Group 29. National Archives, Washington.

______. Twelfth Census of the United States, 1900. Schedule 1 (Population). Record Group 29. National Archives, Washington.

______. Thirteenth Census of the United States, 1910. Schedule 1 (Population). Record Group 29. National Archives, Washington.

______. Fourteenth Census of the United States, 1920. Schedule 1 (Population). Record Group 29. National Archives, Washington.

______. Fifteenth Census of the United States. Schedule 1 (Population). Record Group 29. National Archives, Washington.

______. Department of War. Compiled Service Records of Confederate Soldiers Who Served in Organizations from Texas. Record Group 109. National Archives, Washington.

______. Compiled Service Records of Volunteer Soldiers Who Served During the Mexican War in Organizations from the State of Texas. Record Group 94, National Archives, Washington.

______. Department of War. Adjutant General's Office. Case Files of Applications from Former Confederates for Presidential Pardons, 1865–1867. Record Group 94. National Archives, Washington.

______. Bureau of Refugees, Freedmen and Abandoned Lands. Records of the Assistant Commissioner for the State of Texas, Letters Received, 1867–1869. Record Group 105. National Archives, Washington.

______. Records of the Sub-Assistant Commissioner for Seguin, Texas, Letters Sent. Record Group 105, National Archives, Washington.

______. Office of Civil Affairs. Records of the District of Texas, Fifth Military District, and Department of Texas, Correspondence, 1867–1870. Record Group 393, National Archives, Washington.

______. Works Progress Administration. Historical Records Survey. Center for American History, The University of Texas at Austin.

Vertical Files. Dolph Briscoe Center for American History, The University of Texas at Austin.

Williams, Thomas J. Family Papers. In possession of Mittie Williams [Mrs. Fred] Anderson, Floresville.

Published

Abstract of Titled and Patented Lands Compiled from the Records of the General Land Office, of the State of Texas. Austin: General Land Office, 1860.

Anders, R. B. "Ground-Water Geology of Wilson County, Texas," *Texas Water Development Board Bulletin 5710* (July 1957).

Annual Report of the Indiana University Including the Catalogue for the Academical Year 1881–1882. Indianapolis: William B. Burford, 1882.

Baker, D. W. C. *A Texas Scrapbook*, ed. Robert A. Calvert. Austin: Texas State Historical Association, 1991.

"Banking, Legislative, and Financial News," *The Commercial and Financial Chronicle* 102 (April 22, 1916), 1512–1515.

Barker, Eugene C., ed. *The Austin Papers.* 3 volumes. Washington: Government Publishing Office, 1924–1928.

______, ed. "Journal of Stephen F. Austin on His First Trip to Texas, 1821," *Quarterly of the Texas State Historical Association* 7 (April 1904), 287–307.

"Battle of Chickamauga," *Southern Historical Society Papers* 13 (1885), 384–385.

"The Battle of Chickamauga, 19th and 20th of September, 1863," *Southern Historical Society Papers* 16 (1888), 380–381.

Better Built Homes: What You Have Been Looking For, For Less Money. Houston: Thomas J. Williams House Manufacturing Company, 1915.

"Bexar County Medical Society Active in Exterminating Illegal Practitioners," *Texas State Journal of Medicine* 8 (October 1912), 174.

Bonnell, George. *Topographical Description of Texas.* Austin: Clark, Wing & Brown, 1840.

Bryan, J. P., ed. *Mary Austin Holley: The Texas Diary, 1835–1838.* Austin: University of Texas Press, 1965.

Catalogue of the University of Texas, 1902–1903. Bulletin of the University of Texas, No. 20, June 1, 1903.

Coal Mining Companies and Operators of the United States. Chicago: Mining World, 1905.

"Construction Department: Texas," *Industrial Development and Manufacturers Record* 51 (June 6, 1907), 670.

Cox, Cornelius C. "Reminiscences of C. C. Cox, I and II," *Quarterly of the Texas State Historical Association* 6 (January and April 1903), 113–138, 204–235.

Day, James M., comp. *The Texas Almanac, 1857–1873: A Compendium of Texas History.* Waco: Texian Press, 1967.

Duessen, Alexander. *Geology of the Coastal Plain of Texas West of Brazos River.* Washington: Government Printing Office, 1924.

Dowdey, Clifford, and Louis H. Manarin, eds. *The Wartime Papers of R. E. Lee.* New York: Bramhall House, 1961.

Dresser, Henry E. "Notes on the Birds of Southern Texas," *Ibis* 6 (1865), 312–315.

Edward Alden & Brother's American Newspaper Catalogue, 1882. Cincinnati: Edward Alden & Brothers, 1882.

Ellis, Arthur J. "Mineral Waters," *Mineral Resources of the United States, 1918, Part II* Washington: Government Printing Office, 1921.

Evans, Clement A., ed. *Confederate Military History.* Extended edition, 17 volumes. Wilmington, NC: Broadfoot Publishing Company, 1989.

Fitch, William E. *Mineral Waters of the United States and American Spas.* Philadelphia: Lea and Febiger, 1927.

Fletcher, William A. *Rebel Private: Front and Rear.* Beaumont, 1908; reprint, New York: Dutton, 1995.

Foster, William C., and Jack Jackson, eds. "The 1693 Expedition of Gregorio de Salina Varona to Sustain the Missionaries Among the Tejas Indians," *Southwestern Historical Quarterly* 97 (October 1993), 265–311.

Fourth Annual Report of the Agricultural Bureau of the Department of Agriculture, Insurance, Statistics, and History. Austin: Hutchings Printing House, 1892.

Gammel, H. P. N., comp. *The Laws of Texas, 1822–1897.* 10 volumes. Austin: Gammel Book Company, 1898–1902.

Garrison, Gulnare. "Southwestern Texas as a Health Resort," *The Medical and Surgical Reporter* 44 (Jan. 22, 1881), 91–92.

"General Mining News: Texas, Fayette County," *Engineering and Mining Journal* 65 (January 15, 1898), 83.

George P. Rowell & Company's American Newspaper Directory. New York: George P. Rowell & Company, 1879.

Giles, Val C. "The Flag of First Texas, A. N. Virginia," *Confederate Veteran* 15 (September 1907), 417.

Glover, Robert W., ed. *"Tyler to Sharpsburg:" Robert H. and William H. Gaston (Their War Letters, 1861–1862).* Waco: W. M. Morison, 1960.

Gray, William F. *From Virginia to Texas, 1835.* Houston, 1909; reprint, Houston: Fletcher Young Publishing Company, 1965.

Green, Rena Maverick, ed. *Memoirs of Mary A. Maverick.* San Antonio: Alamo Printing Company, 1921.

Gretchen, Mark. *Slave Transactions of Guadalupe County, Texas.* Santa Maria, CA: Janaway Publishing, 2009.

Gulick, Charles A., et al., eds. *The Papers of Mirabeau Buonaparte Lamar.* 6 volumes. Austin: Texas State Library, 1923–1927.

Haley, J. Evetts, ed. "A Log of the Texas-California Cattle Trail, I, II, and III," *Southwestern Historical Quarterly* 35 and 36 (January- July 1932), 208–237, 290–316, 47–66.

Hamby, William R. "Fourth Texas in Battle of Gaines's Mill," *Confederate Veteran* 14 (April 1906), 183–184.

______. "Hood's Texas Brigade at Sharpsburg," *Confederate Veteran* 16 (January 1908), 19–20.

Hardinge, Sarah A. L. *Views of Texas, 1852–1856*, ed. Ron Tyler. Fort Worth: Amon Carter Museum, 1988.

Hill, Daniel H. "Lee's Attacks North of the Chickahominy," *Battles and Leaders, Volume Two*, ed. Robert U. Johnson and Clarence C. Buel. New York: Thomas Yoseloff, 1956.

Hood, John Bell. *Advance and Retreat*. New Orleans: G. T. Beauregard, 1880.

Hood's Brigade Historical Papers. Privately Published, n. d.

Hutchison, William R., et al., eds. *Aquifers of the Upper Coastal Plains of Texas*. Texas Water Development Board Report 374, October 2009.

Ingmire, Frances T., and Robert L. Thompson, comps. *Bexar County Land Titles*. Privately published, 1980.

Jackson, Jack, ed. *Almonte's Texas: Juan N. Almonte's 1834 Inspection, Secret Report, and Role in the Texas Revolution*. Austin: Texas State Historical Association, 2003.

Jackson, Mattie, comp. *The Rising and Setting of the Lone Star Republic*. Privately published, 1926.

James, Vinton Lee. *Frontier and Pioneer Recollections of Early Days in San Antonio and West Texas*. San Antonio: Privately published, 1938.

Jenkins, John H., ed. *The Papers of the Texas Revolution, 1835–1836*. 10 volumes. Austin: Presidial Press, 1973.

Jordan, Terry G., and Alyson L. Greiner, "The Texas Travel Diary of Henry H. Field, 1853," *Southwestern Historical Quarterly* 99 (January 1996), 351–368.

Journal of the Texas State Convention. Austin: Southern Intelligencer Office, 1866.

Journal of Proceedings of the Forty-Fifth Annual Convention of the Protestant Episcopal Church in the Diocese of Indiana. Madison, IN: M. C. Garber & Company, 1882.

Kennedy, William. *Texas: The Rise, Prospects, and Progress of the Republic of Texas*. 2 volumes. London: R. Hastings, 1841.

Ladd, Kevin, comp. *Gone to Texas: Genealogical Abstracts from the Telegraph and Texas Register, 1835–1841*. Bowie, MD: Heritage Books, 1994.

Lasswell, Mary, ed. *Rags and Hope: The Recollections of Val C. Giles, Four Years with Hood's Brigade, Fourth Texas Infantry, 1861–1865*. New York: Coward-McCann, 1961.

Law, Evander M. "On the Confederate Right at Gaines's Mill," *Battles and Leaders of the Civil War, Volume Two*, ed. Robert U. Johnson and Clarence C. Buel. New York: Thomas Yoseloff, 1956.

"Lee's Farewell to Texas, February 9, 1861," *Military History of Texas and the Southwest* 14 (1978), 244–245.

"The Machinery Markets: Texas," *Iron Age* 90 (August 1, 1912), 283–284.

Matson, George C. "Mineral Waters," *Mineral Resources of the United States, 1912, Part II*. Washington: Government Printing Office, 1913.

McLean, Malcolm D., ed. *Papers Concerning Robertson's Colony in Texas, Volume 16: August 10, 1837, through November, 1838*. Arlington: University of Texas at Arlington Press, 1990.

Mearse, Linda, comp. *Confederate Indigent Families Lists of Texas, 1863–1865*. Privately published, 1995.

Medical and Surgical Directory of the United States. Detroit: R. L. Polk & Company, 1886.

Minutes of the Annual Conference of the Methodist Episcopal Church for the Year 1874. New York: Nelson & Phillips, n.d. [1875].

"Miscellaneous Enterprises," *Industrial Development and Manufacturers Record* 52 (January 2, 1908), 104.

Mullins, Marion D. *The First Census of Texas, 1829–1836*. Washington: National Genealogical Society, 1959.

Nail, Olin W., ed. *Journal of the Rio Grande Mission Conference of the Methodist Episcopal Church, South*. Privately published, 1938.

Nail, Olin W., et al., eds. *Texas Methodist Centennial Yearbook: The Story of Methodism During the Last One Hundred Years in Texas*. Elgin, TX: Privately published, 1934.

Nance, Joseph M., ed. "Brigadier General Adrian Woll's Report on his Expedition into Texas in 1842," *Southwestern Historical Quarterly* 58 (April 1955), 523–552.

"New Coal Trade Enterprises," *Fuel Magazine: The Coal Operators National Weekly* 19 (August 13, 1912), 549.

"New Enterprises," *Fuel Magazine: The Coal Operators National Weekly* 9 (June 11, 1907), 193.

"Official Reports of the Battle of Gettysburg," *Southern Historical Society Papers* 4 (1877), 162–164.

"Official Reports of the Battle of Gettysburg," *Southern Historical Society Papers* 13 (1885), 190–191.

Olmsted, Frederick Law. *A Journey Through Texas*. New York: Dix, Edwards & Company, 1857.

"Paroles of the Army of Northern Virginia," *Southern Historical Society Papers* 15 (1887), 160–167.

Pettengill's Newspaper Directory and Advertisers' Hand-Book for 1877. New York: S. M. Pettengill & Company, 1877.

Phillips, William B. *Texas Petroleum*. Bulletin of the University of Texas No. 5, July 1900.

Polley, Joseph B. "About All the Men in Hood's Texas Brigade," *Confederate Veteran* 18 (May 1911), 222.

______. "Another 'Charming Nellie' Letter," *Confederate Veteran* 4 (April 1896), 118.

______. "Battle Described to Charming Nellie," *Confederate Veteran* 4 (June 1896), 185.

______. "Brave Texans in the Virginia Army," *Confederate Veteran* 4 (May 1896), 158–159.

______. "Concernin' of a Hog," *Confederate Veteran* 5 (February 1897), 58–59.

______. "The Gunboat Gen. Taylor Failed to Get," *Confederate Veteran* 15 (June 1907), 281.

______. *Hood's Texas Brigade.* New York: Neale Publishing Company, 1910.

______. "J. B. Polley About Texans in Virginia," *Confederate Veteran* 5 (September 1897), 471.

______. "Polley Lost a Foot—A Furlough," *Confederate Veteran* 5 (November 1897), 570–571.

______. "Polley Off on Furlough," *Confederate Veteran* 5 (May 1897), 218.

______. "Second Manassas," *Confederate Veteran* 4 (July 1896), 218–219.

______. "Simple Justice Asked," *Confederate Veteran* 3 (October 1895), 317.

______. *A Soldier's Letters to Charming Nellie,* New York, 1908. Reprint ed. by Richard B. McCaslin, Knoxville: University of Tennessee Press, 2008.

______. "A Texas Reminiscence," *Frontier Times* 27 (August 1950), 307.

______. "To Charming Nellie—Not So Funny," *Confederate Veteran* 4 (February1896), 44–45.

______. *Wilson County, Texas: Its Description, Resources, Etc.* Floresville: Privately printed, 1888.

Peale, Albert C. *Lists and Analyses of the Mineral Springs of the United States.* Bulletin of the United States Geologic Survey, No. 32, 1886.

Proceedings of the Grand Lodge of Texas, 1913. Fort Worth: Texas Masonic Home, 1914.

"The Propaganda for Reform," *Journal of the American Medical Association* 61 (August 16, 1913), 504.

"Railway News," *Railway Review* 66 (January 24, 1920), 158.

Rawick, George, ed. *The American Slave: A Composite Autobiography, Supplement, Series 2.* 10 volumes. Westwood, CT: Greenwood Press, 1979.

Richardson, Thomas C. *The Autobiography of the Rambling Longhorn.* Oklahoma City: Farmer Stockman Magazine, 1959.

Rock, James, and W. I. Smith. *Southern and Western Texas Guide for 1878.* St. Louis: A. H. Pranger, 1878.

"San Antonio Banks Consolidate," *The Texas Bankers Record* 5 (January 1916), 37.

Scott, Robert N., et al., comps. *The War of the Rebellion: A Compilation of the Official Records of the Union and Confederate Armies.* 128 volumes. Washington: Government Printing Office, 1880–1901.

Smither, Harriet, ed. "Diary of Adolphus Sterne, IV," *Southwestern Historical Quarterly* 31 (July 1927), 63–83.

The Southwestern Reporter, Volume 44. St. Paul: West Publishing Company, 1898.

The Southwestern Reporter, Volume 59. St. Paul: West Publishing Company, 1913.

Stiff, Edward. *The Texian Emigrant.* Cincinnati, 1840; reprint, Waco: Texian Press, 1968.

Sutherland, John. *The Fall of the Alamo*, ed. Annie B. Sutherland. San Antonio: Naylor Company, 1936.

"The Texans at Sharpsburg," *Confederate Veteran* 22 (December 1914), 555.

"Texas," *American Architect* 96 (September 29, 1909), 14.

Texas Agricultural Bureau. *Fourth Annual Report of the Agricultural Bureau of the Department of Agriculture, Insurance, Statistics, and History.* Austin: Hutchings Printing House, 1892.

Texas Almanac, 1867. Galveston: Richardson & Company, 1866.

Texas Almanac and State Industrial Guide, 1904. Dallas: Dallas Morning News, 1904.

Texas Almanac and State Industrial Guide for 1910. Dallas: Galveston-Dallas News, 1910.

Texas Almanac and State Industrial Guide, 1912. Dallas: Dallas Morning News, 1912.

Texas Almanac and State Industrial Guide, 1914. Dallas: Galveston-Dallas News, 1914.

The Texas Almanac and State Industrial Guide, 1926. Dallas: A. H. Belo & Company, 1926.

Texas Almanac and State Industrial Guide, 1931. Dallas: Dallas Morning News, 1931.

Texas Almanac and State Industrial Guide, 1933. Dallas: Dallas Morning News, 1933.

Texas Almanac and State Industrial Guide, 1936. Dallas: Dallas Morning News, 1936.

Texas Almanac and State Industrial Guide, 1941–42. Dallas: Dallas Morning News, 1941.

Texas Almanac and State Industrial Guide, 1945–46. Dallas: Dallas Morning News, 1945.

Texas Almanac, 1958–1959. Dallas: Dallas Morning News, 1957.

Texas Almanac and State Industrial Guide, 1968–1969. Dallas: Dallas Morning News, 1967.

Texas Almanac and State Industrial Guide, 1976–1977. Dallas: Dallas Morning News, 1975.

Texas Almanac, 1980–1981. Dallas: Dallas Morning News, 1979.

The Texas Almanac, The Encyclopedia of Texas, 1984–1985. Dallas: Dallas Morning News, 1983.

Texas Almanac, 1990–1991. Dallas: Dallas Morning News, 1989.

Texas Almanac and State Industrial Guide, 1996–1997. Dallas: Dallas Morning News, 1995.

Texas Almanac, 2002–2003. Dallas: Dallas Morning News, 2001.

Texas Almanac, 2004–2005. Dallas: Dallas Morning News, 2004.

Texas Department of Insurance and Banking. *Fourth Annual Report ... of the Commissioner ... for the Year 1913–1914, Volume 2.* Austin: Von Boeckmann-Jones, 1915.

Texas Court Reporter, Volume 8. Austin: Ben C. Jones & Company, 1904.

Texas Secretary of State. *Biennial Report of the Secretary of State of the State of Texas, 1884.* Austin: State Printing Office, 1884.

______. *Biennial Report of the Secretary of State of the State of Texas, 1910.* Austin: Austin Publishing Company, 1911.

Texas Senate. *Journal of the Senate, State of Texas, Regular Session, Thirty-Ninth Legislature.* Austin: A. C. Baldwin & Sons, 1925.

Texas State Gazetteer and Business Directory for 1884. Chicago: R. L. Polk & Company, 1884.

Texas State Medical Association. *Transactions of the Texas State Medical Association, 1875.* Columbus: Colorado Citizen, 1875.

"Track and Roadway," *Electric Railway Journal* 54 (November 8, 1919), 880.

A Twentieth Century History of Southwest Texas. 2 volumes. Chicago: Lewis Publishing Company, 1907.

White, Gifford, ed. *1830 Citizens of Texas.* Austin: Eakin Press, 1983.

______, ed. *The 1840 Census of the Republic of Texas.* Austin: Pemberton Press, 1966.

White, John P. *Texas Criminal Reports, Volume 55.* Chicago: T. H. Flood & Company, 1909.

Why Not Know Why? Sutherland Springs: Sutherland Springs Development Corporation, 1909.

"Wildcat Tests," *Fuel Oil Journal* 5 (December 1914), 54.

Williams, Villamae, ed. *Stephen F. Austin's Register of Families.* St. Louis: Ingmire Publications, 1984.

Winfrey, Dorman H., and James M. Day, eds. *The Indian Papers of Texas and the Southwest, 1825–1916.* 5 volumes. Austin, 1966; reprint, Austin: Texas State Historical Association, 1995.

Winkler, Ernest W., ed. *Journal of the Secession Convention of Texas, 1861.* Austin: Austin Printing Company, 1912.

Winkler, Ernest W., comp. *Manuscript Letters and Documents of Early Texians, 1821–1845*. Austin: Steck Company, 1937.

"The Writings of Fannie Amelia Dickson Darden," *Nesbitt Memorial Library Journal* 9 (September 1999), 131–194.

Newspapers

Abilene Daily Reporter
Abilene Reporter
Austin American
Austin *Texas State Gazette*
Austin *Weekly Democratic Statesman*
Bastrop Advertiser
Beaumont *Daily Enterprise*
Beaumont Enterprise
Beaumont Journal
Bryan Daily Eagle and Pilot
Clarksville *Standard*
Columbia *Colorado Citizen*
Columbia *Telegraph and Texas Register*
Corsicana *Morning Review*
Cotulla Record
Dallas Daily Herald
Dallas Herald
Dallas Morning News
Dallas News
Dallas *Southern Mercury*
El Paso Daily Herald
El Paso Herald
El Paso *International Daily Times*
El Paso Times
Floresville Chronicle Journal
Fort Worth Gazette
Fort Worth *Star-Telegram*
Galveston Daily News
Galveston *Flake's Bulletin*
Galveston Tri-Weekly News
Galveston Weekly News
Gonzales Reform
Houston Daily Post
Houston Post
Houston *Telegraph and Texas Register*
Houston *Weekly Telegraph*

Lubbock *Morning Avalanche*
McKinney Democrat
Meridian Tribune
Mexia Weekly Herald
New York Times
Orange Daily Tribune
Palestine Daily Herald
Rio Grande Herald
San Antonio *Daily Express*
San Antonio Express
San Antonio *Express-News*
San Antonio Gazette
San Antonio Ledger
San Antonio Light
San Antonio Register
San Antonio *Western Texan*
San Marcos Free Press
Shiner Gazette
Sutherland Springs *Health Resort*
Sutherland Springs *Western Chronicle*
Victoria Advocate
Washington *National Register*
Wilson County News

Secondary

Articles and Chapters

Aycock, B. L. "The Lone Star Guards," *Confederate Veteran* 31 (February 1923), 61.

Barker, Eugene C. "The Texan Declaration of Causes for Taking Up Arms Against Mexico," *Quarterly of the Texas State Historical Association* 15 (January 1912), 173–185.

Bolton, Herbert E. "The Spanish Abandonment and Reoccupation of East Texas, 1773–1779," *Quarterly of the Texas State Historical Association* 9 (October 1905), 67–137.

Buckley, Eleanor Claire. "The Aguayo Expedition into Texas and Louisiana, 1719–1722," *Quarterly of the Texas State Historical Association* 15 (July 1911), 1–65.

Bugbee, Lester H. "The Old Three Hundred: A List of Settlers in Austin's First Colony," *Quarterly of the Texas State Historical Association* 1 (October 1897), 108–117.

Cross, Cora M. "A. H. Polley Tells How He Turned the Western Trail," *Frontier Times* 6 (June 1929), 362–364.

Deshields, James T. "Siege, Defense and Fall of the Alamo," *Alamo Magazine* (December 1913), 4.

Everett, Donald E. "San Antonio Welcomes the 'Sunset'—1877," *Southwestern Historical Quarterly* 65 (July 1961), 47–60.

Fisher, Sterling. "The Rio Grande Conference," *Texas Methodist Historical Quarterly* 1 (April 1910), 346–355.

Freeman, Martha D. "The Sutherland Plantation and the Alabama Settlement: A Study in Cluster Migration," in *The Antebellum Period in the Stephen F. Austin Colony.* Research Report No. 70, Palmetto Bend Reservoir Series, The University of Texas at Austin, 1980.

Garwood, Ellen. "Early Texas Inns: A Study in Social Relationships," *Southwestern Historical Quarterly* 60 (October 1956), 219–244.

Golson, Edward M. "The Polley Family in Texas," *Frontier Times* 22 (July 1945), 313.

Haggard, J. Villasana. "Epidemic Cholera in Texas, 1833–1834," *Southwestern Historical Quarterly* 40 (January 1937), 216–230.

Henderson, Don E. "General Hood's Brigade," *Southern Historical Society Papers* 29 (1901), 300–301.

"A Hero of Texas Independence," *Frontier Times* 5 (September 1928), 492.

"J. B. Polley Was a Texas Pioneer," *Frontier Times* 7 (September 1928), 461.

Jackson, Jack. "Father José María de Jesús Puelles and the Maps of Pichardo's Document," *Southwestern Historical Quarterly* 91 (January 1988), 317–347.

"The John Henry Polley Home Near Sutherland Springs," *Frontier Times* 22 (July 1945), 315.

"Joseph B. Polley," *Bohemian* 1 (1900), 8.

McCaslin, Richard B. "William Longworth, Republican Villain," in *"Still the Arena of Civil War": Violence and Turmoil in Reconstruction Texas, 1865–1874*, ed. Kenneth Howell. Denton: University of North Texas, 2012.

Muckleroy, Anna. "The Indian Policy of the Republic of Texas, I," *Southwestern Historical Quarterly* 25 (April 1922), 229–260.

Murray, Myrtle. "Home Life on Early Ranches of Southwest Texas," *Cattleman* 24 (May 1938), 9–12.

"Necrology," *Michigan Alumnus* 6 (March 1900), 278.

Parent, E. J. "General Lee to the Rear," *Confederate Veteran* 2 (January 1894), 14.

Patterson, C. L. "Wilson County," *Fletcher States Rights Farming* (December 1, 1937), 1.

Pfeiffer, Leslie. "Cibolo Creek Site," *Central States Archaeological Journal* 48 (January 2001), 46–50.

"R. H. Skinner," *Confederate Veteran* 22 (January 1914), 35.

Rippy, J. Fred. "Border Troubles Along the Rio Grande, 1848–1860," *Southwestern Historical Quarterly* 23 (October 1919), 91–111.

Shearer, Ernest C. "The Callahan Expedition, 1855," *Southwestern Historical Quarterly* 54 (April 1951), 430–451.

Smyrl, Frank H. "Unionism in Texas, 1856–1861," *Southwestern Historical Quarterly* 68 (October 1964), 172–195.

Tyler, Ronnie C. "The Callahan Expedition of 1855: Indians or Negroes?" *Southwestern Historical Quarterly* (April 1967), 574–585.

Valenza, Janet M. "'Taking the Waters' at Texas's Health Spas," *Southwestern Historical Quarterly* 98 (January 1995), 427–456.

Williams, Amelia. "A Critical Study of the Siege of the Alamo and of the Personnel of Its Defenders," *Southwestern Historical Quarterly* 36 (April 1933), 251–287.

Wooster, Ralph A. "Wealthy Texans, 1860," *Southwestern Historical Quarterly* 71 (October 1967), 163–180.

______, and Robert Wooster. "'Rarin' for a Fight:' Texans in the Confederate Army," *Southwestern Historical Quarterly* 84 (April 1981), 387–426.

Books

Bailey, Ernest E., ed. *Texas Historical and Biographical Record.* Austin: Privately Published, 1900.

Baillio, Ferdinand D. *History of the Texas Press Association.* Dallas: Southwestern Publishing Company, 1916.

Baker, T. Lindsay. *More Ghost Towns of Texas.* Norman: University of Oklahoma Press, 2003.

Bancroft, Hubert H. *The Works of Hubert Howe Bancroft, Vol. 15: The History of the North Mexican States.* San Francisco: A. L. Bancroft & Company, 1884.

Barr, Alwyn. *Black Texans.* 2nd edition. Norman: University of Oklahoma Press, 1996.

Baum, Dale. *The Shattering of Texas Unionism.* Baton Rouge: Louisiana State University Press, 1998.

Baylor, Orval W., and Henry B. Baylor. *Baylor's History of the Baylors.* LeRoy, IL: LeRoy Journal Printing Company, 1914.

Berg-Sobré, Judith. *San Antonio on Parade: Six Historic Festivals.* College Station: Texas A&M University Press, 2003.

Biographical Souvenir of the State of Texas. Chicago: P. A. Battey, 1889.

Brown, John H. *History of Texas, from 1685 to 1892.* 2 volumes. St. Louis: L. E. Daniell, 1892.

______. *The Indian Wars and Pioneers of Texas.* Austin: L. E. Daniell, 189–.

Buenger, Walter L. *Secession and the Union in Texas.* Austin: University of Texas Press, 1984.

Burnham, W. Dean. *Presidentia1 Ballots, 1836–1892.* Baltimore: Johns Hopkins University Press, 1955.

Campbell, Randolph B. *An Empire for Slavery: The Peculiar Institution in Texas, 1821–1865.* Baton Rouge: Louisiana State University Press, 1989.

______. *Gone to Texas: A History of the Lone Star State.* New York: Oxford University Press, 2003.

______. *Southern Community in Crisis: Harrison County, Texas, 1850–1880.* Austin: Texas State Historical Association, 1983.

Chipman, Donald E. *Spanish Texas, 1519–1821.* Austin: University of Texas Press, 1992.

Corning, Leavitt. *Baronial Forts of the Big Bend.* San Antonio: Trinity University Press, 1967.

Cox, I. Waynne. *Documentation of the San Pedro Acequia at Trevino Street, San Antonio, Texas.* Center for Archaeological Research, The University of Texas at San Antonio, Archaeological Survey Report No. 230 [1995].

Crouch, Barry A. *The Freedmen's Bureau and Black Texans.* Austin: University of Texas Press, 1992.

Crute, Joseph H., Jr. *Units of the Confederate Army.* Midlothian, VA: Derwent Books, 1987.

Culbertson, Margaret. *Texas Houses Built by the Book: The Use of Published Designs, 1850–1925.* College Station: Texas A&M University Press, 1999.

De Leon, Arnoldo. *The Tejano Community, 1836–1900.* Albuquerque: University of New Mexico Press, 1982.

______. *They Called Them Greasers: Anglo Attitudes Toward Mexicans in Texas, 1821–1900.* Austin: University of Texas Press, 1983.

Fay, Mary Smith. *War of 1812 Veterans in Texas.* New Orleans: Polyanthos, 1979.

Ferris, Sylvia V. V., and Eleanor S. Hoppe. *Scalpels and Sabers.* Austin: Eakin Press, 1985.

Foster, William C. *Spanish Expeditions into Texas, 1689–1768.* Austin: University of Texas Press, 1995.

Fowler, Gene. *Crazy Water: The Story of Mineral Wells and Other Texas Health Resorts.* Fort Worth: Texas Christian University Press, 1991.

Gilliland, Maude T. *Wilson County Texas Rangers, 1837–1977.* Privately published, 1977.

Golson, Josephine Polley. *Bailey's Light.* San Antonio: Naylor Press, 1950.

Groneman, Bill. *Alamo Defenders.* Austin: Eakin Press, 1990.

Hardin, Stephen L. *Texian Iliad: A Military History of the Texas Revolution, 1835–1836.* Austin: University of Texas Press, 1994.

Hardy, Dermot H., and Ingham S. Roberts. *Historical Review of South-east Texas.* 2 volumes. Chicago: Lewis Publishing Company, 1910.

Harris, Charles H., and Louis R. Sadler. *The Texas Rangers and the Mexican Revolution: The Bloodiest Decade, 1910–1920.* Albuquerque: University of New Mexico Press, 2004.

Harwell, T. F. *Confederate Biography: Members, Camp Ben McCulloch, U.C.V., and Others.* Privately published, n.d. [1923].

Hogan, William R. *The Texas Republic: A Social and Economic History.* Norman, 1946; reprint, Austin: University of Texas Press, 1969.

Jackson, Jack. *Los Mesteños: Spanish Ranching in Texas, 1721 to 1821.* College Station: Texas A&M University Press, 1986.

Jaeggli, J. T. *The Court House Story.* Privately published, 1971.

Johnson, Allen, et al., eds. *Dictionary of American Biography.* 22 volumes. New York: Charles Scribner's Sons, 1922–1958.

Johnson, Frank W. *Texas and Texans.* 5 volumes. Chicago: American Historical Society, 1914.

Johnson, Sidney S. *Texans Who Wore the Gray.* Tyler: Privately published, 1907.

Jones, Billy M. *Health-Seekers in the Southwest, 1817–1900.* Norman: University of Oklahoma Press, 1967.

Jordan, Terry G. *Trails to Texas: Southern Roots of Western Cattle Raising.* Lincoln: University of Nebraska Press, 1981.

King, Alvy L. *Louis T. Wigfall: Southern Fire-eater.* Baton Rouge: Louisiana State University, 1970.

Lack, Paul D. *The Texas Revolutionary Experience.* College Station: Texas A&M University Press, 1992.

Long, Jeff. *Duel of Eagles: The Mexican and U.S. Fight for the Alamo.* New York: William Morrow and Company, 1990.

Lord, Walter. *A Time to Stand.* New York: Harper & Brothers, 1961.

Lowe, Richard G., and Randolph B. Campbell. *Planters and Plain Folk: Agriculture in Antebellum Texas.* Dallas: Southern Methodist University Press, 1987.

Magill, Robert M. *Magill Family Record.* Richmond, VA: R. E. Magill, 1907.

Meinig, David W. *Imperial Texas: An Interpretive Essay in Cultural Geography.* Austin: University of Texas Press, 1969.

Memorial and Genealogical Record of Southwest Texas. Chicago: Goodspeed Brothers, 1894.

Memorial and Genealogical Record of Texas (East). Chicago: Goodspeed Brothers, 1895.

Moneyhon, Carl H. *Texas After the Civil War: The Struggle of Reconstruction.* College Station: Texas A&M University Press, 2004.

______. *Republicanism in Reconstruction Texas.* Austin: University of Texas Press, 1980.

Moore, Stephen L. *Savage Frontier, 1835–1837: Rangers, Riflemen, and Indian Wars in Texas, Volume 1.* Denton: University of North Texas Press, 2007.

Morgan, Dale L. *Dale Morgan on the Mormons, Part 2: 1949–1970,* ed. Richard L. Saunders. Norman: University of Oklahoma Press, 2014.

Nance, Joseph M. *After San Jacinto: The Texas-Mexican Frontier, 1836–1841.* Austin: University of Texas Press, 1963.

Nixon, Pat I. *The Medical Story of Early Texas.* San Antonio: Mollie Bennett Lupe Memorial Fund, 1946.

Parsons, Chuck. *The Sutton-Taylor Feud: The Deadliest Blood Feud in Texas.* Denton: University of North Texas Press, 2012.

Patterson, C. L. *Wilson County, Texas.* San Antonio: Privately published, 1939.

Phelan, Macum. *A History of the Expansion of Methodism in Texas, 1867–1902.* Dallas: Mathis, Van Nort & Company, 1937.

Polley, Joseph B. *Hood's Texas Brigade.* New York: Neale Publishing Company, 1910.

Pool, William C. *A Historical Atlas of Texas.* Austin: Eakin Press, 1975.

Potts, Charles S. *Railroad Transportation in Texas.* University of Texas Bulletin No. 119, July 1909.

Ramsdell, Charles W. *Reconstruction in Texas.* New York, 1910; reprint, Austin: University of Texas Press, 1970.

Ray, Worth S. *Austin Colony Pioneers.* Privately published, 1949.

Red, George P. *The Medicine Man in Texas.* Houston: Privately published, 1930.

Reed, St. Clair Griffin. *A History of the Texas Railroads.* Houston: St. Clair Publishing Company, 1941.

Richter, William L. *The Army in Texas During Reconstruction, 1865–1870.* College Station: Texas A&M University Press, 1987.

______. *Overreached on All Sides: The Freedmen's Bureau Administrators in Texas, 1865–1868.* College Station: Texas A&M University Press, 1991.

Sibley, Marilyn M. *Lone Stars and State Gazettes.* College Station: Texas A&M University Press, 1983.

Simpson, Harold B., Jr. comp. *Hood's Texas Brigade: A Compendium.* Hillsboro: Hill Junior College Press, 1977.

______. *Hood's Texas Brigade: Lee's Grenadier Guard.* Waco: Texian Press, 1970.

______. *Hood's Texas Brigade in Reunion and Memory.* Hillsboro: Hill Junior College Press, 1974.

Sonnichsen, Charles L. *I'll Die Before I Run: The Story of the Great Feuds of Texas.*New York: Harper & Brothers, 1951.

Sowell, Andrew J. *Early Settlers and Indian Fighters of Southwest Texas.* Austin: B. C. Jones & Company, 1900.

Spurlin, Charles D. *Texas Veterans in the Mexican War*. Privately published, 1984.

Stadler, Louise, comp. *Wilson County History*. Dallas: Taylor Publishing Company, 1990.

Sutherland, Anne. *We Cousins: The Robertsons, the Sutherlands, and the Making of Texas*. College Station: Texas A&M University Press, 2006.

Sutton, Robert C., Jr. *The Sutton-Taylor Feud*. Quanah: Nortex Press, 1974.

Thrall, Homer S. *History of Methodism in Texas*. Houston: E. H. Cushing, 1872.

______. *A Pictorial History of Texas*. St. Louis: N. D. Thompson and Company, 1879.

Timmons, Bascom N. *Garner of Texas: A Personal History*. New York: Harper & Brothers, 1948.

Valenza, Janet M. *Taking the Waters in Texas: Springs, Spas, and Fountains of Youth*. Austin: University of Texas Press, 2000.

Vest, Deed L. *A Century of Light*. Fort Worth: Masonic Home and School, 1959.

Wharton, Clarence R. *History of Fort Bend County*. San Antonio: Naylor Press, 1939.

______. *Texas Under Many Flags*. 5 volumes. Chicago: American Historical Society, 1930.

Wilson County Centennial, 1860–1960. Floresville: Wilson County Centennial Association, 1960.

Winkler, A. V. M. *The Confederate Capital and Hood's Texas Brigade*. Austin: Eugene Von Boeckmann, 1894.

Wooster, Ralph A. *The Secession Conventions of the South*. Princeton: Princeton University Press, 1962.

Zlatkovich, Charles P. *Texas Railroads: A Record of Construction and Abandonment*. Austin: University of Texas Bureau of Business Research, 1981.

Unpublished Manuscripts

Bean, Christopher B. "A Stranger Among Strangers: An Analysis of the Freedmen's Bureau Subassistant Commissioners in Texas, 1865–1868." Ph.D. Diss., University of North Texas, 2008.

Craighead, Ada. "Early Settlers of Texas." B.A. Thesis, Incarnate Word College, San Antonio, TX, 1936.

DeVierville, Jonathan P. "American Healing Waters ... "Ph.D. Diss., The University of Texas at Austin, 1992.

Frost, Jamie P. M. "Descendants and Ancestors of Joseph Henry Polley, 1625–1996." Typescript, 1996. In private collection.

George, Catherine. "The Life of Philip Dimmitt." M.A. Thesis, The University of Texas at Austin, 1937.

Grammer, Shirley. "Doisedo Colony School and Doisedo Colony Cemetery." Typescript, n.d. In possession of author.

Homer, Herschel H. "The Site Location History of the Floresville United Methodist Church." Manuscript, n.d. In possession of Louise Stadler, Floresville.

Hudson, Florence Sutherland. "We Cousins." Typescript, 1957. Dolph Briscoe Center for American History, The University of Texas at Austin.

Hunter, John W. "John W. Hunter Literary Effort." Manuscript, n.d. Texas State Library and Archives, Austin.

Owens, Nora Estelle. "Presidential Reconstruction in Texas: A Case Study." Ph.D. Dissertation, Auburn University, 1983.

Randt, Richard C. "Descendants of George Polly [*sic*] and Elizabeth Winn." Typescript, November 21, 1993. In possession of George B. Everts, Houston.

Valenza, Janet M. "Places Lived, Places Lost: Taking the Waters in Texas." Ph.D. Dissertation, The University of Texas at Austin, 1992.

Online Sources

American Baptist Association History and Archives Committee, "Servants Among Us." http://www.bogardstore.org/images/Servantssample.pdf.

"Biographies of Wilson County, Texas." http://genealogytrails.com/tex/southtexas/wilson/bios1.html.

Casto, Stanley D. "William A. Waugh: Pioneer La Salle County Rancher." http://www. historic district.com/ genealogy/lasalle/waugh.asp.

Cavazos, Michael. "Small Town History: Sutherland Springs." http://www.accd.edu/pac/history/rhines/StudentProjects/2002/SutherlandSprings/mvcfp.htm.

"Chapter One—John S. McGee, Circuit Rider." http://www.so-ky.com/books/mcgee/ chapter-one.pdf.

Cox, Mike. "Tyrant's Gold," *Texas Escapes*. http://www.texasescapes.com/MikeCox TexasTales/ 175-Gold-Sutherland-Springs.htm.

"Deserted Texas: Sutherland Springs, Texas." http://desertedtexas.com/post/120039989558/sutherland-springs-texas.

"The Distinctive and Aerodynamic McKeen Rail Motor Car." http://theoldmotor.com/?p=134946"Everything Seguin." http://johnwayne-thealamo.com/forum/viewtopic.php?f=9&t=31&start=430&st=0&sk=t&sd=a.

Eaton, Lauri Gray. "Carter House: Hidden Jewel of the Concrete Jungle," http://www.mysanantonio.com/community/northwest/news/article/Carter-House-Hidden-jewel-of-the-concrete-jungle-2270578.php.

"The Expulsion Case of Joseph R. Burton of Kansas (1906)." http://www.senate.gov/artandhistory/history/common/expulsion_cases/092JosephBurton_expulsion.htm.

Find-a-Grave. http://www.findagrave.com/.

"Genealogy—Person Sheet: Preston Walter Hobbs," http://heathcock.org/genealogy/ps01/ps01_099.html.

Giving Multiplied: The Semp Russ Foundation Fund. http://www.saafdn.org/HowtoGive/ThePowerofEndowment/TheSempRussFoundationFund.aspx.

"Gravestone for Chauncey S. and Lola Busby Southern," http://www.usgwarchives.net/tx/wilson/photos/tombstones/sutherlandspring/southern17366gph.jpg.

Liles, Maurine. "Texas Ranger Captain Will Wright," http://wilsoncountyhistory.org/Moments/TEXAS%20RANGER%20CAPTAIN%20WILL%20WRIGHT%20doc %20(short).pdf.

Lost Texas Roads. http://losttexasroads.com.

"Patillo 'Pat' Higgins Turns Grass Into Gold," *Wilson County News.* http://www.wilson countynews.com/article.php?id=24931.

"Possibly the Most Prolific Paleo Site: Cibilo Creek." http://www.arrowheadology.com/forums/content/20-possibly-most-prolific-paleo-site-cibilo-creek.html.

"San Antonio and Gulf Shore Railroad." http://www.txtransportationmuseum.org/ SAG.htm

"Southside Place: Incorporated City Preserves Small Town Culture," *Houston Business Journal.* http://www.bizjournals.com/houston/stories/2010/03/22/newscolumn2. html.

Sullivan, Jerry M. "The Ben Leaton Legend." http://tpwd.state.tx.us/news/magazine/ leaton.

"Sutherland Springs, Texas, United States," http://openplaques.org/places/us/areas/ sutherland_springs_tx/plaques.

Texas Department of Transportation. *Highway Designation File.* http://www.dot.state. tx.us/tpp/hwy/US/US0087.htm.

Texas Legislators Past & Present. http://www.lrl.state.tx.us/legeleaders/members/ memberdisplay. cfm?memberID=2327.

Tyler, Ron, et al. *Handbook of Texas Online.* https://tshaonline.org/handbook.

"Western Ghost Towns: Sutherland Springs, Texas." http://www.ohio.edu/people/gulino/Ghosttownweb/Texas/Sutherland%20Springs/sutherland_springs_tx.html.

Wheat, Jim. *Postmasters and Post Offices of Texas, 1846–1930.* http://www.rootsweb. ancestry. com/~txpost/postmasters.html.

Index

-C-

-D-

-E-

-F-

-G-

-R-

-S-